WALTER SMITH
THE IBROX GAFFER

A TRIBUTE TO A RANGERS LEGEND

SCOTT BURNS

With contributions from

Jorg Albertz, Lorenzo Amoruso, Joachim Bjorklund,
Madjid Bougherra, Kirk Broadfoot, John Brown, Terry Butcher,
Alex Cleland, Neale Cooper, Christian Dailly, Kevin Drinkell,
Ian Durrant, Derek Ferguson, Ian Ferguson, Rino Gattuso,
Andy Goram, Dale Gordon, Richard Gough, Mark Hateley,
Pieter Huistra, Nikica Jelavic, Brian Laudrup, Kyle Lafferty,
Gus MacPherson, Stuart McCall, Kenny McDowall, Alan McLaren,
Ally McCoist, Lee McCulloch, Derek McInnes, Dave McPherson,
Pedro Mendes, Charlie Miller, Kenny Miller, Neil Murray,
Stevie Naismith, Jimmy Nicholl, Scott Nisbet, Nacho Novo,
Sasa Papac, Gordan Petric, Sergio Porrini, Steven Pressley,
Davie Robertson, Nigel Spackman, Trevor Steven, Gary Stevens,
Vladimir Weiss, Davie Weir, Steven Whittaker, Ray Wilkins,
Fraser Wishart, Chris Woods and Gregg Wylde.

BLACK & WHITE PUBLISHING

First published 2011
This edition first published 2011
by Black & White Publishing Ltd
29 Ocean Drive, Edinburgh EH6 6JL

1 3 5 7 9 10 8 6 4 2   11 12 13 14

ISBN: 978 1 84502 357 7

A CIP catalogue record for this book
is available from the British Library.

Typeset by Ellipsis Digital Ltd, Glasgow

Printed and bound by CPI Cox & Wyman, Reading

Also Available from Black & White Publishing

Drinks All Round: the Autobiography
(Kevin Drinkell with Scott Burns)

CONTENTS

ACKNOWLEDGEMENTS

I would like to thank my wife, Amanda, and sons, Ross and Aaron, for their support and patience throughout the whole process. It was very much appreciated.

There are also a number of people who I would like to acknowledge for their help and assistance with the book. Can I start by saying thank you to Stuart Darroch for his help and advice and for taking the time to proofread the book. Maybe you'll have time to get back to the family now.

I would also like to thank Kirk Broadfoot, Nuno Dias (Sporting Lisbon Press Officer), Andrew Dickson, Scott Fisher, Mehmet Gerceski (Bursaspor Press Officer), Andy McInnes, Steve Harvey, Stephen Kerr (Rangers Press Officer), Graeme Macpherson and Carol Patton (Rangers Press Officer) for aiding me in the interview process.

Can I also note my appreciation to all the Rangers players, past and present, who gave up their time and Black & White Publishing for showing faith and producing such a top-quality book.

I must also give a big hand to Willie Vass for the picture element of the book. It has played a big part.

Also to the *Scottish Daily Express* for allowing me to work on this project and for giving me permission to use pictures and quotes from their archive libraries. All Walter Smith quotes used in this book are courtesy of the *Scottish Daily Express*.

Finally, I would like to say a massive thank you to Walter Smith for having such a great managerial career and making this book possible.

SB

FOREWORD BY ALLY McCOIST MBE

(RANGERS PLAYER 1983–98,
ASSISTANT MANAGER 2007–11 AND
MANAGER 2011–)

WALTER SMITH is the best manager that Scottish football has ever seen. In my humble opinion, he stands alone, right at the very top. The Gaffer's record is up there beside the greats of our game like Jock Stein, Bill Shankly, Matt Busby and Sir Alex Ferguson. Everybody will have their own personal favourite but what Walter has done in the game is certainly more than enough for him to be included in such illustrious company. I know I am a little bit biased but, for me, the Gaffer stands above them all.

I know I have been extremely honoured and privileged to be able to say I worked under the great man for the majority of my football career. I have witnessed the Gaffer first hand as a player, coach and assistant manager and I know just how good he is. You only have to look at his managerial record. He has been successful wherever he has been whether it has been at Rangers, Scotland or Everton.

He is not only a top football manager but a great man into the bargain. When you speak to any of Walter's players or ex-players then you will find it very difficult for anybody to say a bad word against him, from his coaching right down to his man-management skills. Walter is a man you could only have the utmost respect for.

I think we will really appreciate Walter Smith's true value now that he has left the club, I am not saying anybody at Rangers has taken Walter for granted but he has been such an important part of the fabric of the club in recent years. He gets everything spot on and is a real leader. The fact he has won so many domestic championships and led a Scottish team to a European final, in the current climate, shows just how good a manager he is. He will be virtually impossible to replace.

The great Bill Struth won eighteen titles in thirty years right at the start but I think over the last 100 years Walter's record stands alone above any other Rangers manager. When you look at what he has achieved that's very hard to argue with.

He has earned the right to be called a Rangers and Scottish football legend. Thanks for everything.

1

SIGNING UP FOR THE SOUNESS REVOLUTION

(1986–88)

RANGERS owner Lawrence Marlborough and chairman David Holmes drew up an Ibrox blueprint in 1986 that not only revolutionised Rangers Football Club but helped to create a Scottish managerial legend in the process – although maybe not the one they had initially thought! The Scotland star Graeme Souness was pinpointed as the man they felt could lift the Light Blues out of their nine-year title slumber. The legendary midfielder, who had made his name with Liverpool but, by this point, was now playing out in Italy with Sampdoria, was approached and, after some careful consideration, was persuaded to take up Holmes and Marlborough's headline-grabbing offer to become player-manager of the Glasgow giants. The Ibrox hierarchy felt the appointment could help put Rangers back on top of a domestic scene that had been frustratingly dominated by their bitter city rivals, Celtic, and the emergence of the New Firm, Aberdeen and Dundee United.

Souness may have played at the very top of the game but his lack of managerial experience was a concern and he knew he would need an experienced coach alongside him to help him learn the ropes, especially as he continued to play. Walter Smith was a man he knew well from his time in the Scotland set-up, where he had assisted the likes of Sir Alex Ferguson. Smith had been a tough, uncompromising defender with Dundee United and Dumbarton before he turned his hand to coaching under the guidance of the legendary Jim McLean. Smith had assisted McLean as the Dundee United side lifted the 1979 League Cup and then eclipsed that when they were crowned champions of Scotland in 1982–83.

Smith had built a reputation as a top coach after he had decided to hang up his boots following a solid if not headline-grabbing playing career. He had finely tuned his playing skills on the streets and waste ground in and around the tough Glasgow suburb of Carmyle. It was this working-class upbringing in the East End of the city that helped to keep Smith's feet on the ground and to this day he has never forgotten his roots. Smith's love of the game was there for all to see from an early age and, thanks to his grandfather, it didn't take him long before the institution that is Glasgow Rangers became a massive part of his life. When he wasn't turning out for Chapelhall or Bishopbriggs Amateurs, he would be at Ibrox cheering on his heroes.

Smith and his brother, Ian, were also at Ibrox for the ill-fated Old Firm derby on 2 January 1971 – where sixty-six Rangers fans tragically lost their lives and another 145 were injured. Smith acknowledged he and his brother were two of the lucky ones because they normally congregated on Stairway 13 – where the disaster occurred – although they managed to get out unscathed, without realising the full extent of what was going on behind them.

Smith painfully recalled: 'Coming on buses from Carmyle, it was the Rangers end where we all congregated and my brother and I were both caught on the stairs. It wasn't unusual back then for the crowds to feel the squeeze on that staircase; there was always a bit of a bottleneck at the bottom of it, and the crowds often had to stop. So I didn't think that much of it at the time. We managed to scramble out over a fence so we must have climbed over the top of other people in order to get out onto Edmiston

Drive. We then got on to our bus and went home. Communication back then wasn't what it is today, there was nobody on the bus really talking about it much at all. It was only when we got back to Carmyle, where everybody was congregating and waiting to see if we were all OK, that we realised there had been such a horrible disaster. I can just remember people there telling us that there had been a terrible situation at Ibrox. It was a disastrous day for everyone. We were the lucky ones, the fortunate ones.'

Smith also knew he would need to get another lucky break if he wanted to become a professional footballer. He knew there were no guarantees and embarked on getting himself a trade. He studied for his apprenticeship as an electrician at Coatbridge Technical College. It was then that Smith's footballing career sparked into life after he stepped up to the junior ranks with Ashfield and had managed to secure himself a job at Dalmarnock power station, working for the South of Scotland Electricity Board.

But it wasn't long before football was taking centre stage as Tannadice boss Jerry Kerr gave him the chance to join top-level Dundee United. Smith didn't need much persuading and duly signed, as Kerr also lined him up a job with Louden Brothers in the City of Discovery that would allow him to finish his apprenticeship. He went on to make more than 120 appearances for Dundee United under Kerr and then the legendary Jim McLean in his two spells at Tannadice, with a brief stop off at Dumbarton sandwiched inbetween.

It was when Smith moved into his twilight years as a player that he began to make a name for himself as he started to put what he had picked up from Kerr and McLean into practice as a coach. McLean quickly promoted him to his staff and it wasn't long before he was given his chance to assist with some of the Scotland youth teams. His reputation in coaching circles grew rapidly and that was why Souness wanted him by his side at Ibrox.

The approach was made and, after some convincing, McLean

was persuaded to let Smith fulfil a lifelong dream by becoming the assistant manager of his boyhood heroes, while Phil Boersma was brought in alongside him to combine the roles of coach and physio. Marlborough and Holmes were delighted they had got their men and the Souness revolution was well and truly on its way. Souness and Smith both demanded and wanted the best and what they wanted they got as they went out and stunned British football by signing top England stars like Terry Butcher and goalkeeper Chris Woods. The fact that English clubs were banned from Europe, as a result of the Heysel disaster, also gave Rangers an obvious advantage in the transfer market.

Northern Irish international Jimmy Nicholl, in his second spell at the club, still remembers the immediate impact the pair made on a club that had been guilty of years of under-achievement: 'Graeme Souness knew Walter Smith from his Scotland days and knew how good a coach he was. That was one of the reasons why he obviously made it one of his first tasks to try to get him to Ibrox as his No. 2. It certainly was a canny move because Walter was a well-respected coach and one of the best in Scotland at that time. That was where you have to take your hat off to Graeme. He was clever. He had a plan and he knew how he wanted to execute it. He had been used to being and playing with the best at Liverpool and out in Italy and that was something he was keen to replicate at Rangers. All credit to him because he did just that. He brought in the best.

'He started with Walter as his No. 2 and then brought in top-class players like Chris Woods and Terry Butcher. Graeme and Walter might have had money to spend but there is no doubt they spent it wisely. It would also still have taken a lot of persuading to convince top England internationals like Butcher and Woods to leave Ipswich Town and Norwich, respectively, to join a team who hadn't exactly been setting the heather alight in Scotland. But Graeme and Walter managed to get them up and in the process immediately dragged Rangers to another level.

Graeme and Walter wanted the best. Their philosophy was – I have brought you in because I think you can do a job. Go out and do it and if you don't then we will bring somebody else in who will! The whole club had been totally shaken up by their arrival. Before, under the late Jock Wallace, God bless his soul, we would win the occasional League Cup but we were nowhere near in the league, as Aberdeen, Dundee United and Celtic continued to dominate. Suddenly the Rangers fans really had something to get excited about.'

Butcher had made his name at Ipswich Town and was a stalwart in the late Sir Bobby Robson's England side, often captaining the side in the absence of full-time skipper Bryan Robson. The much sought-after defender also raised a few eyebrows by knocking back Manchester United to make his stunning switch across the border. Butcher admitted he had been convinced by Souness's grand master plan although he knew very little about his No. 2, Smith. That was to change quickly.

Butcher explained: 'Walter Smith might have been the No. 2, but he was still a major influence on the team and the club as a whole. Graeme was the figurehead. He was the one the press and the fans loved because he always had something to say. He was also no stranger to controversy and the occasional outburst. Graeme loved to aggravate and wind people up through the press but Walter was a far different kettle of fish. He was far more low profile and operated more under the radar. None of the English boys knew much about Walter before we came up to Glasgow but as soon as we started working with him we quickly saw what a knowledge he had of the game and he immediately gained all our respect. He just got on with things and made sure the team was ready for the games and different challenges that lay ahead. Walter would concentrate on the set pieces and more of the tactical side because that was new to Graeme, as he had just stepped into the managerial game.'

Midfielder Derek Ferguson had come through the Ibrox ranks

a few years before Souness's arrival. He was tipped to become a mainstay in the new-look Rangers team along with other precocious Scottish talents like Ian Durrant, Davie Cooper and Ally McCoist.

'My recollection of those early years,' says Ferguson, 'was that Walter took care of most of the training. That is not me being disrespectful to Graeme Souness because he was still playing and management was new to him. But Walter's tactical knowledge and know-how was just brilliant. Graeme would do most of the team talks while Walter would offer more of a personal touch. He would go round the players individually and give us more specific instructions and wee pointers here and there, before games, at half-time, full-time or even in training. Walter is a great man-manager and probably turned out to be Graeme's most important signing. In Walter, he had a brilliant man beside him who had the experience and knowledge that Graeme still had to gain when it came to management.'

Souness might have been the main man but Smith quickly made it clear he wasn't a man that was going to be messed with either.

'Walter could also be hard if he needed to be,' Ferguson admitted. 'For me, he had an aura about him and he was definitely a man you didn't want to cross. He was a lovely guy but you also knew he had a real edge to him when it was needed. I remember there was one situation where he completely lost it and went mad with the entire squad. We were in Glasgow airport the night before we were due to fly out to Il Ciocco. We were staying in a nearby hotel. There was a game on the television and Graeme said we could sit and watch it. He also allowed us to have one beer but nothing more.

'So we were sitting at the bar watching the game and we all decided to have another pint in the second half. Walter, somehow, got wind of that back in the hotel. He came steaming into the pub. He was furious and there was almost steam coming out of his ears. He was livid. He steamed right in and booted poor Robert Fleck's pint all over the place. He was raging and you could see he was really disappointed with us. The manager had given us a bit of slack by allowing us a drink and Walter felt we had tried to take advantage of that, especially as we were also in the middle of pre-season training. At the time we didn't really think we had done much wrong but looking back he was probably right. We did push it too far.'

The Souness revolution hardly kicked off the way Rangers had hoped. Their player manager made headlines for all the wrong reasons as Souness was sent off for kicking out at Hibs striker George McCluskey, sparking a twenty-one-man melee in the process, as Rangers crashed 2–1 at Easter Road.

Smith might have been fiery on occasion but a lot of the time he was forced to keep his emotions in check, to help the team in their hour of need.

'Walter was a bit more laid back than Graeme but when Walter growled everybody knew about it,' former skipper Butcher admitted. 'But at times Walter also had to keep a lid on things, especially when Graeme blew a gasket. He had to because there were quite a few times where Graeme got himself sent off and it was left to Walter to take the reins, like in the first game where Graeme got sent off against Hibs. I sometimes talk about Walter to my assistant manager Maurice Malpas and he reckons he must have mellowed because he claims he was always blowing his top when they worked together at Dundee United. But Graeme and Walter were a good partnership and brought everybody together and made sure that at Rangers it was always a big team effort.'

The following week Souness, despite being suspended, saw his side claim their first win thanks to a McCoist penalty in a 1–0 win over Falkirk, although they were brought crashing back to earth by Smith's old team, as Dundee United beat them at home 3–2 the following week.

Jimmy Nicholl is in no doubt that Rangers struggled in those early weeks because Souness and Smith were determined to change the outlook of the Ibrox support and introduce a whole new style of play that was based more on the continental approach rather than the more direct domestic game they had been used to.

'When Graeme and Walter came in they wanted us to play in a certain style and in a way that was probably alien to the Scottish game at that point,' Nicholl acknowledged. 'They wanted us to keep the ball and even knock it about at the back if it needed to be, just to keep possession. It was a more continental approach, something Graeme had been used to in Italy. I remember he told us this was the way we were going to play and we would have to educate our fans in the process.

'Walter was also important in that switchover. Walter could see things from the side that Graeme maybe couldn't because he was in the thick of the action. But between them they would come up with the best tactics and approaches to get points on the board. I remember one game against Hibs they dropped Mark Walters and Davie Cooper. We used to struggle at grounds like Easter Road but that day the midfield included Graeme, John Brown, John McGregor and myself. It was like dogs of war! But we went out and won the game and their tactics worked. The next week proved to be a different challenge and Mark and Davie found themselves back in the team. It showed the tactical awareness and knowledge of the game that Graeme and Walter had. They knew it was horses for courses.'

Eventually, Souness and Smith got their players tuned into their way of thinking and it saw Rangers lift the first silverware of the season, as Rangers beat Celtic 2–1 in the Skol Cup final thanks to goals from Durrant and Cooper. However, their hopes of an extended European run were ended by Uwe Rahn's goal for Borussia Monchengladbach in the 1–1 draw at Ibrox. The Light Blues drew a blank in the 0–0 draw in Germany and crashed out on away goals. It was a setback but it turned out to be the catalyst for a run of results that would suddenly drag them back into the title race.

Another big signing, England international Graham Roberts, also came in to further reinforce the charge. Roberts played his part in the New Year's Day 2–0 win at Parkhead, thanks to goals from Fleck and McCoist, although Souness was also a man inspired that day.

Midfielder Derek Ferguson recalled: 'We were a fair bit behind Celtic and that was probably due to the fact that the manager had brought in so many new players and it took time for everybody to settle in. Eventually we did bed down and we went on a great run. I think we put a decent run together in the second half of the season. An important win for us was the 2–0 Old Firm victory at Ibrox. That helped us claw things back and eventually we managed to turn things around and came out on top.'

Rangers were suddenly on a roll and the title started to seem like a distinct possibility. Souness was more than happy to see himself and his team grab the headlines as his No. 2 went about his job more discreetly.

'Walter was always the one who helped keep everybody's feet on the ground,' Terry Butcher explained. 'Even when we went on that great run and the results just started to snowball. The good thing about Graeme was that he also wasn't frightened to ask some of the more experienced players or the guys who had played down south advice about other players he was looking to sign.'

Keeper Woods, Butcher and Roberts all played their part as Rangers shut up shop, as the team racked up the points and the clean sheets. Woods took his shut-out record to an amazing 1196 minutes before he was finally beaten by one of the most famous goals in Scottish Cup history – when the Ibrox giants were left red-faced by a solitary goal from Hamilton's Adrian Sprott.

Woods admitted: 'It was a great achievement and I still take great pride from that shut-out record. It will live with me forever because it was a real team effort. It was 1196 minutes. It took in thirteen games from half-time against Borussia Monchengladbach to half-time in the Scottish Cup game against Hamilton. To be honest, I didn't really think about the clean sheets until we had gone six or seven matches. Somebody actually asked me what the record was and I mentioned it to Walter Smith and he immediately told me not to even think about it. He said just forget about it and I will tell you if you get close. Needless to say he didn't say anything and four or five matches on it started again when people began to talk about the record then. It was a bizarre day when we finally beat it because we got knocked out of the cup by Hamilton. We should have been celebrating that achievement but I remember we were all in the dressing room sitting in shock due to the fact that Hamilton had knocked us out of the cup.'

It was a result and a performance that neither Souness nor Smith found easy to stomach. The embarrassment and ridicule only fuelled them and their players to go on to bigger and better things. There was a wobble in the title race when they lost 3–1 at Parkhead but their day of destiny finally arrived at Pittodrie on 2 May 1987.

The season was brought to a climax in much the same way as it started for Rangers, with Souness being shown red. This time it was for a reckless challenge on Dons defender Brian Irvine. It didn't stop Rangers though as a Terry Butcher header put them ahead. That was later cancelled out by Irvine's goal but the point was enough to give the Glasgow giants the result they needed to become champions, as Celtic lost to Falkirk, claiming their first title in nine seasons.

Goal hero Butcher said: 'It was beyond our wildest dream to win the title in our first season. It was my first crack at it and I certainly didn't expect to win the league at the first time of asking. Even when the manager signed me he was looking more at the longer term. Also it didn't look like we would be anywhere near it when we lost two of those opening three games. We also had a lot of injuries and it wasn't until that first Old Firm game that we really kicked into gear.'

Even Souness admitted the title hadn't been on his agenda in that maiden campaign. However, with it sitting pretty in the Ibrox trophy room, along with the Skol Cup, it suddenly heaped even more pressure on the shoulders of the Rangers management team. They had set the standard and it was now up to them to maintain it.

The management team knew they had to strengthen again and in came the likes of Mark Falco and the vastly experienced English striker Trevor Francis, although the biggest coup was, probably, persuading top defender Richard Gough to return from Tottenham. Souness had initially tried to sign him from Dundee United but their boss McLean had blocked the move and so Rangers had to bide their time before they finally got their man.

Gough said: 'I probably know Walter better than most. He was actually the guy who picked me up and took me to my first training session when I first went to Dundee United back in 1980. Walter was definitely a big factor, along with Graeme Souness, in me coming back up to Rangers. He was a man who was a top coach and somebody I had an awful lot of respect for. I came up to Rangers because of him and Graeme and it ended up being one of the best decisions I have ever made.'

The champions came out fighting after losing the first Old Firm derby at Parkhead. That fired up the Light Blues for revenge at Ibrox but Woods, Butcher and Roberts took things too far as they clashed with Frank McAvennie. The Celtic striker had instigated things by going in late on Woods. That sparked a furious head-to-head between the pair, before Butcher charged in and shoved the Celtic striker and then Roberts followed up, as McAvennie crumbled to the ground. Woods and McAvennie were red carded for their part in proceedings while Butcher got away with a caution. Roberts had to take over between the sticks while Butcher's day went from bad to worse as he scored an own goal and got sent packing for aiming a kick at Celtic keeper Allen McKnight. Bizarrely, nine-man Rangers rallied and claimed a share of the spoils thanks to goals from McCoist and Gough in a 2–2 draw.

But the ramifications from this bad-tempered game weren't to end there. The quartet, as public figureheads, were made an example of and ended up in court on charges of breach of the peace. McAvennie, rather surprisingly, was found not guilty while Roberts was able to breathe a huge sigh of relief as the case against him was found not proven. That left the courts to deal with Butcher and Woods who were both found guilty and charged £250 and £500 respectively.

Butcher explained: 'It was a bad spell for the club and none more so that for myself and Chris Woods after that Old Firm game on 17 October 1987 when we ended up getting sent off and up in court. We did win the Skol Cup that season but we both missed the final because of our Old Firm sending offs. So that just made things even harder to take.'

Rangers swept aside all the controversy to retain the Skol Cup after an epic battle with Aberdeen. It ended 3–3 after extra-time, with Cooper, Durrant and Fleck netting for the Ibrox side, before they eventually came out on top 5–3 after a nerve-jangling penalty shoot-out.

The Govan giants were then hit by the hammer blow of Butcher's broken leg. Souness was also constantly tinkering with his squad and continued to try and strengthen as Rangers struggled to hit the heights of their first campaign. Former AC Milan and Chelsea star Ray Wilkins, who Souness had come up against during his time in England and Italy, was the next big name to make the move to Ibrox.

The classy Englishman, who had been playing for Paris St Germain, recalled: 'Graeme Souness and Walter Smith both flew out to Paris to meet me. They must have done a good job in selling Rangers and getting me to move to Scotland because I ended up flying back with them the next day to sign. They were a great partnership and the thing about great coaches is they bring in the best players to make their job easier. They let the good players get on with things and that was what happened in those early years at Rangers. Graeme and Walter only really had to tinker with things now and again but most of the time they trusted the players to go out and put on a performance. Graeme and Walter also knew that they would only have to say things once because we would go out and carry out their instructions to the letter. They deserve enormous credit for putting such a strong team together, on and off the park.'

Souness and Smith, in particular, who had spent his entire footballing career in Scotland, knew the importance of maintaining a strong core of home-based players. Ian Ferguson had made his name as a free-scoring midfielder and his exploits in firing St Mirren to Scottish Cup glory went some way to landing him his dream move.

Ferguson admitted that it was Smith who immediately made him feel at ease as he got ready to fulfil a lifelong ambition. Ferguson recalled: 'I remember when I went to Ibrox to sign I was in awe of both Walter Smith and Graeme Souness. Rangers had agreed a fee with St Mirren for me and remember I felt really nervous as I went into the ground to speak to them about my move. I think it was made even worse because I was a Rangers supporter and suddenly Walter and Graeme had given me this chance to fulfil my boyhood dream. I was nervous but I just remember what a feeling it was walking through those front doors at Ibrox for the first time. I still remember that day and it still feels like yesterday.

'I might have been a bit apprehensive and nervous but I have to say Walter immediately put me at ease by breaking the ice with a few funnies. He knew I was from Barrowfield and how you need to take the street lights in there at night! He knew how rough it was and would laugh and say: "When you leave can you take the cutlery and pens back out of your pocket and put them back where you found them." I think Walter realised I was a bit nervous because I was coming from a smaller club to one of the biggest clubs in Britain. I was about to walk into a dressing room that had top stars like Terry Butcher, Ally McCoist, Chris Woods and Souness himself. But to be fair to Graeme and Walter I was treated the same as everybody else from day one. I was immediately made to feel part of things. That was a big thing in helping me to settle.'

Another long-term stalwart, in the shape of John 'Bomber' Brown, checked in from Dundee and he also could see how important the Souness and Smith partnership was for Rangers.

Brown said: 'It was Graeme Souness who signed me for Rangers while Walter Smith was his No. 2. Walter was very much the coach/trainer. We had top players like Ray Wilkins, Terry Butcher and Chris Woods along with a string of top Scottish players. We are talking about guys who had played in World Cup finals and in all the top European competitions. But all the boys had total respect for Walter and that was because he knew what he was talking about.'

There was no doubt there was now even more quality in the Ibrox ranks but things didn't click quickly enough and their bitter rivals Celtic took full advantage to celebrate their centenary season with a league and Scottish Cup double.

Smith is in no doubt that the injury suffered by their captain, Butcher, had a major bearing on Rangers' fall from grace. He said: 'The second season we did not win the league title and much of that was down to the fact Terry was out for most of that season with a broken leg.'

Butcher, himself, admitted that the Ibrox giants were brought crashing back down to earth with an almighty bang. The straight-talking Englishman acknowledged: 'Celtic were a team on a mission in their centenary season. We just expected things to roll on after winning the league the previous season but it didn't happen. We just blew up and Celtic walked away with the title. It was a rude awakening for us all. I think losing that title was a defining moment for Rangers. It got us refocused again and helped to set us on our way to nine-in-a-row.'

Souness and Smith were sent back to the drawing board and as a result there were casualties. Danish international Jan Bartram was sent packing after he continually slaughtered Souness and Scottish football, while Roberts' Ibrox career was also brought to an abrupt and bloody end after a dressing-room set-to with Smith and Souness. The controversial defender refused to accept criticism from Smith for a defeat at the hands of Aberdeen. Souness walked in and, not surprisingly, took sides with his No. 2 and from that moment Roberts' Rangers career was over. The pair showed they weren't to be messed with and no one was going to stop them from taking Rangers to the pinnacle of Scottish football.

2

THE FIRST STEP
ON THE ROAD TO HISTORY

(1988–89)

GRAEME SOUNESS and Walter Smith felt the major surgery needed had been done the previous season and even though they had lost the title they still didn't think they were too far away. There was to be some minor fine-tuning and once again Souness turned his attentions south of the border to land some of its top talent. The ban on English clubs competing in Europe was still giving Rangers further pull and allowed them to bring in England international Gary Stevens and prolific target-man Kevin Drinkell from Everton and Norwich respectively.

Drinkell recalled how it was Smith and first-team coach Phil Boersma who flew down to London to convince him that he was the man who could get Rangers back on the road to glory. 'Ironically, when I first took the call from my agent to tell me that Rangers were interested I instantly dismissed it because I thought it was Queen's Park Rangers,' Drinkell revealed. 'Then I found out it was Glasgow Rangers and suddenly that became a lot more appealing. Walter and Phil Boersma were the first people I met from Rangers. They flew down to Heathrow to meet me when they were trying to sign me from Norwich. It was Walter and Phil who convinced me to sign for Rangers. They convinced me about Graeme Souness's vision for the club and the success they were looking to have in Scotland and in Europe with it. They also told me how much Graeme wanted to sign me and where I was going to fit into his team.

'There was one point where we weren't sure if the deal was going to happen when the Norwich City chairman Robert Chase came up to negotiate the deal. I was becoming more and more frustrated and I was ready to burst into the room and tell Chase to get the deal done because he had messed me about with other possible transfers. In the end it was Walter and Phil who kept me in check. They just told me just to sit tight and be patient and the deal would get done. Eventually it did. I hadn't even spoken to the manager and still I had agreed to sign for Rangers, so Phil and Walter must have done something right. I ended up flying back up to Glasgow with them the next day where they gave me the guided tour and my introductions to my new team mates and manager.'

Gary Stevens had also seen that Terry Butcher and Chris Woods' moves to Scotland had helped them keep their places in the England set-up. 'It was an easy decision for me because Rangers had shown their ambitions signing players like Terry and Chris and also had Souness at the helm,' the talented right back admitted. 'He had definitely put Scottish football on the map. Before then most top English players would probably have preferred to stay in England but suddenly his revolution had taken Rangers to the forefront of British football. I was really impressed with Graeme and Walter Smith's plans for the club. They had just lost the title to Celtic and they were determined to improve the squad and win it back. They were ambitious and desperate to win things and that was exactly what I was looking for in that next stage of my career.'

Ian Ferguson was also getting ready for his first pre-season at Rangers and was well aware the sole focus was on wrestling the title back from Celtic. Second best was just not an option. The midfielder said: 'I had obviously joined the season before when Celtic had won the league and cup double in their centenary season. I remember the following summer Graeme and Walter took us to Il Ciocco for our usual pre-season training camp. You could see they were both hurting. There was a real determination from them both that the title would be coming back to Ibrox. You could see they meant business, with the players they brought in and their desire to get Rangers back to winning ways. For them there was no hiding place if you weren't successful. If Graeme or Walter signed you for Rangers then they believed you could do a job for them. It was then up to you to go and prove it. If you didn't do it then you would be out the door quicker than you came in it.

'It may sound ruthless but they had set standards and they were determined they weren't going to drop. You need that at big clubs because you have to stand out from the crowd and show why you are a big club. You needed to be a strong character to play for a big club like Rangers. Not everybody can do it but during my time the one thing that every Rangers squad had was character in abundance. That went a long way to helping us achieve the success we had.'

Kevin Drinkell also got to work with Smith on the training pitch and he admitted he made an immediate impression, in much the same way as their first meeting at Heathrow airport. 'Walter was always the man who dealt with most of the training,' the former Norwich City striker revealed. 'Graeme would go and identify the players and give the team talks but a lot of the time he let Walter get on with the training. Graeme would get involved with set-plays or that but most of the drills he would leave to Walter while Phil Boersma would do a lot of the fitness work. The trio worked well together and they were a good mix.'

Top England star Ray Wilkins had worked under some of the top names in European football and even he admitted he learned a lot under Souness's No. 2 – some of the skills and techniques he later took into his own managerial career.

Wilkins said: 'I really enjoyed playing under them and all I can say about Walter is that I later went on to become a No. 2 and there were quite a few things which I picked up from him that I tried to adapt into my own managerial career. I think you can always learn from watching the top coaches and Walter definitely falls into that category. The fact Rangers went on to have the success they had after Graeme left shows you that. A lot of teams would have failed to recover after losing a top manager like Souness but Rangers moved on and went on to win nine-in-a-row, which really is a truly remarkable feat. He also came back to Rangers for a second spell to bring even more success to the club in very different circumstances.

'I loved my time in Scotland. I was lucky enough to win the league and Scottish cups and I look back at it as a really happy time in my career and a lot of that is down to Graeme and Walter and the team they put together.'

Rangers hit the new season running with Stevens and Drinkell both netting early goals, showing they were more than welcome additions to an already vastly talented squad. Wins over Hamilton and the Skol Cup victories over Clyde and Clydebank were hardly going to appease the demanding Ibrox faithful. The real proof of the pudding was going to be the Old Firm showdowns. It was the chance for Souness and his players to put down a marker and they did that in some style. For some Rangers fans it will be a game they will never forget as they thumped the champions 5–1.

A double from Ally McCoist and further strikes from Ray Wilkins, Kevin Drinkell and Mark Walters made Frank McAvennie's opener seem like nothing but a distant memory. But for some Rangers players it still wasn't enough.

Former St Mirren star Ian Ferguson said: 'The day we beat Celtic 5–1 was a fantastic day for us. It was just a great occasion because we managed to beat our main rivals so convincingly. We really were on top of our game and had Celtic where we wanted them.

'We were 5–1 up and we really believed we could go on and

equal Celtic's 7–1 win. But suddenly the manager [Souness] put himself on. He tried to slow the game down and was more interested in trying to beat his man or trying little tricks and step-overs. The likes of Ally McCoist, Ian Durrant and myself were fuming because we wanted to continue going for it. We had Celtic on the ropes. There was still twenty minutes to go and we knew we might never get another chance of getting anywhere near Celtic's 7–1 win.' But it wasn't to be.

That was one of the rare occasions where the Rangers management team allowed their players to drop down a gear or two. The team normally had to train the way they played. If things weren't done properly or anybody stepped out of line then Smith would be waiting. Ian Durrant can testify to that after he ended up on the end of one of his assistant manager's right hooks. He explained: 'We had been playing five-a-sides and Walter had been in one of the teams. There was the normal bit of training ground banter. It was all good natured but I took things a bit too far. I started to slaughter him for the way he played in the game. I was pretty derogatory to him and did overstep the mark. The next thing I knew he came up and caught me with a right hook. I just looked and never said anything. I knew I had stepped out of line and I learned my lesson. The next time I said anything to him I made sure I was more than an arm's length away!'

Things were still moving along quite nicely for Rangers although a defeat at Pittodrie was to prove costly in more ways than one. Not only did they drop valuable points but they also lost their talented playmaker Durrant, who suffered sickening cruciate ligament damage after a horror tackle from Aberdeen midfielder Neil Simpson. It was a day that left a bad taste in the mouth and Souness knew it was a situation he had to nip in the bud quickly, especially as the teams were set to meet again in the Skol Cup later that month. Souness and Smith knew the importance of trying to defuse what could have been a potential powder-keg clash. They had already seen what had happened in the Old Firm game the previous season and they knew Rangers and Scottish football couldn't afford to be dragged through the gutter again.

Gary Stevens said: 'There were a lot of us who were upset at what had happened to Ian. It had been a bad challenge and, at that point, there had even been talk that his career might be over. Both Graeme and Walter knew it could be an issue going into the Skol Cup final but they told us that it was no use going out there to fight or gain our revenge. The best thing we could do for Ian was to go out and lift the cup. It was good management from the pair because it allowed everyone to totally focus their efforts and energies in a positive manner.'

It worked as Rangers came out on top 3–2 thanks to a McCoist double and another from Ian Ferguson. It ensured that the Ibrox side kept a hold of their title and also had some silverware to try and lift the fragile spirits of Durrant.

Stevens added: 'It was my first trophy and to get it so early in my Rangers career was great. We played well on the day and although Aberdeen pushed us all the way I think we thoroughly deserved our win. It was a good day and for me, as one of the new boys, gave me my first taste of success at the club and now I was desperate for more. But then even the lads who had won quite a few medals at Rangers also felt the same. I think that was shown over the next nine seasons at the club.'

Rangers continued to push on in all the domestic competitions, despite longer-term injuries to Durrant and McCoist, while Woods was struck down by illness. It meant that the Rangers side often had to be patched up while short-term signings like Neale Cooper and Andy Gray were brought in to try and keep things ticking over.

Cooper had worked under Alex Ferguson and Archie Knox in the golden era at Aberdeen. He reckoned Souness, like Ferguson, knew the importance of having a top No. 2 behind him.

Cooper said: 'For me, Walter Smith was a bit like Archie Knox had been at Aberdeen. They were both assistant managers but they were strong individual characters. You could have a laugh or joke with them but if you didn't do things right then they wouldn't be slow in letting you know. A lot of the time the managers, like Sir Alex Ferguson and Graeme Souness, get all the plaudits but I don't think you could overestimate the part Walter and Archie played in their respective successes at Aberdeen and Rangers. That was why it wasn't really that much of a surprise that Walter asked Archie to become his No. 2 when he eventually became the Rangers manager. He knew, first-hand, the importance of having a good assistant standing beside him.'

Rangers might have been market leaders when it came to buying players but it seemed the club also had its price, as Graeme Souness convinced steel tycoon and top Scottish businessman David Murray to buy the club from Lawrence Marlborough. The Ibrox manager felt the new man, who had earlier failed to buy Scottish minnows Ayr United, had the financial muscle and business accumen to take the club on again. It certainly was a different style to the biscuit tin approach that was being operated on the other side of the city, which in the end was to leave Celtic with nothing but crumbs over the bulk of the next decade.

The news of the takeover boosted confidence on and off the field and Rangers turned on the after-burners and powered away from the chasing pack, although there was still time for another Souness wake-up call to make sure that nobody was to get too carried away. This time it came in the Scottish Cup where they flopped in the semi-final against St Johnstone. Rangers got out on jail after the 0–0 draw and at least would get a second crack at things. The players were told, in no uncertain terms, that if they didn't then their Rangers careers would be on the line.

Kevin Drinkell said: 'It was a sort of good cop, bad cop mix between Graeme and Walter. For example, when the Gaffer came in after our Scottish Cup draw with St Johnstone he read us the Riot Act and told us he would sell every single one of us if we didn't get things sorted in the replay. Graeme walked away and then Ray Wilkins had his say and it was then left for Walter to pick up the pieces and to get the guys going again. He would say, "Don't worry about the Gaffer. You are good players; just go out and play the way you know you can and you will be fine."

'Walter had a good rapport with the players because he was more of the go-between between them and the manager. Everybody had great respect for Walter and even though he was still learning his trade you could see he was a top coach. I am sure it would also have been a good learning curve for Walter as well, working with top internationals like Ray Wilkins, Terry Butcher and Chris Woods. They were all top players and I am sure even Walter would admit they made his job that bit easier.'

It was a warning the Ibrox squad were more than happy to heed as they thrashed the Saints three days later thanks to goals from Walters, Stevens, Drinkell and McCoist in an emphatic 4–0 win at Celtic Park. It set up an Old Firm Scottish Cup final but before then the Rangers team had their eyes on a far bigger prize – the title.

It became more a matter of when rather than if a couple of weeks before the semi-final when Rangers travelled across the city to claim their first win at Parkhead since 1980 thanks to a 2–1 victory. Goals from Kevin Drinkell and McCoist did the damage and left Celtic looking like April Fools that day.

Aberdeen became the main title contenders but Rangers just kept winning and the title was eventually wrapped up with four domestic games to play, as they thrashed Hearts 4–0 at Ibrox thanks to a brace apiece from Mel Sterling and Drinkell. The home fans had expected the wait to go on for at least another week but then the news filtered through that the Dons had slipped up against Celtic, and Rangers were officially champions again.

'I had won titles with Grimsby and Norwich and so it was brilliant to add another title on this side of the border,' said Drinkell, who had finished as the team's top scorer. 'I think we always felt we had the better team. We were buying genuine quality players and we knew if we played well then we would win the games. Over the season we were the better team and our results showed that. It was great to score a couple of goals in the game that saw us win the title against Hearts. We thought the title chase would go on for another few weeks but we were more than happy to hear that Celtic had done us a favour by taking points off Aberdeen. It was great to get over the line but the one thing everybody forgets is that we had a lot of injuries that season and there were spells where I had to play up front on my own or alongside Scott Nisbet, who was more of a defender. But we all mucked in and together we got over the line. I had been in Scotland for a season and I had walked away with a league and Skol Cup winner's medal. It had vindicated my decision to move to Scotland.'

There was also trouble off the pitch for Souness and Smith as they clashed with the authorities at the Scottish Football Association. The pair, for separate incidents, were both banned from the dugout for a year. Smith's came after he had been reported by an official for comments he made during a home clash with Motherwell. Souness was no stranger to the Park Garden beaks, but for Smith the punishment seemed a bit harsh as it was only the second time of note he had stepped out of line in his coaching career.

Striker Drinkell said: 'Walter Smith was certainly a strong character but it was normally Graeme Souness who was the more confrontational. He would be the one out in the press defending his players or having it out with opposition managers. I remember after a game at Motherwell that Graeme basically had Tommy McLean by the throat in the tunnel but Walter was a lot calmer, most of the time. There were times when he got into trouble with the authorities but that was pretty infrequent. It was quite funny because both Walter and Graeme got banned from the dugout at the same time. That left poor Phil Boersma in the dugout and he would spend most of the games on the radio getting instructions from Graeme and Walter up in the stands.'

The Rangers team, without their management team in the dugout, were able to free-wheel out their league campaign, although that would later to come back to haunt them as a combination of injuries and a failure to get back up the gears denied them a domestic treble.

Celtic stood between them and the clean-sweep. Souness's biggest problem was finding enough players to start as Ray Wilkins and Derek Ferguson missed out and Richard Gough was laid low by a virus the night before. It wasn't until the Rangers team got to Hampden that they knew Gough had shrugged off the virus and was able to start. But, like their key defender, the rest of the team were left feeling under the weather as their arch-rivals salvaged something from what had been a disastrous season for everyone in green and white. Rangers had a goal disallowed before a disastrous mistake from Gary Stevens at a throw-in let Joe Miller in for the only goal of the game.

A disappointed Stevens admitted: 'Graeme Souness came up to me after the game and said, "You were the best player out of the pitch, apart from that f****** pass back!" I have to say it didn't make me feel any better. I didn't need to be told that my throw-in had gifted Joe Miller his goal. It is bad enough when you lose a goal in the league but to gift a goal that costs you a cup final is almost indescribable. In the end to win the title and the League Cup was great for me but what happened in the Scottish Cup final took a wee bit of shine off things.'

Smith was adamant Rangers were undone by a number of controversial decisions that day, at both ends of the park. The Ibrox No. 2 recalled: 'There's not much I remember apart from this – it was never a throw-in. Roy Aitken took it yards away from where the ball went out to set up Joe Miller and then right at the end Terry Butcher scored and it was chalked off. Not that I'm biased!'

Smith may have been assistant but he had a major say in all the big decisions. Souness would regularly send him out to look at players and signing targets and would run everything by him, including his tactics and team selections. The set-up, which also included Boersma, was very much centred round the management 'team' and the work they were doing would be invaluable to Walter Smith in the future.

3

RANGERS FIND THEIR TITLE MO-JO

(1989–90)

THE 1989–90 campaign was one that rocked Scottish football and Graeme Souness, David Murray and Rangers were bang at the heart of it. Not content with grabbing headlines for their football and their already high-profile signings, they wanted to bring someone on to tackle the deep-rooted social problem of bigotry. Rangers had hardly been known for playing Roman Catholic players and that was something Souness was keen to address. He had initially tried to break that mould by signing the Republic of Ireland midfielder Ray Houghton, who was born in Glasgow, but that move failed to come off. Souness then turned his attentions to a more controversial target. Former Celtic star Maurice Johnston had only weeks earlier verbally agreed to return to Parkhead and had even posed at Parkhead in a Celtic strip and scarf. Before Souness made his move he ran things past his trusted assistant Walter Smith – who took seconds to agree that Johnston would definitely enhance their double-winning squad. The wheels were then set in motion before the 1988–89 season had even been played out.

Kevin Drinkell explained: 'After the Scottish Cup final, Graeme Souness came into the dressing room and told us not to be too downhearted to have lost. He said to let [Celtic] have their moment of glory because he knew something that would wipe the smile from their faces. He didn't say anything else. We were all still a bit down after losing the cup final and we never thought much more about it.

'It wasn't until we returned for pre-season that we got the full jist of what the manager had been talking about. We were on our way out to Il Ciocco in Italy and the morning before we left the transfer broke on the back pages. It had come out that Rangers had signed Mo Johnston. I think the club wanted to get us out of the way before they announced the deal. Mo was to meet the media that day while we headed out to Italy. Mo and Graeme later flew out by helicopter to join us.

'It was big news. Nobody could quite believe it. Mo was a good player but took things to another level. The madness erupted back home with Rangers fans burning scarves and throwing season tickets away, while Celtic fans were even more furious that Johnston had posed in the Celtic strip and then after being offered a few more pieces of silver acted, so they thought, like Judas. We couldn't even park our cars in the street outside of Ibrox because of all the threats. We had to park inside the ground and it was like a military exercise to get back out, as armed police guards checked under our cars for bombs or any suspect parcels. It really was madness.'

Souness made several other additions to his squad, like former Liverpool player Nigel Spackman, and he headed for the other side of Merseyside to land another England international from Everton, in the shape of Trevor Steven.

Steven said: 'It was an easy decision for me to join Rangers. They were a team who already had a number of established English internationals and it was a club where I felt I could win even more silverware. I had already won things at Everton and felt I could achieve even more in Scotland. I was also very impressed by Graeme Souness's plans for the club.'

The new boys came in with big price tags and even bigger reputations but that counted for nothing in the opening weeks of the season as they struggled to bed in. They were bought to make the Scottish champions even stronger but they, along with the rest of the squad, struggled to find their feet. The first two league games were lost to St Mirren and Hibs, although they continued to progress in the Skol Cup past Arbroath and Morton. It was hardly the ideal preparation for the first Old Firm game of the season which, of course, was dominated by Mo Johnston's return to Celtic Park for the first time as a Rangers player. That game and the following week's clash against Aberdeen proved instrumental in Johnston's bid to win over his doubters and, more importantly, the Rangers support.

Kevin Drinkell recalled: 'The build-up to that first Old Firm game was even bigger than normal because it was Mo's first visit to Celtic Park. There was extra security and it really was massive. It was bad enough for the rest of the boys but it must have been even worse for Mo, having to go to Parkhead worrying that some idiot might try to get to him. It must have been a big worry but to be fair he just went out and tried to play his game. You have to give him credit for that. Getting through that game was a big hurdle for Mo and he knew after surviving that he could survive anything.

'In the next game Mo then got his goal against Aberdeen. It proved to be the winner and I still remember it. The ball hit the net and there was this big roar and then there was a wee bit of a muted silence when the fans had realised that it was Mo who had scored.'

Johnston was helped through those difficult early months by the likes of Souness and Smith because he knew they had total faith in him. That was a forte of the Rangers management team, especially Smith who was the real link between the dressing room and the manager's office.

'When I first came in Walter was obviously the assistant manager, but even then you could see the qualities he had,' England star Steven recalled. 'He was always good at managing individuals. He knew how to handle players on an individual basis. He knew who he needed to have a quick word with or who just to leave to their own devices. I fell into the latter category and I didn't really have that many one-to-one discussions with Walter throughout my time at Rangers. I am sure if I had needed one then I could have gone to him. I certainly saw the influence he had on many of my team mates and he definitely managed to get a lot more out of some of the boys. Walter was always certainly very ambitious and even as No. 2 he wanted to win. That burning desire for success just got stronger when Walter became the main man.'

Ex-Liverpool midfielder Nigel Spackman added: 'I first worked with Walter as Graeme Souness's right hand man. They were a good team and I can only describe Walter as a top-class person. Graeme was very vocal and full on like he was as a player. Walter was more tranquil but when he said something you always took notice. He had the respect of all the players as a person and as a top-class coach. He was also somebody who was a good go-between for the players and the manager.'

Speaking to the majority of players who played under Souness it is clear that Smith was the one who kept things on the level. That was important when Rangers dropped points against Dunfermline and Dundee.

Right back Gary Stevens explained: 'Walter was initially the man behind Souness and he was certainly a very important man at that time. Graeme, as everyone knows, could blow hot and cold and when he did explode it was normally left to Walter to try and get things back on an even keel. There is no doubt Graeme learned a lot tactically from Walter while it is also to be fair that Walter would also have learned a bit from working under Graeme.'

Souness was far from happy as his side failed to kick into life and his mood was hardly helped by another European nightmare. This time their campaign lasted all of two games as they crashed out to the might of German giants Bayern Munich.

They lost the first game at Ibrox 3–1, which all but put them out of the running although the Light Blues were severely hand-icapped by suspensions to Ally McCoist and Drinkell. The second leg needed an almighty turnaround but Souness again, like in the first-leg, started with one sole striker and that was to be the death knell for Drinkell's Ibrox career.

'When Mo Johnston signed for Rangers it suddenly meant there were three of us, Ally, Mo and I, fighting it out for two spots,' Drinkell revealed. 'I had concerns and I went to see the manager and he was honest and up front. He told me that I would play in the big games against the likes of Aberdeen, Celtic and Hearts, etc and Mo and Ally would play against the so-called lesser teams like Dunfermline, Dundee and Motherwell, etc. The manager was trying to introduce a squad rotation system. It is all the rage now but back then it was pretty alien. I had been used to playing as the main striker every week and so I found it hard to get my head round the fact that I wasn't going to play every week. I just wanted to play. I was really frustrated that I hadn't started in that second leg against Bayern Munich. I was pretty annoyed and then we had got back home in the early hours when the phone went. It was the manager telling me he had agreed a fee with Coventry City and it was now up to me if I wanted to join them. I went and spoke to Graeme and he said, "You have to do what is best for your family." I was being offered more money and the chance to play every week so it looked a decent move – it was also back to the English top flight and it wasn't long after Coventry had won the FA Cup so the move had a lot going for it. I decided to go but within weeks I knew I had made the wrong move and leaving Rangers, when I did, turned out to be the biggest regret of my career.'

Inconsistency continued to be Rangers' biggest problem. They lost to Motherwell, surrendered the Skol Cup final to Aberdeen and then lost to the Dons again at Pittodrie. They did beat Celtic at Ibrox, with a certain Mr Johnston scoring the only goal of the game. Souness was keen to get a title charge up and going again. His team did precisely that putting together a great run from December into the New Year, where Nigel Spackman's goal beat Celtic and Mark Walters and Ally McCoist took care of Aberdeen.

The champions were back in the groove and the team unity was there for all to see – on and off the pitch. Midfielder John Brown explained how their management team made sure of that.

Brown explained: '[Graeme] always encouraged the boys to go out and socialise and have a drink. Once a month we would head off to a restaurant in Kelvinbridge and he would let us have a few beers and glasses of wine so we could relax and unwind. Graeme would have a few drinks and would leave us, but most of the time Walter stayed out to the death. Those nights were great and forged the team spirit that the nine-in-a-row success was built on. All the players would come out and it brought us closer together. When it came to the football on a Saturday we all knew the guy sitting on either side of us would go out and run that extra yard for you. That was a big thing. We did go out a lot socially but only when the time was right and, to be fair, we also had a lot to celebrate during that period.'

Smith also wasn't one for missing a night out with the boys whether it be Saturday Night at the Movies or Under the Board Walk. Ian Ferguson admitted: 'Walter also liked a night out. I remember one night Walter and I took our wives to the Edmiston Club to see the Drifters. It was a great evening and at one point Walter was up standing on the chair singing and dancing. Here was our Gaffer who had delivered all these trophies and titles up there like every other punter. That is the good thing about Walter – he knows how to separate work from his social life – although I am not so sure Mrs Smith will, maybe, agree with me!'

Rangers also still had plenty to toast in the run-in – although a Scottish Cup exit to Celtic did put a bit of a dampener on things. Aberdeen struggled to keep up with the league leaders and the title was eventually wrapped up at Tannadice thanks to Trevor Steven's goal in a 1–0 win over Dundee United.

The hero said: 'I still believe the Rangers side that I played in will go down as one of the greatest in the club's history. I know at that time that Graeme Souness and Walter Smith had an open cheque book but you still have to buy the right players and they did that superbly well.'

John Brown still remembers the title celebrations and how he almost blew his Rangers career after getting on the wrong side of Smith. 'We had some big characters back then and we could all dish it out when it came to pranks and dressing-room banter,' Bomber explained. 'I remember I stepped over the line one day and nearly threw my Rangers career away. We had just won the league at Tannadice thanks to Trevor Steven's goal. On the way back down the road the manager got the team coach to stop off at a hotel to stock up on champagne and beers for the remainder of the trip. We were all mucking about and I took one of the bottles out of a metal ice bucket and, as I did, one of its handles came down and cracked Walter on the head. He was absolutely raging and he said: "You will be playing for Stranraer by Monday morning, ya b******!" Reading it now it might have sounded like a wind-up but back then he was being deadly serious. He hardly spoke to me the rest of the night and I knew I was in trouble. I honestly feared I would be out the door but it wasn't until Phil Boersma sat me down later on that I realised that he wasn't really being serious. Needless to say I apologised and never did anything like that to upset Walter again. We all got a bollocking at some point but that didn't stop us having the utmost respect for Walter.'

4

FOUR GAMES TO WIN THE TITLE – WELCOME TO THE IBROX HOTSEAT, MR SMITH

(1990–91)

THE EARLY headlines of the summer were once again hogged by the highly controversial Maurice Johnston. This time it wasn't so much his high-profile arrival at Rangers but his early departure from the club's Italian pre-season camp in Il Ciocco. The Scotland star was disciplined and sent home by manager Graeme Souness after some drunken high jinks. It was hardly the ideal preparations for a team who were looking to win a third consecutive championship.

Defender Scott Nisbet recalled the famous night that evoked the wrath of Walter Smith before Souness sent him packing. Nisbet said: 'The manager let all the boys who had been at the World Cup stay up a bit later to have a few more drinks and sent the rest of us up to our beds. Mo was obviously a bit worse for wear and suddenly appeared at our bedroom door and tried to get in. I was rooming with Ian Ferguson so we decided to bolt the door to keep him out. Fergie and I were big lads and the beds were too small and so we had thrown the mattresses on the floor and slept there. The next thing we knew there was water and bubbles coming under the door. Mo had decided to relief himself. He then, somehow, forced the door open and came flying in. He didn't realise my mattress was in front of the door and he went flying into it and got himself in a right mess because he went right through it and head first into the springs. He had obviously hurt himself and when he got up he was absolutely furious. I think he thought we had set it up as a bit of a trap for him, but we didn't. He was raging and started throwing bottles of water everywhere.

'Walter was sent up to calm him down and he left Mo without a name. He gave him a right dressing-down and then sent him back to his room. Mo was sharing with Ally McCoist but when he got back there he woke everybody up again, as he started to throw lamps and furniture about. Walter was sent up again and by all accounts he didn't miss Mo. The next day Mo apologised to all the boys but by then the damage had been done. The manager felt he had crossed the line and sent him home early.'

Johnston knew he had over-stepped the mark and had to try and appease Souness, Smith and the rest of his team mates. He was also aware that competition for the two striking berths was as fierce as ever with Ally McCoist and new signing Mark Hateley, who was checking in after an injury-hit time in Monaco. To be fair to Johnston, he took his punishment on the chin and responded in the best way possible – by sticking the ball in the back of the net. Johnston netted four goals in five games as the Light Blues made an impressive start to the 1990–91 campaign.

Former England cap Hateley arrived with a huge reputation thanks to successful spells in France and then in Italy with AC Milan. The big striker was desperate to get his career back on track but admitted his early months at Ibrox were actually harder mentally than physically. Souness decided that Hateley with his strength and aerial physique was going to be his main striker, with Johnston and McCoist scrapping it out to partner him. More often than not it was Johnston who got the nod and that upset the Ibrox faithful as their favourite 'Super Ally' was given more of a cameo role from the bench.

Hateley explained: 'That first season was the hardest one in all my time at Rangers. I had been out for nearly two years at Monaco before I agreed to join Rangers. I had struggled in my last couple of seasons in France after four operations on my knee but I was fit when I joined Rangers. I played a lot of the season up front next to Mo Johnston and it upset some sections of the Rangers support because Ally McCoist was being left out. People blamed me for keeping Ally out but it wasn't me, it was Mo. Mo was a similar sort of player to Ally while I was more of a physical presence. The manager told me it was either going to be Mo and me or Ally and me.'

A lot of people believed that it was a simple personality clash between Souness and McCoist but Smith is adamant that wasn't the case. Smith later said: 'As a manager, you have choices to make, and that first season Mark Hateley did very well for us. People thought it was a personal thing between Graeme and Ally, but it wasn't. At that time nobody could be guaranteed a game every week at Rangers. It would be almost impossible to play in every game because, if we were successful, then some of our international players would have ended up having to play around seventy games.'

Hateley, Johnston and McCoist were also helped as promising Dutch winger Pieter Huistra was brought in from Twente Enschede to supply the ammunition for Rangers' goal-hungry strikers. The new boy added competition alongside Mark Walters and made an instant impression. He admitted it was Smith and Phil Boersma who really helped him settle in.

Huistra said: 'At the time Graeme was the main man and everybody looked up to him but I always found it difficult to go and speak to him. He was more distant and Walter was more of the link between Graeme and the players. It was also Walter and Phil Boersma who did most of the everyday training because Souness was still playing at the time. There is no doubt the three of them worked well as a unit.'

The new-look Rangers were scoring goals for fun and playing

well although Smith also muscled in on those headlines after a frustrating goalless draw against St Johnstone at McDiarmid Park. Smith and Saints manager Alex Totten got involved in an ugly clash which saw both end up in court. Totten was done for a breach of the peace while the charge against the Rangers No. 2 was found not proven. Smith, throughout his career, has never been scared of confrontation – whether it be one of his players, an opposition manager or even the press. That stems back to his coaching days at Dundee United where he was widely viewed as Jim McLean's enforcer. He has always had a reputation for standing up for himself and what he feels is right. He has also frequently demonstrated that he is loyal to the core and will defend his team and his players to the end.

The Ibrox side were showing just as much fight on the pitch although there was to be more European heartache. Maltese minnows Valletta were easily swept aside but Yugoslavian outfit Red Star Belgrade proved to be a far different proposition in the second round of the European Cup.

The damage was done in the first game out in Yugoslavia where goals from an emerging Robert Prosinecki, Darko Pancev and a John Brown own goal all but made the Ibrox return something of a non-event. It was another sore one for Souness, who was keen to win the competition and the cup he had so gloriously lifted as a player with Liverpool.

Spirits were lifted before the second leg, as Rangers saw off Celtic 2–1 at Hampden, thanks to goals from Walters and Richard Gough, to get their hands on the Skol Cup once again. Those celebrations were, however, quickly dampened when a disappointing 1–1 home draw with Red Star sealed their European exit. Once again they had to make do with domestic bliss, although Aberdeen pushed them all the way.

Rangers were moving along quite nicely although their hopes of a domestic treble were wrecked by Celtic in the quarter-finals of the Scottish Cup. At that point, Rangers had more pressing concerns. English giants Liverpool were on the lookout for a new boss after the legendary Kenny Dalglish had decided to step down. Anfield eyes suddenly started to turn to Ibrox and one of their favourite sons.

Souness knocked back the first approach but Liverpool refused to give up and eventually got their man. Souness and Boersma both agreed to the switch and wanted Smith to join them. Rangers midfielder and former Liverpool star Nigel Spackman admitted: 'I had to say that Graeme's departure came as a bit of a shock. Graeme had signed me from Liverpool and I just didn't think he would ever leave Rangers. I think if anybody else other than Liverpool had come in for Graeme then he would have turned them down. I think the emotional pull and tie that Graeme had with Liverpool was just too much for him to turn the Anfield job down.'

Dalglish, Terry Venables and even Alex Ferguson were all tipped to replace Souness at the Ibrox helm. Chairman David Murray, however, was looking a little closer to home and was in no doubt that Smith was ready to step out of the shadows and become the main man.

Smith admitted he was lucky and honoured to be handed the top Ibrox job at that time. He said: 'When Graeme left, I had no track record as a manager and Sir David Murray could have gone anywhere to get someone who had that. He took a chance on me and it couldn't have been an easy decision for him. I will always be grateful to him for that opportunity. Graeme had offered me the opportunity to go with him, but there were too many people at Liverpool at that time and I didn't want to. There was no guarantee I'd get the Rangers job and no guarantee of employment after that, so I don't know where I would have ended up. I might have been back at Dalmarnock power station, I don't know.'

Scott Nisbet recalled the announcement. He said: 'When Graeme Souness went to Liverpool I remember all the players were called into a meeting. Sir David Murray was there and he gathered us all together and told us Walter was going to be our new manager. I still remember it because all the boys were absolutely delighted. We all knew Walter well, respected him and knew he was a top coach. He had done most of the training during Souness's time anyway. He also loved to referee the Scotland v England matches during training on a Friday afternoon. They were full-blooded battles and I don't know how he managed to name a team on a Saturday with some of the challenges that were going about.'

Smith also inherited a well-oiled team that he had been instrumental in building. His side had a wealth of experience and he wasn't slow in giving the more experienced heads like McCoist, Spackman and Hateley an input into things.

Spackman said: 'The good thing for Walter was he was taking over a group of players who already had a winning mentality. Graeme and Walter had installed that in us and we were able to just get on with it. Whoever took on the job wasn't going to need to do a lot of work. If any. In the end Sir David Murray decided to give Walter his chance and I think history shows that he couldn't have made a better appointment. Walter stepped up and built on the blueprint that Graeme and he had put in place for the long-term success of Rangers.'

The new manager, who recruited Archie Knox as his No. 2, was handed the reins with just four games of the season remaining and kicked off with a hard-fought win over St Mirren, thanks to a Sandy Robertson goal, while Dundee United were also beaten by an Ian Ferguson goal. Aberdeen, on the back of an eleven-game unbeaten run, kept up the pressure and awaited a slip. It came in the second last game of the season at Fir Park, as Rangers were smashed 3–0 by Scottish Cup finalists Motherwell, while the Dons won to climb top of the table. Alex Smith's side knew that a draw on the final day at Ibrox would be enough to see them crowned champions.

The match was massive and just four games in suddenly Walter Smith was facing a game that was going to make or break his managerial career. Looking back, John Brown said: 'The biggest thing when Walter took over was all the unrest caused by Graeme's departure but to his credit he knuckled down and did brilliantly to turn things around. It all came down to the final game, which was only Walter's fourth as our manager. Everything that could have gone wrong seemed to go wrong for the Gaffer during that early period. The team failed to settle and we had injuries galore. The pressure was really on the Gaffer going into that last game against Aberdeen. We needed to win while Aberdeen only needed a draw for the title. Looking back the Gaffer had a thankless task. If we had won the league then it would have been Graeme's team and if we had lost it then people would have questioned whether or not he was up to the job.'

Smith not only had that pressure but he could probably have contemplated pulling on his own boots again, such was the injury crisis that hit his title-chasing squad. Battling Brown was one who shouldn't have played but was determined to dig deep for his team mates and Smith. Brown explained: 'I was really struggling with an Achilles problem for that Aberdeen game. We were down in numbers and Walter came to me and asked if I would play. He said something like, "I know you will break down at some point but I just need you out there." I took a painkilling injection to get through the game. I played my part although I did end up rupturing my Achilles and being sidelined for the next four months. It was worth it just to win the title. I don't regret it and that title was probably the biggest one for me. I know how much it also meant to Walter. He still shakes my hand to this day because he knows how big a game it was for him and Rangers.'

Ally McCoist and Ian Durrant were also far from fit but Smith believed their sheer presence on the bench could give Ibrox a lift if needed. Nigel Spackman said: 'Results didn't go the way Walter had hoped initially but that had nothing to do with Walter. It was down to the fact we had an absolutely horrendous injury list. Guys like Ally McCoist, Mo Johnston, Richard Gough and Ian

Ferguson were all out for long spells. It was no wonder we struggled, losing players of that ilk out of our squad. I was one of Walter's more senior players and in Richard Gough's absence I was given the captain's armband. I was the captain going into the final game of the season title decider against Aberdeen. I remember Walter pulled me in and showed me his team and asked me for my thoughts. Coisty and Durrant weren't 100 per cent fit but he told me he was going to name them on the bench because they were still capable of producing a bit of magic or grabbing a goal. He also knew seeing them step on to the pitch would give the fans a big lift because they were both firm favourites with the Ibrox faithful. It turned out to be a masterstroke on the day.'

Such was the quality of Smith's squad that he was still able to disappoint Pieter Huistra, who had been desperate to play, not just to seal the title but because of the huge Dutch contingent that been instrumental in pulling Aberdeen back into the title race. Players like Hans Gillhaus, Willem van der Ark and goalkeeper Theo Snelders. Huistra recalled: 'Aberdeen had a good team and also had a lot of Dutch players. So it was interesting for me as a fellow Dutchman going into that game. I was really looking forward to it and so it was a bit of a blow when I found out I wasn't involved. But there was always a lot of competition for the left-wing position during my time at Rangers, whether it was Mark Walters or Alexei Mikhailichenko. I had been in and out of the team and so when the team was pinned up my name wasn't in the team or amongst the substitutes. It was a disappointment but I was still quite young and just had to accept the manager's decision. I just went to the game to cheer the boys on and although I was a bit down personally the manager's decision proved the right one.'

The hero of the day was a man who on an afternoon of destiny delivered and finally won over his Ibrox doubters, as Mark Hateley netted a dream double to lift the championship he so desperately wished for.

Hateley said: 'Aberdeen only needed to draw to become champions. We just got up and at it from the first whistle and we got the win we needed. I was lucky enough to grab the goals. The first came when Mark Walters swung in a cross and I managed to rise above the Aberdeen defender Alex McLeish to head the ball home. People say it was a typical Mark Hateley strike! It proved to be a big goal that day and we went on to seal the title thanks to my second goal – a tap-in. It was great to get the goals that day but over the course of the season it had been a real team effort and that was our strength throughout all my years at Rangers. I also think that day went a long way to me winning over the Rangers support. It is certainly a day I will never forget.'

Smith, speaking at the time, was full of praise for Hateley and all his players as they helped him to step out of the shadows of Souness. He said: 'Mark Hateley had to battle all season and I hope the fans appreciate the job he has done for us. I can't praise him enough. We've had our troubles all the way through but against Aberdeen the players showed their determination to succeed. It was not one of our best performances in terms of football, but in terms of character it was the best of the four Championships wins since I came here.'

The victory was even more remarkable due to the fact that Brown and Tam Cowan both had to limp off. So it really was a case of last man standing for Smith and his men.

Scott Nisbet explained: 'We were clear and when Walter took over we went on a really bad run and it came down to the final game of the season against Aberdeen. It was a real "winner takes all" game. I remember John Brown snapped his Achilles and Tam Cowan also broke his nose. It was a real battle but we ended up coming through on the day 2–0 to win the title.'

Ian Ferguson was delighted to finally get over the line but knows Rangers should never have let Aberdeen back into the title race. Ferguson conceded: 'We were probably very fortunate to win the title that season. Aberdeen pushed us all the way and if we hadn't have won that final game then we wouldn't have won that title. Aberdeen had a good side and had done brilliantly to get back into the position they did. I think they were maybe something like thirteen points behind and they had managed to claw it back. I don't know why we dropped off so badly. I don't know if we took our foot off the pedal or we were just off form and in the end injuries and suspensions just caught up on us. In the end it helped to make it such an exciting title race, although I am not sure the Rangers fans would agree with me.

'If I am being honest I never thought we were ever going to lose that game. That is not me being blasé but there was such a belief in our dressing room that we were going to win it. It was only heightened when we walked out on to the pitch because the stadium was packed and the atmosphere was just electric. Even during that game Aberdeen had a couple of chances before we even had a shot on goal but I still felt confident that we would do it. Sometimes you need a stroke of luck and we probably got it in that title race but we also went out and did the business when it really mattered. I still have some fabulous memories of that game when the whistle went, knowing we were champions again.'

John Brown insisted that Walter Smith deserves enormous credit for patching up his squad and being able to put out a team that was strong enough to make one final stance. 'That day the spirit he managed to muster got everything out of a team that was on its last legs,' the long-serving midfielder insisted. 'For me that game just typified Walter Smith as a person, a motivator and a man-manager. That, for me, was the making of Walter Smith the manager. He sent the fans home happy with another title and proved he could do the job. Look at the success he went on to have. Would he have got the chance if he hadn't won that title? Who knows? But he did and now the rest, as they say, is history.'

Ian Durrant also believes that Smith deserved all the credit for that particular championship. The midfielder said: 'As far as I am concerned it was the Gaffer who won us that league. Graeme Souness might have been in charge for ninety per cent of the season but it was the Gaffer who brought us together and got us over the line. He got us the wins when it really mattered. Beating Aberdeen that day was the start of everything.'

Ally McCoist has pretty much seen it all in his Ibrox career but even he admitted that he had never experienced a game like that Aberdeen one – where the winner really did take all!

The Scotland star recalled: 'The final day victory over Aberdeen was incredible. It was such an emotional occasion. I have never experienced anything like it in my life – one game where everything was at stake. It was one we had to win because we knew a draw would have been no use. What is even more amazing was that maybe five of the players who were in the starting XI or even on the bench shouldn't even have been there. They were all injured and in normal circumstances they wouldn't have been involved but we all knew how important this game was. I don't mind admitting that I actually broke down in tears after the game that day. It was just such a great feeling and an emotional day.'

It was left to stand-in skipper Spackman, in the absence of Richard Gough, to lift the championship trophy and hand Walter Smith the first of his managerial titles.

A proud Nigel Spackman beamed: 'As captain I was handed the SPL trophy and I knew I was a very lucky man to lift the trophy aloft and it gave me almost as much satisfaction passing it on to Walter. It was his first trophy as Rangers manager and a big moment in the club's history. I am sure that day was as special to Walter as it was to me.'

5

THE GOALIE, THE REAL McCALL
AND WALTER'S EASTERN BLOC

(1991–92)

THE 1991–92 season was always going to be a massive challenge for Walter Smith. Now the buck stopped with him. He was the one making all the big decisions, buying and selling players. Smith now had Rangers' destiny in his hands.

It was his first full season as manager and Smith admitted he initially found it hard to distance himself from the same players he had worked and bonded with in his position as assistant to Graeme Souness. He explained: 'I had to take a step back and I found that difficult. I knew I was now going to have to make decisions that some of the players would not like. We had a high standard of players at the club and none of them were ever going to be happy at being left out of the team. That was something I had to learn to handle after so long as a coach. For thirteen years I've had closeness with the players. I'd worked with them, trained with them and chatted to them every day. My duties were suddenly very different.'

Smith decided to make changes. He also had to consider the new foreigner rule that was introduced to the Champions League and, as a result, had to try and bring in more home-grown players. One of his first targets was a new goalkeeper to replace the long-serving Chris Woods. He didn't have to look far, just along the

M8 where he believed the Hibs goalkeeper Andy Goram was the man to fill such legendary gloves.

Goram admitted: 'There was a lot of pressure on me when I signed for Rangers. The Gaffer had paid £1 million to sign me from Hibs and I was also replacing a big fans' favourite in Chris Woods. They were big shoes to fill and I hardly helped with my first few performances. I thought the Gaffer was actually going to ask Hibs for his money back at one stage because I was that bad!'

Smith also moved for Scottish international midfielder Stuart McCall, who came in from Everton, and raided title rivals Aberdeen to land highly-rated left back David Robertson.

Robertson, who cost just under £1 million, explained: 'My last game for Aberdeen before I joined Rangers was the title decider on the final day at Ibrox that cost us the title. So it was strange to suddenly be making the move to Ibrox.

'After Aberdeen had accepted Rangers' offer Walter Smith actually drove all the way up to Stonehaven and I met him in a lay-by, beside the old Commodore Hotel. There and then I knew he was a guy I wanted to play for. Then when I went to Ibrox for the first time I was greeted by the commissioner and I could see all the trophies and traditions that came with a club like Rangers. It really was something else and I hadn't experienced anything like it before even though Aberdeen were a great club. Also when I walked into the dressing room I was given my training kit by Jimmy Bell. It had the No. 6 on it. Jimmy said, "That used to be Terry Butcher's so there's no pressure on you!"'

The rivalry between Aberdeen and Rangers has always been fierce but it was stoked up as a result of the climax of the previous campaign. The Dons were left to harbour a summer of heartbreak and the departure of one of their star assets, Robertson, hardly helped the strained relationship between the bitter rivals. It also seemed that not everybody approved of the transfer and the new boy was sent chilling death threats. Robertson was shocked but determined it wasn't going to stop him making a name for himself.

'When I first arrived at Rangers I actually received death threats through the post,' Robertson admitted. Whoever sent them had cut letters out of a newspaper and stuck them on a piece of paper and mailed them to Ibrox. I was young and naive. I was only twenty-one and I didn't give it a second thought. I didn't even tell Walter or anybody at the club. I just got on with it. I don't even know who sent them but it didn't stop me going out shopping in Glasgow, etc. Maybe if it had happened now then I would have taken it a lot more seriously, but back then I didn't really bat an eyelid. Looking back it really was madness because anything could have happened to me and I hadn't even told anybody.'

Most of the money that Smith spent during that period was recouped by the big-money sale of Trevor Steven to French champions Marseille, in a £5.5 million switch.

Steven said: 'That was the thing about Walter, he wasn't afraid to make big decisions. He sold me to Marseille and then bought me back again. What Walter had was this great ability to manage his squad. He had an abundance of top players and knew when and how to use people. Also to his credit he, somehow, managed to keep even his top players happy. You also have to remember Walter was under a lot of pressure both domestically and especially on the European front. He couldn't afford too many mistakes in the transfer market and to be fair he didn't have many.'

Rangers continued to hold their position at the top of the Scottish game but there were also a few wake-up calls along the way, especially in the Champions League. Rangers crashed out 1–0 in Czechoslovakia to Sparta Prague while there were to be other costly defeats before the Ibrox second leg. They lost the Skol Cup as they gave way in the last four to eventual winners Hibs, and then Aberdeen came to Govan and won 2–0 to prove they would be genuine title contenders once again. Smith's response was to delve into the transfer market again and in ground-breaking style brought in a couple of USSR internationals to Scotland. He signed talented midfielder Alexei Mikhailichenko from Sampdoria and cultured defender Oleg Kuznetsov from Dynamo Kyiv, but even the new arrivals couldn't spark an extended European run. A double from McCall put Rangers in the driving seat against Sparta Prague before another late twist again crushed Ibrox hopes, thanks to Horst Siegl's last-minute goal cruelly sending Smith's side spinning out on away goals.

'The Goalie' also found himself in the firing line after some sub-standard performances. His manager could see things weren't right and threw an arm of support around Goram by bringing in the keeper's mentor, Alan Hodginson, to try and get him back to the form he showed at both Oldham and Hibs.

Goram recalled: 'I got us knocked out of the League Cup, I also threw one in against Hearts and I was also far from convincing as Sparta Prague knocked us out of the Champions League. It was a nightmare!

'The Gaffer called me into his office to talk about things. He said he wasn't a goalkeeper but didn't think I was doing too much wrong. I also felt I was doing the basics right and it was only down to a wee run of bad luck. I certainly looked at every aspect of my play and there was nobody more self-critical about their performances than me. Walter asked me if there was anything he could do to help me. We didn't have a goalkeeping coach at the time and I asked if there was any chance he could bring Alan Hodgkinson up. I had lost my dad a few years earlier and Alan had coached me and became my father figure and somebody who I looked up to in the game. Walter told me to leave it with him and he went and had a word with the chairman [David Murray]. Then the next thing I knew Alan was being employed, initially on a part-time basis, as Rangers' goalkeeping coach. It was a great gesture from the manager and the club and goes to show the lengths he goes to for his players.'

David Robertson also admitted that he struggled with the sheer weight of expectation that came with playing for a big club. 'The

Skol Cup semi-final defeat was the match where the manager really slaughtered me and rightly so,' Robertson candidly admitted. 'I didn't play well and Walter didn't waste any time in telling me. He said I had been hiding and didn't want the ball. My confidence was probably a wee bit down but even when things weren't going for you Walter always wanted you to show character. He said, "I don't care if you keep getting the ball and losing it or you keep putting the ball into the stand. We can't afford to play with ten players, we need everybody out there pulling in the right direction. I want you to keep showing for the ball."

'It didn't matter if you kept making mistakes because Walter would always encourage you to get over them. That was a wee bit of a bad spell for the club because a few weeks later we also went out of Europe when we lost to Sparta Prague. The other low points were the defeat at Hearts and my Old Firm sending off later that season but, fortunately, there were a lot more highs than lows.'

Smith lost the attacking wing talents of Mark Walters who decided to return south to work with Souness again at Liverpool. The signing of Mikhailichenko would help but the Rangers boss also felt he needed another winger and his search led him to sign Norwich City's Dale 'Disco' Gordon.

Gordon explained: 'I was aware Rangers were watching me and it was under Graeme Souness I had first come on to their radar. I had heard they had been down to watch me five or six times but then Souness left for Liverpool and I thought nothing more about it. Then Souness took Mark Walters with him and suddenly I was told that Norwich had accepted a bid from Rangers for me. I went to Heathrow to meet Walter. That was my first meeting with him. I also knew very little about Rangers although my Norwich team mate Robert Fleck had spoken a bit about them and Chris Woods and Kevin Drinkell had also made the same switch, successfully, before me.'

England B cap Gordon cost Rangers in excess of £1 million and instantly proved his worth with two goals in a five-goal rout of Dunfermline before he made a winning start in his first Old Firm clash. He also helped to make it a decent end to the year with a 3–2 win over Aberdeen and a 3–1 New Year's Day win over Celtic, as Ally McCoist, Mark Hateley and John Brown all got on the scoresheet.

Gordon said: 'I remember my first few games. Things couldn't have gone any better as I scored twice in a 5–0 win over Dunfermline. Then my Old Firm debut on New Year's Day was special as we beat Celtic 3–1 at Celtic Park. That was an unbelievable day. That was the first time I had played an away game where we had 25,000 fans cheering us on. At Norwich we would have had 1,000 to 1,500 if we were lucky. Richard Gough came up to me before the game and said as soon as you get the ball get rid of it, don't try to do anything fancy. So a couple of minutes in I controlled the ball on my chest and took it down and suddenly the Celtic defender Tom Boyd smashed right into me. I thought, "What has happened here?" and then seconds later Richard was right up at me with his finger in my face telling me I should have got rid of the ball earlier. We played well and Coisty and John Brown scored while Mark Hateley scored a penalty after, let us just say, a dubious stumble from Coisty.'

Celtic, once again, faltered over the longer term and this time the gauntlet was taken up by Hearts. But even then their championship charge couldn't be sustained as the Light Blues pushed away to stamp out any thoughts of a capital rising. A McCoist goal at Tynecastle in early February was enough to kill off their stubborn resistance.

'That was the season where Hearts were our main challengers for the title,' Gordon recalled. 'They weren't far away around that hectic early year period and I remember we beat them at Tynecastle in the February. It was a big result, which not only boosted our own hopes but had a real damaging effect on Hearts.

I really enjoyed that season because the team did well and I contributed with a few goals which, personally, was nice.'

The following week a hard-fought win over St Mirren kept Rangers in top gear, although Smith proved a hard task master as he demanded not only results but top-drawer performances into the bargain.

Nigel Spackman painfully recalled falling foul of his manager after that trip to Paisley. He explained: 'The only time Walter really lost it and got cross with me was in a game away at St Mirren. He came in and just started having a go at me because he felt I hadn't done my job properly. He was so angry that he turned and kicked one of the metal kit hampers that was beside him. He really smashed it and right away I could see he had hurt his foot but I certainly wasn't brave enough to say anything. Then the Gaffer went into the shower and at one point I actually thought he might have broken his ankle but I just kept my head down. I had already upset him enough. We ended up winning the game and a couple of days later I asked how his ankle was. He said, "You didn't see that I had hurt my ankle, did you?" I said yes and he said: "It was your f*****' fault!" It was the only real incident where Walter actually lost it with me. That was down to the fact he was such a great man-manager. He didn't need to shout and scream that often to get his point across.'

Scott Nisbet got it in the neck the following week for a sub-standard performance in the Scottish Cup win over Motherwell. Nisbet admitted: 'The good thing about the manager is that he always treated his players with respect, but when he lost it he really lost it. He was one of the most passionate guys I have seen in all my time in football. I remember him losing it with me at half-time in a match with Motherwell. We were struggling and he let me have it for an awful clearance. It didn't cost us a goal but let's just say I struggled to get the ball in the stadium! He, quite rightly, was far from impressed.'

But Smith's fury wasn't exclusively reserved for the first team.

He wouldn't be slow in coming down hard on his second string either if they weren't pulling their weight or maintaining the immaculate standards he had set for the club.

Pieter Huistra explained: 'My biggest dressing-down from Walter actually came in a reserve game against Airdrie. I didn't play well and Walter came in at half-time and gave me pelters. He just gave it to me straight. I hadn't worked hard enough and he wasn't shy in letting me know. Walter might have been an easy-going guy but that front would quickly disappear if he didn't see players giving him their all.'

It was the Scottish Cup semi-final against Celtic where Nigel Spackman reckoned he saw Smith at his motivational best. Rangers went down to ten men after David Robertson's early red card but still managed to go in ahead at the break thanks to a McCoist goal. Smith rallied the troops again and they saw the game out and booked their final place against Airdrie.

Spackman acknowledged that the inspirational night had Walter Smith's fingerprints all over it. 'There were so many Walter Smith moments but the one that probably stands out for me was the Scottish Cup semi-final with Celtic,' explained the Englishman. 'David Robertson got sent off early in the game and we played the majority of the game with ten men. I actually had to drop back to centre half and help us get a result. I still remember Walter's team talk. It was so inspirational and we actually walked back on the park feeling as if we had eleven men again. We managed to get the result we needed through Ally McCoist's goal.'

Robertson admitted he could have little complaint over his red card. He explained: 'I got sent off six minutes in against Celtic. Terry Butcher was doing the co-commentary that night and he thought I had been harshly treated, but if I had made the challenge I did on Joe Miller today then I would have probably ended up in jail. He was my old Aberdeen team mate but I just body-checked him and took him straight out. Walter came in at half-time and he asked me what had happened. I was expecting a right blast but he said that was a joke [talking about the referee's decision]. He backed me when so many other managers would have quite easily hung me out to dry in front of my other team mates.'

Pieter Huistra recalled how Robertson's early departure forced him to curb his natural attacking tendencies in order to cover for his missing team mate. 'The semi-final win where we beat Celtic was the one outstanding Old Firm moment for me,' Huistra beamed. 'David Robertson, our left back, had been sent off after four or five minutes and that left us up against it. I ended up playing up the left hand side myself and we managed to dig in to get a 1–0 win. Old Firm wins were always good but in the circumstances that we won that one was even better for me.'

The Light Blues had built up a commanding lead at the top of the table and allowed Smith to hand a debut to another of his Ibrox protégés. Steven Pressley was at that time an emerging central defender, dubbed as the new Richard Gough. Pressley remembers his early years and how Smith and Knox turned him into a polished performer.

'Walter gave me my debut at Motherwell and it was great,' Pressley recalls. 'He showed a lot of faith in me to throw me in at such an early age. I was only eighteen at the time. I had played in the Glasgow Cup as a fifteen-year-old and I think that was maybe the first time I had caught the manager's eye. As a young-ster I had a few tasks and one of my regular jobs was to clean the Gaffer and Archie's cars. I also had to do little things like clean their shoes. A lot of the young players would complain and refuse to do it but not me. I think it gave me a great grounding and looking back Walter and Archie probably used it as a gauge of your character. I was more than happy to do what I was told and to get on with things. I saw it as an education that would hopefully help to make me a better person. I think that discipline is something that is sadly lacking in the modern game, especially amongst some of the younger players. I certainly have a lot to be grateful to Walter and Archie for.'

The title was eventually won at a canter and was clinched in some style as St Mirren were thrashed 4–0 at Ibrox. A double from a rejuvenated McCoist and further strikes from Gary Stevens and Huistra ensured the league was wrapped up with an impressive three games to play, well ahead of Hearts and Celtic, who finished second and third, respectively.

Smith was delighted. His team had won the title and this time there could be no accusations or fingers pointed that it wasn't all his own work. 'That was an extra special day for me,' Smith admitted. 'To lift the biggest prize in Scottish football in my first full season as manager was so important. I was just delighted to be able to continue the success that had been brought to this club in those early years.'

An overjoyed Andy Goram was also glad he was able to help repay the faith his manager had shown in him. He said: 'It was amazing when we won the league. It was my first medal as a Rangers player and my first senior medal in football. I had played at Hibs and Oldham before but I had never won anything so when we clinched the title it was just amazing. It also meant that I had something to show my kids. I didn't want them thinking I know you were a decent goalkeeper and you played for Scotland but what did you ever win? So that first title was a big one for me.'

It was the same for Stuart McCall and was one of the main reasons why he was persuaded to swap England for Scotland and a whole new family.

'Every single one of my title successes at Rangers was huge but the big thing for me was signing for Rangers,' McCall insisted. 'It was a dream come true the day I signed for the club. Players judge their careers by the number of titles they have won or the amount of money they have pocketed. At Rangers I won a lot of things and earned some decent money but the biggest thing for me was the amount of friends I made at Rangers. We are still close today and I think that team spirit was one of the first things that struck me when I first signed for Rangers. I was just fortunate into the bargain that I also played in what was a golden era for the club. I know how lucky I am to have played for Rangers when I did.'

There was to be one more remaining fixture as Rangers signed off their season by making it a dream double with their 2–1 Scottish Cup final win over Airdrie. McCoist and Mark Hateley were the Hampden heroes and finally enabled the Light Blues to bury their long-running hoodoo in the competition.

David Robertson recalled: 'Winning the league for that first time was just brilliant. I had been so close with Aberdeen so to finally win the league was such a big thing for me and also to come away with a Scottish Cup winners medal just made it even more memorable. Ironically the Scottish Cup was the one thing I was able to give most of my team mates stick about that season. I had won the competition with Aberdeen but up to that point that Rangers team were still waiting for their first Scottish Cup. I had a bit of fun with that. So to win those first two medals really was something I will never forget.'

Rangers were now well clear as the top team in Scotland. The gulf was widening with every big-money signing but Smith was never going to let anybody get carried away. He wasn't interested in what the outside world had to say. He just wanted to keep his side focused on the job at hand, knowing nothing less than 100 per cent would keep them at the top of the Scottish game. That was shown as he barked this warning to his squad: 'If our players listen to the media, their friends and relatives saying that Rangers will win the championship without having to play for it then we could come unstuck.'

That was something he was determined wasn't going to happen under his watch.

6

SMITH SINKS A GLORIOUS TREBLE

(1992–93)

AFTER an SPL and Scottish Cup double-winning assault, the nucleus of Walter Smith's squad was now in place to have a genuine go at all three domestic competitions and the ever-elusive Champions League. The likes of Andy Goram, Davie Robertson, Stuart McCall and Alexei Mikhailichenko had all proved to be quality additions and there was very little for Smith to tinker with. The one area he did feel needed to be strengthened was his back line. He felt another quality defender would allow him to put the finishing touches to an already formidable side. Scottish international Dave McPherson was coming out of contract at Hearts and having played previously at Ibrox, when Smith and Souness first arrived, he now felt ready to be a first pick in the Rangers' back line.

McPherson recalled the chain of events that saw him head back to Ibrox five years after he had upped sticks and headed to Tynecastle. He said: 'Walter brought me back in 1992. I was coming to the end of my contract at Hearts, although it was before the days of Bosman. So if anybody wanted to sign me then they would have needed to agree compensation with Hearts. I remember I went away with Scotland to Norway and it was there that Richard Gough told me Rangers wanted to sign me and Walter also spoke to me not long after that. I was a Rangers fan as a boy so as soon as I heard Walter was interested there was only going to be one place I was going and that was back to Ibrox. Hearts knocked back Rangers first offer but eventually a deal was struck. It wasn't really much of a surprise because both clubs did quite a lot of business together back then, so it was a deal that left everybody happy.'

The central defender had always hoped he would get his dream return. 'I also felt I had a bit of unfinished business at Ibrox,' McPherson admitted. 'I first left when I was twenty-three and I went a wee bit too early. I had primarily played for the club when they were going through a bit of a transitional period, under the likes of John Greig and Jock Wallace before Souness came in. I had been a young player coming through the ranks but I decided it was time to leave when maybe I should have stayed on under Souness.'

Mark Hateley is in no doubt that Smith had an eye for a player. He not only looked for quality but guys who had the characteristics to blend into the team ethos that was at the heart of his team's success.

Hateley explained: 'The Gaffer has a brilliant knack of knowing when to bring in new players. He would normally make three or four signings in the summer and add another couple at the turn of the year. He seems to know when to freshen things up and at the same time get them to fuse with his existing squad. He knows how to manipulate people and to get the best out of them, regardless of their reputations or price tags. He has done it again in his second spell although he has hardly had any money to spend and had to operate with a far smaller squad of players.'

But even in that first spell, where he had an embarrassment of riches, there were times when he had to make do and mend. That was shown when Dave McPherson was forced to play out of position to compensate for the loss of crocked right back Gary Stevens.

McPherson said: 'When Walter signed me he took me in as a

central defender. I had been out at the European Championships with the likes of Ally McCoist, so we all got some extra time off. That meant that when we came back we were almost straight into the competitive games. By that point Stevens had suffered a bad injury and suddenly we were left without a recognised right back. Walter called me in and said, "I know I have signed you as a central defender but I need you to play right back for me. How do you feel about that? Is that okay?" I just told Walter that I had come back to play for Rangers and if that was what it was going to take then I was more than happy to do it. I had worked with Walter before and even when he was No. 2 you could see that he was eventually going to progress into management in his own right. His man-management, tactics and attention to detail were there for all to see. By that point I had been away from Rangers for five years and in that time Walter had obviously gained even more experience and also matured in a managerial sense.'

Smith went back to the future again by bringing in another Ibrox old boy to strengthen his squad, as Trevor Steven came back in a cut-price deal from Marseille.

The signs were good as Rangers built up the confidence with good early season wins over St Johnstone, Airdrie, Hibs, Dumbarton, Dundee and Stranraer in the league and Skol Cup. The first real test came in the first Old Firm showdown. Rangers came through that unscathed although they were left slightly disappointed after the 1–1 draw, where Ian Durrant had got on the scoresheet.

The team's confidence was clearly up and they continued to steam-roller everyone who dared cross their path. Possible title challengers Aberdeen and Hearts were also put in their place while Dundee United and St Johnstone were disposed of on the way to the Skol Cup final.

They were matched against the Dons in what had become a regular occurrence when it came to the League Cup showpiece. Rangers, in the main, had the upper hand and weren't about to let that slip, as a strike from Stuart McCall and a Gary Smith own goal helped the Ibrox giants come out on top again. The 2–1 win was enough to see Smith and his men pick up the first trophy of the season.

That only whetted the appetite for even more success. This was a team that was thirsty for glory and for once was able to juggle the crippling demands of Scotland and Europe. Their unbeaten surge continued as they took care of Celtic home and away while a Mark Hateley goal at Pittodrie was enough to plunge a dagger through the heart of chasing Aberdeen.

The next big test was to come at Celtic Park in March, where Rangers' hopes of going through the season unbeaten were brought to an abrupt end. Full back David Robertson was rushed back for that game. 'I had missed the win over Brugge with a hamstring injury and the next game was against Celtic at Parkhead,' Robertson explained. 'I came in on the Saturday morning with my track suit on to get treatment. One of the physios asked me to go for a run. He then kept telling me to push it until I was running flat out. I thought that's strange, what's he up to? Then I went into the shower and Archie Knox came in and asked me how I was. I said I felt fine and then he said: "That's good, can you go up and join the players for the pre-match. You're playing – is that okay?" I said, "that's fine but I have a problem. I only have a tracksuit and the dog is outside in the car." He said that's nothing to worry about. The next thing I knew he had somebody driving my dog back to the house and I was up getting my pre-match looking like a right scruff as all the other boys were suited and booted. I would have loved to have said it was worth it but we ended up losing the game and that brought an end to our unbeaten run.'

They say all good things must come to an end but every Rangers player and supporter would have preferred it to come against any other team. For defender Scott Nisbet it was a game that was to be more painful than most. Not only had their record gone but he suffered a cruel injury, which was to prematurely end his top-level career.

'We went forty-four games unbeaten in the league and Champions League that season,' the Edinburgh-born star recalled. 'I played against Brugge in the midweek and then Celtic on the Saturday. I got injured in a challenge with John Collins and ended up doing my hip. That was to be my last game for Rangers. I have to say it was a hard time but Walter was absolutely brilliant to me. He took me to one side and said he would do whatever he could to help me. He and Sir David Murray, who also took me through to Edinburgh, were absolutely brilliant to me and have been every day since. That sums up what good men they both are.'

That defeat turned out to be a minor blip and the team quickly got back to winning ways. Not even the loss of talismanic hitman Ally McCoist, with a broken leg while playing for Scotland, could derail them. The team continued to gun for glory in the Scottish Cup, as wins over Motherwell, Ayr United, Arbroath and Hearts saw them set up another Hampden set-to with their old adversaries Aberdeen.

Before that the title was clinched at the start of May as promising young striker Gary McSwegan, who had come through the youth ranks, hit the only goal of the game at Broomfield to sink Airdrie and seal the fifth Scottish Premier Division title in a row. A relieved David Robertson explained: 'The first title win was special but the second one wasn't quite as enjoyable. The first time I remember the joy but after that the pressure was on as we tried to go for nine-in-a-row. In the end each title became more of a relief than anything else.'

Stuart McCall admitted a big factor in their success that season had been Smith and his back-room team, Archie Knox and Davie Dodds.

'I was lucky to win a few titles in a row,' the ex-Scottish international acknowledged. 'A lot of our success was down to our coaching staff of Walter, Archie Knox and Davie Dodds. They installed a really good spirit within the team and I think that is also a big thing in the success Walter has had second time around at Ibrox. His man-management skills are second to none. He just knew how to treat you properly. He won your respect and made you really want to play for him. As a team we also believed in each other and we knew when we went out and crossed that white line we would die for each other.'

The Gers title party went a bit flat when they were thumped by Partick Thistle at Firhill. It was a defeat which was to cost Dale Gordon his cup final slot.

'I tweaked my medial ligament in that game and I had to come off,' revealed the former Norwich star. 'I hobbled back on to the park at the end for the celebrations but it just didn't feel the same as the previous season because of the injury. It was a blow because I was touch and go for the Scottish Cup final with Aberdeen. I worked hard to get fit and I was convinced I was going to be fit enough to be involved or even be on the bench. But I didn't make either and I was just so disappointed.'

The remaining league games were seen out before their Scottish Cup final farewell. Gordon missed the game while McCoist and John Brown both struggled to make a game which they knew could see Rangers clinch a memorable treble.

'I played through the pain barrier for Walter but I have to say he paid me back ten-fold for that,' Brown acknowledged. 'When I was struggling for big games through injury he would always tell me: "Don't worry, I will make sure you get the win bonus." I always used to tell him I was not worried about the money, it's the medals I was after. I also told him if I couldn't go out and do myself justice on the pitch then I wouldn't go out for the sake of it because I would never put myself in that position and deny somebody else a medal. I just couldn't have done that to one of my team mates. Going into that cup final I was touch and go right to the last minute. Thankfully I managed to pass my fitness test although Ally McCoist failed his and didn't make the game.'

Smith was often criticised for not giving youth a chance but the likes of Gary McSwegan, Neil Murray and defender Steven Pressley were all given their chance at critical stages throughout that season. Two of them also got early Hampden appearances in the Scottish Cup final.

Murray scored Rangers' first goal before Mark Hateley added a second to seal a 2–1 win and a domestic clean sweep.

Murray admitted: 'The 1992–93 season was probably my personal best because it was my first full season. We managed to do well in Europe and win a domestic treble. I also played in the Scottish Cup final win and managed to get a goal in our win over Aberdeen, so that was massive for me, but I have to say every championship was absolutely brilliant at Rangers.'

Young defender Pressley came off the bench to pick up the first medal of what was to be a long and distinguished playing career. 'I was only nineteen so to be involved in a Scottish Cup final was great and to win it was even better,' he proudly explained. 'It was my first real senior trophy and a real memorable one.'

The delighted manager still looks back on that season's achievements with great pride. Smith explained: 'If you look at the teams that have dominated in Scotland over the years and look at Celtic's nine-in-a-row run, you'll see it is not easy to win a treble. You need a fair share of good fortune to do it. At Rangers, there's a pressure on you to win all the games you play. That means when you start out in a season you've got to be looking to win cups and leagues. If you're not featuring in them, you've got a problem.'

The success and one of the best seasons in Rangers' history only helped justify Dave McPherson's decision to come and play under the managerial master who was Smith.

McPherson said: 'It turned out to be a great return. I played most of the games. We won the treble and had ten games in the

Champions League – even though I had played at right back. To be fair to Walter he was brilliant and was really grateful that I had done him a turn by playing out of position. There were a lot of highlights including the Leeds United games but the big one for me was the Scottish Cup final, knowing we had finally clinched the treble. It was some achievement to win all three domestic trophies while also doing so well in Europe.'

Dutch winger Pieter Huistra also reckons the 1992–93 campaign will go down as his best ever. He admitted: 'Walter's second full season was a great one for me and the rest of the boys. We went undefeated in the Champions League, including those Battle of Britain games against Leeds United, and we also walked away with a domestic treble. I don't think things could have gone much better. It was just a brilliant, brilliant effort. I also played in two cup finals. What stood out for me that season was the fighting spirit we showed. There were quite a few matches where we went 1–0 down but we came back and won the games. We didn't stop when we got level, we just kept going until we got our noses in front.'

It was an ethos instilled in Rangers history and which was to be reinforced by Walter Smith throughout his time at the club.

7

CHEATED OUT OF CHAMPIONS LEAGUE GLORY?

(1992–93)

THE 1992–93 domestic treble may have filled the Ibrox trophy cabinet but it was in the Champions League where Walter Smith's side finally came of age. Prior to that, Europe had read like an Ibrox Hall of Shame. Bayern Munich, Steaua Bucharest, Sparta Prague and Red Star Belgrade had all put paid to their hopes over previous campaigns.

It was a constant cause of frustration first for Souness and then Smith. Chairman David Murray was also keen to see some success on that front because he had been desperate to turn the Glasgow giants into a European superpower.

They had been perennial under-achievers and that was something Smith was anxious to put right. He also knew he would have to deliver success to destroy the myth that he was simply a cheque-book manager who bought success in Scotland but was unable to deliver when it really mattered – in the money spinner that was the newly formed Champions League.

The Scottish champions got off to the perfect start when they beat Danish outfit Lyngby 2–0 at Ibrox, as Mark Hateley and Pieter Huistra settled the early competition nerves. The return leg saw Ian Durrant net the only goal in Denmark to see the Light Blues breeze through the qualifying round 3–0 on aggregate.

Smith still had to steer his side through one more qualifying round before they could even think about the group stages. The draw wasn't kind although it was one that engrossed and gripped the entire United Kingdom, as Rangers were drawn against English champions Leeds United. It was a genuine Battle of Britain. The match was also given a bit of added spice as Howard Wilkinson's squad also boasted a heavy Scottish influence, including Gordon Strachan and Scottish international Gary McAllister. They also had the mercurial talents of Eric Cantona, Lee Chapman and the grit and fight of David Batty.

Rangers came back from an early McAllister strike when an awful blunder from Leeds keeper John Lukic, who punched into his own net, let Smith's men back in. Ally McCoist then became the hero of the night with his winner.

It was a massive result for Rangers and Scottish football but they were still written off, especially by the English press, who claimed the Elland Road return leg would be a formality. Keeper Andy Goram admitted that the English tabloid headlines helped to fire the passion in Smith's men.

'I remember the Battle of Britain clash with Leeds at Elland Road,' Goram admitted, with more than a wry smile. 'We won 2–1 at Ibrox but the English newspapers still wrote us off as no-hopers. They all predicted that Leeds would give us a good battering down there. So when it came to the Gaffer's pre-match team talk he didn't have to say much. He came in with a big pile of press cuttings from the English newspapers and threw them into the middle of the floor. He said, "If this doesn't motivate you then nothing will." In the end it worked a treat because we not only went out and qualified but we also beat Leeds 2–1 at Elland Road to progress into the next round of the Champions League.'

Mark Hateley netted before a second half goal from Ally McCoist killed off Leeds, despite Cantona's late consolation. McCoist reckons getting through, over those two games, was as big as anything he achieved in his long and distinguished Ibrox career.

McCoist explained: 'The two Leeds United games were amazing

games. Looking back I feel really proud to say I was part of those Rangers teams. I have to say there were so many highlights for me during my Rangers career but those Leeds United games were definitely up there.'

Captain Richard Gough admitted that was a major achievement to be crowned the pride of Britain.

'I had so many highs at Rangers under Walter,' Gough admitted. 'The two games where we beat Leeds United in the Champions League were massive. I think over the two games that nobody could argue that we deserved to go through. It was also the first time we had qualified for the Champions League group stages so those results were absolutely massive.'

Left back David Robertson later went on to play for Leeds United although he never hit the heights as he did at Elland Road with Rangers. Robertson admitted: 'That season in the Champions League we maybe didn't have the greatest team in the competition but we had a real spirit and will to win. That was what took us places. We went out and gave it a real go and that got us results that maybe surprised some people. I know I was fortunate to play for Rangers during such a successful era. When I was at Aberdeen and Rangers, playing football for me was something of a hobby. I didn't feel pressure going out on the park because the likes of Walter Smith would take all that away. It wasn't until I went to Leeds United it became a job and I didn't have the same enjoyment. In fact the only time I think I actually got a standing ovation in my time at Leeds was when I was with Rangers when we beat them at Elland Road. We were clapped off the park but when I played for Leeds I think I was mainly booed off.'

Suddenly Europe was no longer seen as a weight around the neck. Rangers could now look forward to another guaranteed six games in the group section of Europe's premier club competition. The draw wasn't to disappoint as big-spending Marseille came out as top seeds and joined Belgian side Club Brugge and the relatively unknown quantity that was CSKA Moscow, who had seen off the might of Barcelona to get to this stage.

The first game saw the visit of Marseille. They rolled out their big guns and immediately blasted a big hole in Rangers' hopes. They raced into a 2–0 lead thanks to goals from German legend Rudi Voller and Croatian Alen Boksic. That would have been a bridge too far for many teams but Rangers were unbeaten domestically and also had a manager whose own motto could well have been 'no surrender'.

Young Gary McSwegan gave Rangers hope before Mark Hateley brought every Rangers fan off their seat with his late equaliser. It not only proved to be a valuable opening day point but it also showed that Smith's side could hold their own against the very best. Ian Durrant said: 'The Champions League run was amazing. We got some really big results against Marseille who went on to win it so that shows just how well we did. It was also at a time when the "three foreigner" rule was still in place so it made things even more difficult for the Gaffer. But he did well, going out to buy some of the best players in Britain. He also installed a real camaraderie amongst the boys, which was also like having another man out on the pitch with us. The manager got us playing in a real British style. We were hard to beat and teams definitely didn't like playing against us. That was down to the way the manager organised us and the way he set up the team. He also brought players in that could play in that system.'

Home-grown midfielder Neil Murray, who was thrown in against the French giants, recalled: 'I made my debut against Stranraer in the cup and a couple of months later I was running out against Marseille. That was a great boost and showed Walter had faith in me. He knew the type of character I was coming through the ranks and felt I could handle Marseille. But Walter was a great man-manager and he always made you feel like he believed in you. His man-management is second to none. He would never complicate things. He made things very simple. He just wanted you to go out and play your game. It didn't matter if you were playing Stranraer or Marseille. That was a big thing, especially for a young player coming through the ranks at Rangers. I was up against Didier Deschamps but the manager spoke more about me than Deschamps or any of the Marseille players. Thankfully it worked. I went out and just did my job and it went quite well. To be part of that team who did so well in Europe and won the league was amazing in my first season at Rangers. It was amazing.'

The feel-good factor continued as an Ian Ferguson strike was enough to give Rangers their first win in the section away to CSKA Moscow, with the match played in Bochum, Germany.

Next up was a trip to Belgium, where Huistra's goal was enough to salvage a draw and keep the impressive unbeaten run going. 'I scored a goal against Brugge with my right foot,' the Dutchman proudly revealed. 'That was probably my best European memory at Rangers. We won a point so it proved to be a big goal for us.'

The next game in the double-header was at Ibrox and Rangers knew if they could get one over the Belgians then they would have a real chance of making it to the knock-out stages. Ian Durrant had turned into a bit of a Euro specialist and hit the opener although the real moment of controversy came when Mark Hateley was wrongly sent off after a rather timid clash with a Brugge defender.

Hateley, who also claimed to have received a call offering him a bribe if he failed to play against Marseille earlier in the tournament, admitted, 'The sending-off was hard to take because I really didn't do anything. I couldn't believe it when the referee showed the red card. I was totally stunned because I knew I hadn't done anything. But looking at things philosophically now, everything happens for a reason. I think my red card galvanised the team. They felt a sense of injustice and as so often happens when you have ten men you get a reaction because every player digs in even deeper. The boys went on to win that game. Maybe we wouldn't have got the same reaction and result if I hadn't been sent off.'

Every single one of Hateley's team mates felt he had been harshly treated. Straight-talking Scott Nisbet said: 'Mark was sent off for absolutely nothing. I am certain the Marseille officials had bribed the Russians and a number of referees over the course of that Champions League campaign.'

That sense of injustice moved to galvanise Rangers, even after Brugge equalised through Lorenzo Staelens. The Scottish side rolled up their sleeves and dug out the win thanks to Nisbet's now famous long-range strike. Nisbet recalled his moment of glory. He said: 'It was bucketing down. A cross came in from Trevor Steven and it came off Stuart McCall's back and bounced. I went into a challenge with their player and he pulled out. The ball went flying and it must have hit the driest patch on the pitch because it bounced up over the keeper and into the net.'

It was a great result but the leg-weary Ibrox side walked off the pitch to hear that CSKA Moscow had uncharacteristically collapsed in the Velodrome and were on the end of a 6–0 thrashing from Marseille. Now the French side had an obvious advantage if it was going to come down to goal difference.

Pieter Huistra admitted he was left totally dismayed when he learned of Marseille's overwhelming victory. 'There were some question marks over Marseille during that campaign even at that point,' the Rangers star insisted. 'I remember everybody was really shocked and surprised with their result against CSKA Moscow. Nobody had expected them to win by so many goals and it just didn't feel or look right. That 6–0 defeat also had a major impact on our own European hopes. It made it virtually impossible for us to qualify for the next stage.'

But the good thing was that Rangers' destiny was still in their own hands and if they were to beat Marseille in France then they would be back in the driving seat to upset the odds and qualify from Group 1. Franck Sauzee stunned Rangers before Ian Durrant responded again but Smith's team was unable to churn out that all-important win.

Durrant said: 'I probably played my best football under Walter. He had faith in me and gave me a confidence. He has a great ability because he knows your strengths and weaknesses. He just asked you to go out and give your all and do what you're best at. There was never any pressure on you to do something he knew you weren't capable of.'

Suddenly it came down to the final fixtures with Rangers entertaining CSKA Moscow and Marseille set to travel to Belgium to take on Brugge.

Rangers knew a win would see them through but all of a sudden CSKA Moscow displayed a steely determination not to lose, which was in complete contrast to their spineless efforts in France. They saw out a goalless draw in Glasgow while Boksic scored in Belgium to help Marseille qualify for the final, where they eventually saw off AC Milan thanks to a goal from a certain Basile Boli, who was later to become a Rangers player.

Stuart McCall said: 'Maybe I am naive but I didn't really believe that corruption and cheating really went on within the game. But then everything came out and looking back you start to view things in a different light. Our last Champions League game was a 0–0 draw against CSKA Moscow at Ibrox. After the game the CSKA players were celebrating as if they had won the Champions League, never mind getting a draw at Ibrox. It was strange and maybe, just maybe, there might have been some financial reward behind their actions. It was disappointing not to progress but looking back it was still a fantastic achievement to go ten games in Europe unbeaten. We definitely exceeded expectations although it was disappointing not to go through. The bottom line is we didn't win enough games in the group. We only won two and had four draws in the group section and that was what let us down.'

It later emerged that Marseille president Bernard Tapie had been guilty of fixing matches and offering bungs. He was jailed for his underhand antics – much to the disgust of Smith and his men.

Smith said: 'Marseille in 92–93 does still grate a wee bit. That was a chance for Rangers to make a European Cup final. It was frustrating at the time and then, afterwards, we found out something of what that club had been up to. We'd an opportunity to get to the final if we had won in France, and we very nearly did in the game that finished 1–1. I met the CSKA Moscow manager a few years after that and he told me a few things but we did not need to be told – it had already come out what happened with Bernard Tapie and Marseille. We had Mark Hateley sent off at home to Bruges and I could never quite get my head around that. There was a kickout from the keeper, Mark went up for a header and the next thing I knew he was red-carded and out of the game in Marseille. That didn't sit right at all with me.'

Winger Pieter Huistra also still finds the events of that Euro campaign hard to get over. He recalled: 'I was a bit annoyed when it came out a few years later what Marseille had been up to but what we achieved in Europe that season was still special for me. Even if we didn't end up with what we deserved at the end of it.'

Mark Hateley, who had suffered first hand, wasn't entirely surprised when the revelations were finally uncovered. The Englishman admitted: 'I was disappointed when the news eventually came out about all the corruption surrounding Marseille's involvement in that season's Champions League campaign. If I am being honest it didn't really surprise me. I had been used to stories of corruption during my time out in Italy. It was always flying around so it wasn't really a shock that it was also going about in the Champions League. Some people will go to any lengths to win – whether they are legal or not! I wouldn't be surprised if it still goes on today.'

Ian Ferguson believes that Smith and his squad can still look back on that entire season, domestically and in Europe, with enormous pride. 'Winning the treble in 1992–93 was special,' Ferguson insisted. 'We not only did well domestically but went the entire campaign undefeated in the Champions League. That season we really had a never-say-die spirit. Even when we fell behind in games we always believed we would pull it back and a lot of the time we did. You only have to look at our European run. We took on teams like Marseille and Leeds United in the Battle of Britain and we still went unbeaten. Looking back I think everyone who was involved in that Rangers team can take great pride in what we achieved that season, especially in the Champions League.

'It is a bit of a disappointment when you heard what came out about Bernard Tapie, during his time in charge of Marseille. Seeing Tapie go to jail for what he did at Marseille did leave a sour taste in the mouth. But all I can say, from a Rangers point of view, is that I don't think we could have done any more. We threw everything at it, including the kitchen sink, but it just wasn't to be. Too many draws, in the end, killed us, but even so we were still only, maybe, one goal away from making the Champions League final. If we had managed to find a winner out in Marseille then who knows, we might just have made it. That is the thin line between success and failure. But that season will always have a bit of magic round it for me.'

Scottish international Dave McPherson was in no doubt that Rangers would never have had the success they had that year without their main man, Smith, at the helm.

McPherson admitted: 'We certainly felt we played well enough and were good enough to make the Champions League final. If we had maybe have got a wee bit more luck against CSKA then we might have made it. I think that season Walter really showed his qualities. He showed he was tactically aware and could get the best out of his players and, more importantly, knows what it takes to beat quality teams. He has shown that throughout his management career with Rangers, Everton and Scotland.'

That amazing run certainly helped to put Rangers back on the European map.

8

JAIL, AWOL STARS
AND A DOMESTIC DOUBLE

(1993–94)

HOW DO you top a season that saw Rangers wipe the floor in Scotland and go unbeaten in the Champions League? That was the conundrum that Walter Smith faced. The only way that could realistically be done was to try and get to the Champions League final. That, however, was easier said than done as they were hardly heavyweights when it came to European competition. The previous season had seen the team buck the trend, in some style, although this was a team who were still trying to establish themselves as a major force again.

Smith was once again backed to the hilt by David Murray who sanctioned the near £4 million purchase of renegade striker Duncan Ferguson from Dundee United. There was no question the big hit man was going to have a big future in the game but there were striking similarities between him and Mark Hateley, who was still very much the main man up front along with Ally McCoist.

Smith's other main problem was trying to keep his top stars fit. Andy Goram struggled with fitness problems for most of the season, meaning the Motherwell cup-winning keeper Ally Maxwell was to be the main Ibrox custodian. Smith also felt he was a bit light when it came to the full back positions and decided to plunder the bargain basements to bring in a player he had long admired, Fraser Wishart, who was without a club after Falkirk's relegation from Scotland's top tier.

'It is funny because I only found out recently that Rangers had first tried to buy me in 1987 when I had still been at Motherwell,' Wishart revealed. 'It was Phil Boersma that told me. He said that he and Walter had been sent out to watch me on numerous occasions. Phil said they had gone to Motherwell and said to them, "Write down a number and tell us how much you want for him," but Tommy McLean told them I wasn't for sale. So it took me more than twenty years to find out about it. Tommy McLean never cracked a light to me and managed to keep Rangers' interest under wraps.

'I then had a few ups and downs and thought the chance of playing for a big club had passed me by. I had a short spell at Falkirk in the 1992–93 season, which helped me get my confidence back, but then they got relegated and were unable to offer me a contract. So I went on trial with Middlesbrough. I did quite well on trial down there and then I got a phone call telling me that Walter wanted to speak to me. I spoke to Walter and he told me he was keen to get me in because he had so many injuries. His first choice full backs Gary Stevens and David Robertson were out injured and he needed some short-term cover. He asked me if I would help him out by signing a short-term contract for a couple of months and that was how it started. I was coming in on a free transfer just weeks after they had paid £4 million for Duncan Ferguson.'

Wishart knew he wasn't going to play every week if Smith had his strongest side available to him. He admitted that the straight-talking Rangers boss didn't try to lure him in with a string of lavish promises and that refreshing honesty was a big factor in his decision to move to Ibrox.

The defender explained: 'What struck me from Walter's point of view was there was no pretence or kid on. He said you might play out of your skin for every game in those two months and you might still not get another contract at the end of things. We have two international full backs but they are injured and I am bringing you in because you can provide cover for either the left or right back positions. You will play in the short term but the good thing is that when you leave you will be leaving having played X amount of first-team games for Rangers. That should help you find another club at a high level.'

It certainly wasn't the summer signing frenzy that the transfer-hungry tabloids had predicted. Smith, however, was also aware that the club couldn't keep spending and he needed to play his part in helping to generate funds. That was one of the reasons why Dale Gordon was sold to West Ham United.

Gordon, when asked about his departure, said: 'I went off in the summer and I came back fighting fit. I was really looking forward to getting going again and getting over the disappointment of the injury and missing the cup final. Then West Ham, who had just been promoted back to the English top-flight, came in for me. Walter told me that he didn't want me to go but I could go and speak to them if I wanted, although he expected to see me back in training the following day. I went down and I stupidly decided to make the move. Looking back now my decision had nothing to do with football. West Ham were only a couple of hours away from where I was from, my wife was expecting and I just felt it might be better to move closer to home. West Ham were also offering me more money so yet again that was another non-footballing factor behind my decision to move. It turned out to be the biggest regret of my career. I should never have left Rangers. I left far too early. I was two years into a four-year contract at Rangers and I should have seen that deal out. I might also not have picked up the injury that in the end forced me to retire. But hindsight is a wonderful thing. The good thing for me is that every time I go back to Rangers it feels like it was only yesterday I left because Walter, the rest of the lads and the fans are all so welcoming.'

With the new team lined up by Smith, Rangers started the new campaign the way they had signed off the last – by churning out wins. They beat Hearts and St Johnstone in the league before the first real test came when they headed to Celtic Park. Wishart came through his Old Firm debut unscathed after the goalless draw but then feared that was going to be his last game in light blue.

Wishart recalled: 'We played Celtic at Celtic Park three or four games in. We drew 0–0 and I thought I had done quite well. David Murray came in and shook everybody's hand. He got to me, shook my hand and said: "It is up to you, isn't it?" I thought I had done okay but those comments left me a bit baffled. I then played in the following game, a cup-tie against Dunfermline, and then Walter called me into his office. He said, "I have some good news and bad news. What do you want first?" I told him to give me the bad news. He said, "You are not playing against Kilmarnock today, you are a sub, but I want to offer you a new two-year-contract. Come and see me on Monday." I was absolutely delighted especially when you look back to where I had been the previous summer – on trial down in England without a club.'

There was then a frustrating run of league slip-ups with defeats to Kilmarnock and Aberdeen and further dropped points against Partick Thistle and Dundee.

Wishart explained: 'I was on the bench for a game we lost at home to Kilmarnock. I didn't even get on and Walter came in after the game and went mental. I think he was having a go at the midfield players. He was giving it both barrels and it was unlike Walter because to be fair he rarely raised his voice. As he stormed out of the room he turned and launched this big litre-bottle of water towards me. I had to duck out of the way. It hit the wall and burst everywhere. It soaked me and all my clothes. At the back of my mind I wanted to stand up and say to the Gaffer that I didn't even play. But I then thought to myself just keep the head down. Very rarely did he lose the place like that but when he did you knew about it.'

The one positive from the defeat at Pittodrie was the debut appearance of promising youngster Charlie Miller. He had come through the youth set-up and Smith thought he was ready for his first taste of top-team action.

Miller admitted: 'I have a lot to be thankful to Walter Smith for. He brought me through the ranks and played me, basically, for two years solid. It wasn't until I started to get into trouble off the park that I lost my place. Looking back now I know I was young and stupid with some of the things I got up to when I should have been totally focused on my football. I had to do all the usual chores like clean the Gaffer's office, his shoes or even go and make him toast. I would openly try to blank him and ignore him wherever I could until I was given a clip round the ear or was given a roasting from one of the other coaches to get it done.

'Walter was brave enough to give me my debut at seventeen. I remember one of my early games was against Aberdeen. I played centre forward up against Alex McLeish and Brian Irvine and what an experience that was. I certainly was surprised when the Gaffer told me I was playing. But he obviously had faith in me and felt I could do him a job.' Miller's performance at Pittodrie was one of the few highlights from that day as the Light Blues slumped. It showed the youngster was ready to make an impact at the top level.

The mood within the Ibrox camp was lightened when they beat Levski Sofia in the first leg of their qualifying round of the Champions League at Ibrox – although the 3–2 win was far from convincing. A Dave McPherson goal and a Mark Hateley double got them the win although the two away goals gave the Bulgarians an unlikely lifeline.

There was also progress in the Skol Cup as Rangers saw off Celtic in the last four but the big game for all concerned was the second leg against Levski. Nasko Sirakov put the home side ahead before Ian Durrant levelled. The Scottish champions looked to have done enough until Smith and his men were to suffer the cruellest of European exits – as Nikolay Todorov netted a stoppage time rocket to put them out on away goals.

Fraser Wishart admitted: 'Nikolay Todorov's name is one I will never forget. We won at home and out in Sofia it was 1–1 going into injury time. They really battered us and the boy Todorov got the ball thirty-five yards from goal and smashed this unstoppable shot past Ally Maxwell. I turned to the dugout to see Archie Knox lying flat out on the track, battering the track in sheer frustration. There was such enormous pressure on us to do well in Europe and to go out in that way was just heartbreaking.

'Then after the game we were sitting in the dressing room. It was an old concrete bowl of a stadium and we were all just sitting in the dressing room with our head in our hands. There was hardly a word said because we were all so disappointed. Then suddenly we heard this thudding noise and Walter was laying in to this metal hamper. I think it was harder to take because the team had done so well the previous season.'

It was left to the talismanic McCoist to lift the spirits after a serious leg break. The Scotland star came off the bench to net a glory winner in the Skol Cup triumph over Hibs. The Light Blues came out on top 2–1 with Durrant netting their opener.

However, bad luck struck Wishart ahead of the final and cost him his one and only winner's medal. He explained: 'I had played in every round of the League Cup and I think I would also have played in the final, the one where Ally McCoist scored the overhead kick against Hibs. But I got injured the week beforehand and so I didn't even get a medal from that.'

The cup victory was a timely boost as Duncan Ferguson was sidelined for the first part of the season through injury. Smith still felt he needed more firepower and went out and bought Gordon Durie from Tottenham Hotspur.

By that time Rangers looked to be back on the straight and narrow after their Celtic Park set-back at the end of October. They went on an unbeaten run which saw them take care of nearest challengers Aberdeen and Motherwell until they were brought crashing back down to earth with a 3–0 defeat against Dundee United at Ibrox.

Dave McPherson still remembers that afternoon where his manager wasn't about to take any prisoners. 'We were playing Dundee United at Ibrox and they came flying out of the traps,' the defender admitted. 'They were 2–0 up after ten minutes. We were struggling and I ended up getting injured midway through the first half and I had to get off. I went in and I was getting treatment on the physio's table when I heard the roar go up and realised that Dundee United had gone 3–0 up. So at half-time Walter came up the corridor. The treatment door was lying half open and he saw me on the table. He was fuming. There was steam coming out of his nose and ears, he was so angry. He came flying in and shouted at me: "Where were you for the third goal?" He then turned around and realised I had been substituted. He gave me a wry smile, turned and headed for the dressing room.'

There was no doubt that rocket was all Rangers needed to get back to winning ways as they pieced together another long, unbeaten run. That included an impressive New Year's Day win at Celtic Park, where the manager had popped the champagne corks ahead of the game.

'We were in the hotel and the manager let us stay up,' Neil Murray revealed. 'When it came to the bells he allowed us a glass of champagne. It was a good touch because it really relaxed us and the next day we went out and beat Celtic 4–2. Normally whoever wins the New Year derby goes on to win the league and that was what happened that season. That result allowed us to lay down a marker.'

The match had a very Soviet feel about it as Alexei Mikhailichenko netted a double while compatriot Oleg Kuznetsov also scored after Mark Hateley's opener.

Captain Richard Gough still remembers that game and how it

emphasised the gulf in class between the two sides of the Old Firm. The seasoned defender said: 'I remember going to Parkhead and being 3–0 up after fifteen minutes. Even Oleg Kuznetsov scored, that's how bad it was. During that period I would go out with Paul McStay, who I knew from playing beside him for Scotland in World Cup games. I loved Paul and thought he was the best player Celtic had for years, but I felt sorry for him. I was playing with maybe the best of British at that time and even in the tunnel I would look at him as if to say, "You've got no chance here, pal." And he would look back and you could tell he knew that as well.'

The team went on another convincing undefeated charge, beating Kilmarnock, Partick Thistle, Hibs, Raith Rovers, Motherwell, Hearts and St Johnstone along the way. That impressive run also coincided with Andy Goram's return to fitness. 'The Goalie' recalled: 'When we got to that stage the pressure was really on us. We were beginning to edge closer to nine-in-a-row. We knew we had to try and win nine-in-a-row because the club might never get another chance to achieve it. A lot of us were also Rangers fans. We knew what it meant to play for the club. We were also good players and that along with the Gaffer and Archie's drive, enthusiasm, determination and know-how helped us achieve what we did although there is no doubt the Gaffer's drive rubbed onto the players and the team.'

It was always levelled at Smith that he was simply buying success but that season he showed he could deal with almost anything that was thrown at him. He steadfastly backed David Robertson when he decided to turn his back on Scotland, having grown sick of leaving his family for long spells and not really getting anywhere near the action.

'Walter would also defend his players to the hilt,' Robertson said. 'I remember the time that I decided to quit Scotland. I was really frustrated because I had travelled here, there and everywhere with Scotland but I only ever got involved if we were really struggling for players. It was hard being away from my family for so long, knowing that I was unlikely to get a game. So I spoke to Walter Smith about things and he agreed with me and backed my decision all the way. I told Craig Brown that I wanted to play for Scotland but I didn't want to keep travelling all over the world for nothing. I wasn't turning my back on my country and I told him if he needed me I would be there, but I was no longer prepared to just go to make up the squad numbers. Also one of my last games was against Holland. I came back with a hamstring problem and missed the next three or four weeks and although Walter never said anything to me I knew he was far from impressed.'

Steven Pressley also had Smith to thank for guiding him through one of the most difficult periods of his life.

Pressley explained: 'I have to say I absolutely loved my time at Rangers. I was just impatient and frustrated. I thought I was a better player than I really was. I still felt I should be playing every week and I wasn't. Walter had even offered me a two-year extension but I thought I knew better and turned it down. I thought I would be better leaving. Looking back I had lost my father and I didn't have anyone to give me the guidance I needed at that time. It was a tough time for me. I had played a lot of football in the first half of the season and then I lost my father. I then fell out of the team and it really did get to me. Looking back Walter took me out of the side to help me get over the loss of my dad but I didn't see it. I just wanted to play but looking back Walter was just trying to help me and look out for me. That shows his great man-management skills.'

But for the Rangers boss this was very much the calm before the storm. Unwanted headlines became the norm for Rangers for most of that season and they had absolutely nothing to do with football.

Duncan Ferguson sparked the controversy in a league game against Raith Rovers at Ibrox when during the routine victory he went face to face with Jock McStay and head-butted the visiting defender. It led to the Scottish international being jailed for three months for his assault.

Fraser Wishart admitted: 'That did affect the squad. The players weren't happy with what had gone on. It was an incident that was wrong but we had also seen much worse out on the park. Duncan was just unlucky because there was a government campaign at that point to really clamp down on football. I think we were all saddened by what had happened and it did really affect us when he was jailed. He was one of our team mates and now he was being sent to jail for something he did on the park. He did receive a lot of support from Walter and all the players. I think quite a few went up to see him and show their support.'

Ferguson and Rangers felt let down by the punishment and it spelt the beginning of the end of the striker's Ibrox career. He later joined Everton and Smith admitted his departure had nothing to do with football. Ferguson had every right to feel aggrieved and even turned his back on Scotland after the SFA had failed to show him enough support. Smith explained: 'I bought Duncan Ferguson for Rangers and the reason I sold him was nothing to do with football. There were just circumstances that made it difficult for him to stay at a Scottish club.'

But Smith managed to keep his other stars focused and they continued their long unbeaten run, which included a Scottish Cup semi-final win over Kilmarnock after a replay.

Just when Smith thought the negative headlines couldn't get any worse, 'The Goalie' went AWOL on a family holiday to Tenerife. Smith had agreed to let Andy Goram get away to try and recharge the batteries and give him a fighting chance of getting fit for the Scottish Cup final with Dundee United.

Goram explained: 'The day I never came back from Tenerife was the one where I really felt the wrath of the Gaffer. I went out to try and get fit for the Scottish Cup and ended up going on the bender which almost ended my Rangers career. As soon as I got back he dragged me into his office and said: "This is it. Your Rangers career is over." I don't mind admitting that I burst into tears but I had done wrong and there was no way the Gaffer was going to back down. I knew that if an offer came in then I would be sold there and then. The Gaffer wasn't a man to be messed about with. Once you crossed that line that was you and I knew I had done that in some style. I didn't want to leave Rangers and I am just thankful that nobody else came in for me or I would have been off. The manager then relented because there had been no interest and brought me back for pre-season. I worked hard, got my weight down and did everything he asked of me. He then took me off the transfer list and gave me a second chance and that is something I am eternally grateful to him for.'

There was also a wind of change on the other side of the city. Celtic had fallen deep into crisis and were on the verge of closure when the Canadian-based Fergus McCann stepped in to save them. It was to build the long-term foundations for their rivals although it was left to Aberdeen and Motherwell to lead the title chase.

The Fir Park outfit did stoke things up with a 2–1 victory against Rangers at the end of April but they were still unable to delay the inevitable. A draw with Celtic and then the title was clinched despite a loss to Hibs at Easter Road – as Motherwell also lost to Dundee United. Aberdeen were eventually to finish second, well behind the Light Blues.

Fraser Wishart said: 'I was part of two title-winning seasons but I didn't play enough games to get a medal from either of them. I don't have the medals but I do have my memories in winning those leagues. I actually could have joined Hearts at the end of that first season but I didn't. It just didn't feel right. I had slipped even further down the pecking order but I still fancied a wee tilt at things.'

There was still the chance of back-to-back trebles but there was one remaining hurdle – Dundee United. It was expected that

Rangers would wipe the floor with Ivan Golac's side, who had finished a lowly sixth in the table. That didn't happen as Craig Brewster scored the only goal of the game to wreck their hopes of consecutive trebles.

Smith knew his side came within a whisker of creating their own unique piece of history. He admitted: 'We won a treble in 1993 and lost in the final of the Scottish Cup the following year, but we would have been the first team in history to win back-to-back trebles. It would have been a great achievement but it wasn't to be.'

Defender Dave McPherson added: 'It was the same treble-winning squad that had been enhanced with another couple of signings. It was a hard feat to try and achieve back-to-back trebles. It was maybe slightly easier because we didn't do as well in Europe. We did well to win the league and the League Cup but it ended up being a real disappointment losing the cup final to Dundee United. In most other seasons a domestic double would have been seen as a major success but as I said there was a wee tinge of disappointment that season.'

It was to be a night of even bigger disappointment for Gary Stevens even though he didn't even kick a ball at Hampden.

Stevens explained: 'I was lucky to play for Rangers at a time when we dominated Scottish football although my time at the club did end a wee bit bitterly. I had struggled with the injury and I remember the night after the cup final. I hadn't been involved and had a few drinks. Walter pulled me across midway through the night and told me that the chairman was putting me up for sale. I was disappointed but I hadn't played a lot and I was still probably one of the higher earners at the club. Maybe I should have dug my heels in and stayed but I was the type of guy who just wanted to play football. I came back the following season but I was still a bit short and had a bit of a nightmare against AEK Athens, as we crashed out of the Champions League, and I knew then it was the beginning of the end of my Rangers career.'

Experienced campaigners like John Brown admitted there was

huge disappointment over the Scottish Cup final defeat but it was still a period that the club and Smith can look back on with great pride.

Brown said: 'We won five out of six trophies in those two seasons. Our record was second to none at home and also in Europe. It was during that time that Walter's man-management really came to the fore. To go ten games unbeaten in Europe was an amazing feat. Walter had been the one who had masterminded it and had pushed us on. Even in the Old Firm games that was clear for everyone to see. You only have to look at the Gaffer's record. He recently surpassed Jock Stein's record as the most successful manager in the Old Firm games. He knew how to get the best out of his teams in the big games.'

Those feelings were also expressed by Trevor Steven. 'Walter and Rangers were under pressure to win things,' Steven claimed. 'To keep that run going took a lot of hard work because to win five or six titles in a row was a great achievement. Of course, Walter went on to make it to nine titles in a row, which really was incredible.'

For free-scoring Mark Hateley, the medals and silverware didn't end there. He was named as the Scottish Football Writers' Association player of the year. He collected that trophy and also the golden boot for finishing top scorer.

'It was a great season for me,' claimed Hateley, who had by that point firmly established himself as an Ibrox favourite. 'I was named the football writers' player of the year – and the first English player to win the award. I also walked away with the golden boot and so that year could not have gone any better even if I had scripted it myself.'

Five out of six domestic trophies was certainly an impressive run and showed how dominant a force Smith had built at Rangers. He had players at their peak, like Hateley, and they were desperate and hungry for even more success.

9

WALTER'S GREAT DANE HELPS RANGERS WALK TO THE TITLE

(1994–95)

WALTER SMITH knew it was going to take something special to take Rangers on again and he produced it in some style with the financial backing of David Murray, in the summer of 1994. The signing of Danish superstar Brian Laudrup and European Cup winner Basile Boli certainly did that. French international Boli was no stranger to Rangers having come up against them in Europe with his infamous Marseille side. But it was the shock capture of Laudrup, who arguably turned out to be Rangers' greatest signing of recent seasons, that really caught the imagination.

Laudrup said: 'I had a few options but most of the interest was from teams wanting to take me on loan. That was something I wasn't really interested in. I had been at AC Milan for the season on loan and I decided if I was going to leave Fiorentina then I wanted to do it on a permanent basis. I waited and that is when Rangers came in for me. I have to admit I had reservations about moving to Scotland. I didn't know a lot about Scottish football but I was aware it had a reputation of being an overly physical league. That was something I was unsure about but Rangers had offered the money that Fiorentina were looking for and so, out of courtesy, I flew to Scotland to meet with Rangers.

'When I arrived in Scotland to talk to Rangers, I remember

Walter Smith took me for a ride in his car. He showed me the stadium and some of Scotland's main sights. He even drove me down to Loch Lomond where we stopped off at Cameron House. He obviously had big plans and hopes for Rangers and he felt I could help take the team on. He made it clear that he was willing to give me the liberty to go out and do what I do best, which was trying to create and run at defences. That was a big factor in my decision, having a manager who believed in me and was willing to let me go out and play my natural game. I had been out in Italy with Fiorentina and then I had a loan spell at AC Milan, but I have to say I never really played my best football in Italy. That was down to the fact that Italian football is very tactical and the attacking players have to fit into systems rather than maybe being allowed the creative freedom to try and produce something different. So that was a big thing for me. I felt that I could play good football under Walter and that, in the end, was what convinced me to sign for Rangers. I put pen to paper and it turned out to be one of the best moves of my career. I ended up having four really top years at Rangers.'

There was no doubt Laudrup and Boli had the abilities but keeper Andy Goram, who was still fighting to save his Ibrox career at that point, knew that Smith looked beyond their on-the-field talents.

Goram said: 'Walter didn't just buy good players; he also looked deeply into their backgrounds and their characters. There was no point in bringing in a good player if he was shy in our dressing room. He would never have survived because we had a really lively dressing room. There was a real aggression and will-to-win in there and if you didn't show your character then you just would never have made it at Ibrox during that time.'

The A-list signings raised Champions League hopes but again it proved to be another false dawn, as the SPL champions were caught cold in the red-hot heat of the Greek capital. The problem was that Rangers launched their European campaign before a domestic ball had even been kicked and Smith's side were left short. They crashed 2–0 to AEK Athens. Dimitris Saravakos netted both goals and Smith had to hold his hands up and take the blame for his side's defensive collapse. Rangers needed to turn the tie on its head at Ibrox but a Toni Savevski goal was enough to see them off, quite convincingly, over the two legs. The crisis headlines were reserved for Ibrox and weren't helped by Boli's outspoken attack on Smith after their Champions League exit. That pretty much spelt the end of Boli's short and undistinguished Ibrox career as Smith took a no-nonsense approach with the former Marseille star. It, once again, proved that reputations and price tags counted for nothing under his reign.

The European hangover left Ibrox on a downer, as they crashed 2–0 to Celtic and bombed out the Coca Cola Cup at home to Falkirk. By that time the critics were out in force and there were serious doubts whether Smith's side could continue their domestic domination. There were fleeting moments of their old magic but it wasn't as consistent as Smith and Archie Knox demanded.

John Brown admitted being written off just made the Rangers players even more determined. He said: 'From our second or third title in a row we really believed that we were strong enough and good enough to make it nine-in-a-row. Celtic were in a bit of a state and our main challengers were Aberdeen, although Motherwell and Hearts also pushed us at times. Aberdeen came closest but the good thing was that whenever we needed to push on the manager was able to go out and buy more quality, thanks to the full backing of the chairman. So from that point of view we were always confident although we also knew that money didn't always buy you success.

'Also we were picking up the papers every couple of weeks and the former Celtic captain Billy McNeill would be saying Rangers will never make it five-in-a-row and then it was six-in-a-row and so on. People like Billy and the rest of our doubters just made us even more determined to go out and prove them wrong by keeping our unbeaten title run going. I think Billy, as a Celtic man, was just fearful that we were going to equal or break his old club's record.'

Smith felt he had to bolster his defence and he turned to Hearts again. This time Scottish international centre half Alan McLaren was the target. The big defender revealed the on-going moves behind the scenes.

McLaren explained: 'When Rangers were trying to sign me, what struck me was Walter Smith's determination to get the deal done. He was instrumental in getting me to Rangers. There was a point where I didn't think I was going to move. Rangers had agreed a fee and then Hearts moved the goal posts. Chris Robinson [Hearts chairman] knew the club were struggling financially and felt he could use Rangers' interest to get a better deal. He knew Rangers wanted me and he knew I wanted to go so he tried to use those factors to his advantage. He started by asking for money and Dave McPherson. Then when Rangers agreed that deal for a second time he chanced his arm and tried to get another midfielder into the bargain. There was a bit of stand-off and I wasn't sure if the deal was going to happen. The way Hearts handled things was farcical. Even when the deal was in the balance and looked like it wasn't going to happen Walter Smith went that extra length to assure me that the deal would be done. He came through to Edinburgh to meet me personally. He made it clear that he wanted to sign me and spoke at length how I was going to fit into his Rangers team. Up to that point, Rangers had been playing with a flat back four but he wanted to change that to a back three because he felt that could really benefit the team, especially in Europe. I had been more used to playing with a back three at Hearts and so it was a system I was more than used to. He told me that he thought I could play a big part in the changeover and he really sold Rangers to me, although playing against them I knew all about them.'

McPherson, on the other hand, admitted moving back to the capital was something he felt would enhance his Scotland career.

'I was still playing out of position at right back so I was keen to move back into a more central position,' McPherson admitted, as he explained the reason behind his shock departure. 'So when the bid for Alan McLaren was made it became clear that Hearts wanted me back as part of the deal. I thought it would be a good move because I had some good times at Hearts and I also felt it would help with my international career going back to Tynecastle. To be fair to Walter he didn't try to push me out the door. He left the decision up to me and when I told him I wanted to go he shook my hand and thanked me for all my efforts.'

The deal was eventually brokered but McLaren, by his own admission, left Rangers wondering what they had bought in those opening few days. Fortunately, when the real action started, he proved he was more than up to the task, starring against Celtic and on his return to Tynecastle.

McLaren recalled: 'Eventually the clubs agreed a deal and I signed for Rangers on the Thursday and my first game was on the Sunday, a real baptism of fire, against Celtic. I started training with the Rangers team and I had an absolute shocker in those opening few days. I was that bad I would have struggled to get a game for the Rangers youth team, never mind the first team. The team trained at such a high intensity. It was totally different to Hearts but Walter had the team training exactly the same way as his players approached games. I played alongside Basile Boli and thankfully I managed to raise my game a bit and we came out with a 3–1 win thanks to a couple of goals from Mark Hateley and another from Brian Laudrup.

'I had played in quite a few Edinburgh derbies with Hearts but I have to say that game was a bit more ferocious. It was a decent start and the games came quick and fast. A couple of weeks later I found myself back at Hearts. Not surprisingly, I took a fair bit of abuse from the Hearts fans. They gave me stick and booed me every time I touched the ball. I expected it. We drew 1–1 and the Hearts fans were more than delighted. They were also pleased that I hadn't come back to Tynecastle and got the win.'

The signings of Boli and McLaren, however, were the death knells in the Ibrox career of Steven Pressley. The young defender was already frustrated he wasn't getting enough top team action and the new arrivals would once again leave him cooling his heels on the Ibrox fringes. So he decided he wanted out and eventually left for Coventry City.

Pressley admitted: 'Walter, to be fair, tried his hardest to give me advice but I didn't listen. He told me I should sign my extension, but I knew better and decided it was time to leave. Looking back I should have listened to his advice and signed the contract. I had been in and out of the team and I was always knocking on Walter's door. I was impatient and felt I should be playing every week. I would go in and play well but as soon as Richard Gough or Dave McPherson was fit I would be back out the team again. I didn't have an understanding of the situation and it wasn't until I actually moved to Hearts and found myself an experienced player that nine times out of ten I would go back into the team if I was fit. It was only then I realised that the manager would always go with their tried and trusted players. It is only now I realised that the manager couldn't leave out Gough for this young budding centre half, but that only comes with maturity and experience. Looking back I now know I was the one who was in the wrong although, at the time, I thought the manager was the one who was wrong. You learn with experience.'

It took another Old Firm set-to to spark Rangers into life. Goals from Brian Laudrup and a Mark Hateley double helped Rangers to an impressive 3–1 win at Celtic's temporary Hampden home. The Ibrox big-spenders kicked on and put together an impressive fourteen-game unbeaten run together.

The team had clearly gelled on and off the pitch. 'What struck me was how close-knit the dressing room was,' Fraser Wishart admitted. 'I think that is what Walter Smith tries to foster. He doesn't like individuals who don't want to be part of a team. He'd rather have somebody who would play for the team than themselves. Guys like Brian Laudrup were fabulous players but they also loved playing for Rangers. There were no airs or graces in that dressing room. If anybody got too big for their boots then they would be hauled back into line. You had to be a strong character in that dressing room.'

Young Charlie Miller was also impressing although some of Smith's other protégés didn't polish up the same way. 'The one story that stands out for me with the Gaffer involved one of the younger boys we had at Rangers called John Douglas,' Miller revealed. 'He was from Northern Ireland. The Gaffer told him to clean his shoes and when he came back he wanted to see his face on the soles. John took him, quite literally, at his word. He polished his shoes top and bottom put them down and left them for the Gaffer. He put them on and drove home. He had light upholstery in his car and then he had jumped into the house and walked the polish right into a really light carpet. By all accounts the carpet was wrecked and Mrs Smith was far from happy. So the next day we could see the Gaffer was fizzing. He came in and shouted for John. He went into his office and we heard the Gaffer going right through him. He was absolutely furious.' It maybe came as no surprise that Mr Douglas failed to make a name for himself at Ibrox.

Summer signing Alan McLaren was still keen to impress Smith and the rest of the management even though his next move, by his own admission, went down like a lead balloon with the rest of his team mates.

'I ended up getting suspended and missed three or four games around the Christmas period,' McLaren recalled. 'Around that time the players had arranged a Christmas get-away to Monaco for all the boys. I felt a bit guilty that I had missed a few games through suspension so I told the manager that I would stay behind and play in a few reserve games to top up my fitness. Looking back I think to myself what a plonker, and I am sure my team mates probably thought exactly the same about me. My situation was made even worse because all the reserve games ended up being cancelled and all I ended up doing was training while my team mates were living it up in Monaco. I knew I would get very little sympathy and I only had myself to blame for being so stupid.'

Things were going well but it still wasn't enough to keep Pieter Huistra at Ibrox. He had been signing short-term contracts and although he was playing regularly he still felt he was in the shadows of Laudrup and decided to quit for pastures new that January.

Huistra explained: 'Rangers had offered me a new four-year contract but I wasn't getting as many games as I would have liked. I actually played more games even although I was on a short-term contract but I also knew I was likely to be sold if the right offer came in for me. I don't know, maybe I could have stayed but Sanfrecce Hiroshima came in for me and offered me quite a good deal. My fellow Dutchman Wim Jansen was also the coach there and that was a big thing for me. In the end that was probably the deciding factor in me swapping Rangers for Japan. I left Rangers with a heavy heart but it is always a period of my life and career that I look back on with great fondness. It was also the most successful time of my career where I won trophies and picked up medals. I also met some great people in Glasgow and that is why I look back at Rangers with such fondness.'

Smith still felt his squad was a bit light, especially in terms of squad cover and he made a shock double raid to sign Alex Cleland and Gary Bollan from Dundee United. It was a bolt out of the blue for the pair as well. Cleland said: 'It was a real surprise for me and Gary because we didn't hear anything about things until the day we actually signed for Rangers. We didn't even know if we were going to Rangers to play or just to be cover for the squad.

'Our first game was due to be against Dundee United but as

part of the transfer we were unable to play until the following week, so that was frustrating sitting in the front reception watching all my old Dundee United team mates troop in to get ready for the game. It can normally be a big transition going to a top club like Rangers but the Gaffer played a big part in getting us settled. It can often take months, but I think within six weeks I felt a part of things and that was all down to the manager, his coaching staff and the players. Gary and I were made to feel a part of things from the day we walked in the door. Also, with every day that passed I felt more confident within myself that I could play with the top, top players that were at the club. I had to play them three or four times a season but now I was asked to play to that level every week. I eventually made my debut up at Aberdeen and it was hardly a debut to remember. We lost 2–0 at Pittodrie and bang went the team's long unbeaten run.'

Rangers were then knocked out of the Scottish Cup by Hearts. The Jambos beat them again in the league but that was their only other defeat as they cruised away from Alex McLeish's Motherwell, who finished a creditable second.

There had been a lot of pressure on Brian Laudrup but he had produced the goods and was delighted to play his part in what was to be his first league triumph. The Dane admitted: 'To win the title in my first season was great. We played well and we thoroughly deserved to win the league that season. It was also another step on the road to nine-in-a-row. I was also a big-name signing and I knew the pressure was on me to make sure Rangers continued to be successful in Scotland. We managed to do that and the fact it was my first league winner's medal in Scotland made it even more special.'

A big part of Rangers' success had been down to the goal-hungry partnership between Ally McCoist and Mark Hateley. 'I look back at my partnership with Ally McCoist with great pride,' Hateley admitted. 'We scored just under 300 goals between us in five and a half seasons. It really was an incredible record to score so many goals in Scotland and in Europe.'

The title may have been safely back under lock and key at Ibrox but Smith demanded standards were maintained. So a 3–0 defeat at Hampden Park against Celtic in the second last game of the season was never going to be simply brushed aside by the Rangers boss.

Alex Cleland recalled: 'My Old Firm debut came at the end of that season. I was really looking forward to it because I had seen a lot of the games and I knew how big they were. We had already won the league but it hardly went the way I had hoped. The team and I didn't play particularly well and we lost 3–0. That was probably the first time I saw the manager far from happy. You always knew the Gaffer wasn't happy when you saw him clench his fists. Fortunately he didn't have to do it too often. But when you saw the fists then you knew he wasn't happy and you'd better buck up your ideas.'

That was one particular afternoon that Neil Murray also saw his Gaffer in full flow. Murray said: 'We had already won the league when we went to Hampden and lost 3–0 in a league game to Celtic. The manager came in after the game and I have to say that was the one and only time where I saw him really, really angry. He didn't shout and scream but you knew he was very, very upset. We had won the league but he demanded the highest standards from his players at all times.'

Versatile defender Cleland played his part in the title win but still didn't play enough games to get the medal he craved. Cleland explained: 'I ended up playing ten or eleven games that season as we won the league. I was actually wondering if I had done enough to win a medal. I remember Archie and Walter going round with the medals and I never got one. I had been just short of the number of games you needed to have played. I don't even know if I had played in that first match against Dundee United if that might have been enough! Anyway, knowing Walter the way I do now then I am sure Walter would have given me a medal if he felt I deserved it. I certainly was never going to chap on his door and ask him for one.'

There, however, was to be some additional silverware for Charlie Miller, who had impressed immensely in his first full season as a top-team regular. He not only helped to win the title but also walked away with Scotland's best young player award.

Miller, who recalled it with great pride, said: 'I won the Scottish PFA young player of the year award. The Gaffer had me well warned before the ceremony. He told me I'd better not be drunk when I went up to accept my award. There was no way I was going to upset him that night and I didn't even have a drink. It was a great night and was the perfect end to a great season. I know I have my team mates, Walter and all the coaching staff to thank for helping me to win that award.'

10

A GEORDIE GENIUS
HELPS TO MAKE IT EIGHT-IN-A-ROW

(1995–96)

THE 1994–95 championship might have been won by an impressive fifteen points from Motherwell but that was the only piece of silverware that ended up at Ibrox. Major disappointments in the Coca Cola Cup, Scottish Cup and Champions League hadn't been part of Walter Smith's major plan. So, once again, he delved into the transfer market with stunning effect. The next big signing was even to eclipse the previous summer capture of Brian Laudrup. The signing of Geordie genius Paul Gascoigne not only caught the imagination of Scotland but also the world game. 'Gazza' was known for his madcap antics but the one thing that nobody could question was his ability. The silky playmaker had been dogged with injury since the day he made the move from Tottenham Hotspur to Lazio. Smith and chairman David Murray had got wind the Italians were about to sell and tried to strike a deal before England's top clubs became aware of Gascoigne's situation. The chance to return to the UK, outwith the constant glare of the paparazzi, was also something that appealed to the troubled England international and it allowed both parties to get together and thrash out the daring £4.3 million transfer.

A delighted Smith, when he unveiled his latest arrival, said: 'This is yet another important signing for us as we continue our policy to bring the best players available to Scottish football. Paul has the top quality every player needs. Last year we brought in Brian Laudrup from another Italian club, Fiorentina, and he went on to have a great season. Now we are hoping that Paul can make a similar impact and strengthen our team both domestically and in Europe.'

There was also to be a bit of a changing of the guard. Mark Hateley had been troubled by injuries and so Smith turned to Russian international Oleg Salenko to get the goals. He had starred at the World Cup the previous summer and arrived at Ibrox via an indifferent spell with Spanish giants Valencia. There was also a splattering of Scottish-based signings including talented full back Stephen Wright from Aberdeen and Dundee United's imposing Serbian defender Gordan Petric, who had looked set to move to Celtic.

Petric said: 'I was really surprised that I ended up at Rangers. It was never really discussed in the newspapers and it looked more likely that I would be going to Celtic because their late manager Tommy Burns always spoke highly of me and I think he even confirmed that he wanted to sign me. I honestly don't know how my move came about. I know Jim McLean had a relationship with Walter so maybe that was the deciding factor, but I don't really know. It wasn't until I signed for Rangers that Walter told me that he had actually been tracking me for a year before he finally got me. I think Dundee United were trying to get as much money as they could for me because I was going into the final six months of my contract and I told them I wanted to keep my options open to see if I could try and win a move to a bigger club or to a more high-profile league. Jim McLean was far from happy with me and had a go at me in the press and so I think he was just happy to have got a decent deal from Rangers for me and by doing so he could also make me look like the bad one for not signing a new contract.'

Gazza's first competitive debut was met by a frenzy of media activity as he made his bow in the Champions League qualifier against Anorthosis Famagusta. Gordon Durie got the only goal. Gazza then netted in the Coca Cola Cup second round clash against Morton at Ibrox. Legendary marksman Ally McCoist also netted his 300th goal for Rangers but even that wasn't going to knock Gazza off the back pages.

This time round there were no big problems as old and new hit the ground running and a 0–0 draw with Famagusta was enough to get them back into the Champions League. The bad news for Smith was that his team was drawn in the so-called Group of Death with Borussia Dortmund, Juventus and Steaua Bucharest. But Rangers also knew they had strength in depth.

Gordan Petric admitted: 'The first thing that struck me about Rangers was the real togetherness they had within the dressing room. There were so many great players and they all wanted to win. A lot of that was down to the longer-serving players like Richard Gough, Ally McCoist, Ian Ferguson, Ian Durrant, Davie Robertson, John Brown and Andy Goram. Most of them had come through the ranks with Walter and they knew what it took to win titles and to have success under the manager. We didn't always play well but we always fought hard for everything. There were guys like Brian Laudrup, Paul Gascoigne and Oleg Salenko, so there was a real abundance of quality in the Rangers squad I had just joined with a top manager at the helm. We had twenty-odd top players and the fact Walter managed to keep everyone happy showed just what a great coach and man-manager he was.'

The group campaign kicked off in the Romanian capital against Steaua Bucharest and ended up being a nightmare night for Rangers and in particular Alan McLaren. The big defender got sent off along with Damian Militaru after he went for the Steaua player who had spat at him. The frustration and anger were then multiplied when a certain Daniel Prodan, who later infamously signed for Rangers, netted the only goal of the game minutes from time.

McLaren admitted: 'I had a lot of high points at Rangers but my lowest was probably the Champions League clash against Steaua Bucharest. I got sent off and we lost to a wonder strike from Daniel Prodan. I got sent off because I elbowed the Steaua player twice in the face. I had no complaints. It was a straight red card. I just lost it. The player spat at me and the red mist just came down. I couldn't get a punch at him and so I went at him with the elbow. I left the referee with no option but to show me the red card. We both got sent off. The manager came in after it and asked me what had happened. I just showed him my shirt. The phlegm was still all over the collar. I fully expected him to go mental because he had every right. I had been stupid and let the team down badly and on top of that we had lost the game. I felt like rubbish and I think he knew I felt bad enough and he wasn't about to add to my disappointment by slaughtering me in front of my team mates.'

That disappointment was lessened as an Ally McCoist goal knocked out Celtic and booked Rangers a place in the semi-final of the Coca Cola Cup. The Light Blues followed that by picking up their first Champions League point in a 2–2 Ibrox draw with big-spending Germans Borussia Dortmund. Richard Gough and Ian Ferguson got the goals although the result came at a cost as Laudrup suffered an injury that saw him miss the next thirteen games. Rangers weren't too troubled by that loss and built on that with a fine 2–0 win over Celtic at Parkhead in the league.

It was a game that will live forever with Alex Cleland. He explained: 'After the disappointments of my Old Firm debut one of my highlights was scoring in our 2–0 win at Parkhead. Celtic battered us that day and we spent long spells defending but we produced a real good counter-attacking display. I managed to get the first goal that day when I managed to get on the end of an Oleg Salenko cross to get my head on the ball. It was some feeling to see it skid off the surface and under the Celtic keeper Gordon Marshall. I then ran off in front of the dugout to do the old Ally McCoist high knees celebration. It was a great moment for me and then Gazza sealed the win with a great, great goal. Everyone always remembers Gazza's goal but if you ask them who got the first one they can't remember. Fortunately it is a goal and a game I will never forget.'

It was also a night where Ian Ferguson ended up on the wrong side of Smith and took a Parkhead pummelling.

'In that game against Celtic I probably got one of my biggest rollockings from Walter,' Ferguson embarrassingly recalled. 'I came in at half-time and he left me without a name. He sat me down and let me know in no uncertain terms that I'd better buck up my act in the second half. I actually thought I had played quite well but he claimed I had been more of a headless chicken, who was more interested in going out to kick people. Looking back at the DVD, he was right. I lost my discipline and I was everywhere on the pitch whether it be out on the left, on the right or through the centre.'

The next big test was to come in the shape of Italian giants Juventus in Turin. Richard Gough scored but on a treacherous night Rangers were easily thrashed 4–1. The only man to come away from that game with any credit was goalkeeper Andy Goram.

Goram admitted: 'We played Juventus away in the Champions League and they absolutely thumped us 4–1. They were a top team and had guys like Alessandro Del Piero and Fabrizio Ravanelli and that night they were all on top of their games. They gave us a real going over. I thought the Gaffer would go mental after the game but he came into the dressing room and never really said much. Then on the flight back I was sitting next to Richard Gough while Ally McCoist and Ian Durrant were sitting across from us. Normally the Gaffer would let us have a drink on the plane on the way back from European games. I said to the boys there is no chance we are getting a drink tonight after that. Then as soon as we took off, the curtain opened up and sure enough there was the drinks trolley. Walter then stood up and said, "If I see any of you are sober by the time we arrive back in

Glasgow then you are getting fined." He just wiped the slate clean and it worked because we had a big game on the Saturday and we went out and battered Hearts in the league.'

However, they lost the Coca Cola Cup semi-final to struggling Aberdeen and were then thrashed again by Juventus, 4–0, with Alessandro Del Piero once again at his best. It meant Rangers were sitting embarrassingly with just one point from their opening four games. They needed to produce something special but the campaign ended in disappointment with a 1–1 draw with Steaua Bucharest and a 2–2 draw in Dortmund that was marred by Paul Gascoigne's sending off.

The league race wasn't quite as challenging although a revitalised Celtic made more of a fist of things under Fergus McCann's tight financial rein. Rangers drew their next two Old Firm games although the highlight was a 7– 0 thrashing of Hibs just before those games.

There was also to be a shock departure for Mark Hateley, who had struggled with injury and returned to England with QPR. It was a hasty decision which came back to haunt the big Englishman.

Hateley admitted: 'There is no doubt leaving Rangers was the worst decision of my professional career. I was stupid. I had been out for quite a while after knee and ankle operations and I decided then I was going to leave Rangers. Looking back I should have listened to people's advice that you should never make a major decision when you're feeling low. I was thirty-three, almost thirty-four, when QPR came in for me and offered Rangers something like £1.5 million for me. I think David Murray looked at the deal and thought for a player of my age it was a great bit of business. Looking at it from his point of view it probably was. It was a chance to return to England with a decent club and I decided to take it but within ten days of moving to QPR I knew I had made a major mistake and I should never have left Rangers.'

Smith swooped into the transfer market again to sign Morton's highly rated midfielder Derek McInnes. There were a host of top teams who were after his signature but the chance of joining his boyhood heroes was one he wasn't going to turn down.

McInnes recalled: 'I was absolutely delighted when Walter Smith came in for me. I had done reasonably well at Morton and although Rangers had a vast array of talent I was still confident that I could force my way into his team. I felt I was at the top of my game when I left Morton and believed if I could play at the same level at Ibrox then I could make more than an impact. The good thing about Walter was that I immediately felt like I had his trust and confidence. I think that showed because whenever I was fit and training then I was either playing or on the bench while there were other players who were better than me who weren't involved at all. If you went out and did all you could for Walter then there was no doubt you earned his trust and when you do that the man is very loyal to you.

'Also Walter showed his true class the day I went to Ibrox to sign and have my medical. It was a dream come true for me because I was a Rangers fan and that day I also took my dad along with me. My dad spent most of the time in the office chatting to Walter and having a beer with him. It was a great touch. I wasn't a big-name signing. I was coming from Morton but the Gaffer still took the time out to make sure everything was all right and to make me and my dad very welcome. He realised it was as big a day for my dad as it was for me and Walter taking the time out made it even more special for him.'

The team continued to go goal crazy and hit an impressive ten-goal haul in the Scottish Cup at Pittodrie. However, it wasn't Aberdeen but Highland Keith who were put to the sword.

Alex Cleland, who was an unlikely hat-trick hero, along with Ian Ferguson, said: 'Another big highlight of that season was my hat-trick at Pittodrie. I always joke that there aren't many Rangers players, especially defenders, who have scored a hat-trick up at Aberdeen. People always say I can't remember you scoring three goals against Aberdeen and it is then I have to tell them it was in the Scottish Cup against Keith. I scored my hat-trick and then Ian Ferguson got another one. I remember after the game I went looking for the match ball. I went to see the referee and Fergie heard me and chipped in that he wanted it as well. I told him I was getting it because I had been the first one to get to three goals. I went to see the referee and he told me that the Keith boys already had the ball in the dressing room. He told me it was their big day so why don't I just let them have it? I said it is my first hat-trick as a Rangers player and who knows if I would ever get another one. Later on I eventually went into the Keith dressing room and I eventually got the ball. All the Rangers players that day signed it and it has some lovely dedications on it like "great hat-trick big head". I still have it and it is still proudly displayed upstairs in my house.'

Rangers continued to soldier on despite being continually chased by Celtic – who had been inspired by Tommy Burns's three Amigos – Pierre van Hooijdonk, Paulo Di Canio and Jorge Cadete. Smith also continued to look to the foreign markets and swapped Peter van Vossen for the ineffective Salenko, while Danish striker, Erik Bo Andersen, nicknamed the Red Romario, arrived from Aalborg.

Celtic, however, just couldn't beat Rangers when it mattered. At times they played Rangers off the park but always seemed to come up against a man inspired – 'The Goalie'. The late Celtic manager Tommy Burns once said that he wanted 'Andy Goram broke my heart' inscribed on his tombstone because of the amount of times he had helped to humble the Hoops. That led to the well-versed 'Smell the glove' stories, where it had been claimed that 'The Goalie' had thrown one of his gloves into the Celtic dressing room and told them to 'Smell the glove'. Goram, however, denies that and is adamant it is nothing more than an Old Firm myth.

John Brown admitted: 'Celtic came back with a vengeance for a couple of seasons under Tommy Burns. They were a decent side who not only played some good football but also had some top attacking players. They took us right to the wire and they were probably unlucky not to win the league. In one of the seasons I think Celtic only lost one game but somehow we managed to get our noses over the line. We had the determination and will to win. We were also street-wise and knew what it took to win the league and at the end of the day that might well have been the difference.'

A lot of the success in those big games was down to the belief Smith instilled in his troops.

'Everybody says Walter is a fantastic manager and there is no doubt he is,' Alan McLaren admitted. 'I can vouch for that through my own personal experience. He always had time for you and maybe when your form took a wee bit of a dip he was always there for a word or a wee pick-me-up or a quick two-minute chat on the way out to training. He would ask how the family were and would give you a few words of reassurance about your own game. It always made you feel that you were a big part of his plans.'

Ian Ferguson also reckons their boss was a major factor in humbling the Hoops in both his spells at Ibrox. That season Rangers also saw off Celtic in the Scottish Cup semi-finals 2–1, thanks to goals from Ally McCoist and Brian Laudrup.

'The Gaffer that season proved how good a manager he was,' midfielder Ferguson acknowledged. 'I don't think he actually got the credit he deserved during our nine-in-a-row run. A lot of his critics claimed he had the success he had because he was able to buy success and spend more money than anybody else. People tend to forget that money doesn't always buy you success. Even when you buy top players you still have to manage them and get the best out of them, as well as trying to keep the team in the trophy haul. I am now a manager and although I have had nowhere near the level of success that Walter has had I now fully appreciate what a great job he has done throughout his entire managerial career.

'I mean look at it – during our time Celtic also threw plenty of money at it but he still managed to come out on top. But there is so much more to Walter than just buying players. You only have to look at his second spell at Rangers. He wasn't able to buy a player for two years. For a club the size of Rangers that is unheard of but he still managed to regularly win silverware. That proves he is a top manager whether he has money at his disposal or not. I don't think there would be many other coaches, if any, who would have had the success the Gaffer has had during his two trophy-filled spells at Ibrox.'

A slip-up against Hearts gave Celtic a fighting chance but Rangers continued to keep them at arm's length and were able to seal the title in the second last game of the league season. Gazza went some way to establishing his big money price tag with a brilliant hat-trick in that win over Aberdeen.

It was to be the final title for long-serving John Brown as too many days of putting his head on the line finally caught up with him and he had to call time on his first-team adventures.

'I did the first eight titles in a row before I broke down in the ninth,' Brown admitted with more than a little hint of disappointment. 'The eighth was a big one. We sealed it with a 3–1 win against Aberdeen thanks to a Paul Gascoigne hat-trick. Celtic were right on our tails and if we hadn't beaten Aberdeen then we would have had to go to Kilmarnock in the following game and that was a potentially tricky fixture, so I was glad we wrapped things up before that point.'

Derek McInnes admitted by that point everybody was now talking about equalling Celtic's nine-in-a-row run. McInnes said: 'There is no doubt that coming up to seven- and eight-in-a-row the pressure grew, but it also built up on Celtic as well because they were the team who had to try and stop our nine-in-a-row. We were lucky because we had a core of really good players who had been over the course of the previous four or five seasons. They along with Walter and the new signings helped to drive us on.'

Rangers eventually saw off Celtic by four points before they headed to Hampden to take on Hearts in the Scottish Cup final. The Tynecastle side had finished fourth in the league and fancied their chances but that proved misguided as a virtuoso perform-ance from Laudrup, who grabbed a brace, and a hat-trick from Gordon Durie saw Rangers thrash them 5–1. Laudrup recalled: 'It was a tremendous team effort. I scored two goals and a lot people talk about my display but Gordon Durie was also bril-liant for us that day. For me, personally, that was probably my best performance in all my time at Rangers. When I look back at my display over a ninety-minute spell, it was my greatest perform-ance because I was full of confidence and I was able to go out and play to the best of my ability. To finish it by lifting the cup just made it the perfect day for me and Rangers.'

Defender Alan McLaren knew the impressive win over his old club was a big one and down to two certain individuals. McLaren said: 'It was a magnificent performance with Gordon Durie and Brian Laudrup taking centre stage with their performances that day.'

Gordan Petric walked away with two winner's medals and justified his decision to make the switch from Tannadice to Ibrox.

Petric was delighted with his first season's exploits. He said: 'That first championship win was probably my favourite. I played a lot of games and showed after my move that I was a good player. We also went on to win the Scottish Cup by beating Hearts. Gordon Durie and Brian Laudrup were marvellous in that game and it helped to make it a great first season for me at Rangers.'

For two of Smith's squad, the season didn't end on such a high, as the rapid rise of Charlie Miller was brought crashing back to earth. His off-the-field reputation was growing almost as quickly as his footballing abilities.

'It was at the end of that season that I had got into trouble away from the club and I lost my place,' Miller recalled. 'I had been playing just about every week and suddenly I found myself out on my ear. It was hard to take because suddenly I wasn't involved. I also missed the Scottish Cup final win over Hearts. It was tough but the Gaffer was only trying to help me out and keep me on the straight and narrow. We had umpteen run-ins through the years but I still love him to bits and respect him for what he did for me and my career.'

Also, fellow Ibrox graduate Neil Murray, who had started to spend more time on the bench or the sidelines, decided, for the sake of his career, that it was time to move on. Murray, who won four titles during his Ibrox stay, explained: 'I was out of contract and I was offered a new deal but I wanted to keep my options open.

'I didn't want to leave Rangers but I knew I needed to play more football. I think the manager appreciated the predicament I was in. He offered me month-to-month contracts and that was the case when we went out to Il Ciocco but when I came back I received an offer from Sion in Switzerland. It was a very good deal and I went to see Walter and he was great with me. He asked me if I really wanted to leave. I told him I did. He said that if I felt it was the right move then he wouldn't stand in my way. He shook my hand and wished me all the best. I remember walking down the stairs for the last time and going to get my boots. It was strange but it was time to move on because the face of the team was starting to change. Some of the young boys I had come through the ranks with were no longer there and there were more foreign players. I didn't feel it was the same although the foreign boys were all very good players. But, perhaps, they didn't realise what it meant to play for Rangers, compared to the Scottish boys who came through the ranks at Ibrox.'

Title days also brought out another side of Smith. Long-serving Goram said: 'Everyone talks about Walter's man-management and rightly so. He was great to his players and staff but he also appreciated the supporters. There used to be this guy we called "The Copland Nutter". He was a fan who would run up and down the steps during the games, starting the singing and getting the crowd going. He was mad but I remember after we won the title the Gaffer went straight up to the Copland Road end and shouted him down. The next thing we knew the Gaffer was taking off his trademark navy waistcoat and gave it to him. It was a great gesture and showed the Gaffer appreciated the efforts of everybody in helping the team to win the title. But when it came to the trophy celebrations and laps of honour you will always see the Gaffer in about things. You still see that wee sparkle in his eye when you win a trophy. He loves it and you can see what every trophy means to him.'

Smith, remarkably, had suddenly amassed an amazing six titles as manager, but more importantly for Rangers and every one of their supporters was the fact that he had led the club to their eighth consecutive title. Celtic's record was very much in their sights and was almost within touching distance.

11

THAT ALL-IMPORTANT
NINE-IN-A-ROW

(1996–97)

SUDDENLY Rangers were on the verge of something very special – something that had haunted their supporters for more than twenty years. Walter Smith's all-conquering side were just one championship away from equalling Jock Stein's nine-in-a-row heroics at Celtic Park.

Smith knew his team also faced their stiffest test. Celtic were now breathing down their necks and, like in their centenary season of 1987–88, they were desperate to drag the title back across the city. They certainly didn't want to see Stein's record equalled. There was also a massive weight of expectation on Smith and his team to finish what they had started. He knew more than anyone that the previous eight titles would count for nothing unless they could get to nine.

He also had to open up without inspirational defender Alan McLaren, who had paid the price for playing through the pain barrier at the end of the previous season. The injury cost McLaren his Scotland place at Euro 96.

McLaren explained: 'I thought I would be out for two or three weeks but it ended up taking three or four months to get over it. I only went in for an exploratory operation and ended up missing Euro 96, which was a real disappointment. I was struggling and I was hardly training the season we made it eight-in-a-row. I was only training one day a week. I would spend the week in the gym and swimming pool and then on a Friday I would come in and train with the team. I wasn't training flat out but the Gaffer knew I would always go out and give it my best shot. Fortunately my performance levels on the pitch didn't drop too much. I was told that I wouldn't do the injury any further damage. I don't know if it did or didn't. I know I played in some games when I shouldn't have but I was more than happy to play for the club and the Gaffer. Quite a few of us put our bodies on the line and I think the manager appreciated that. The Gaffer also repaid us and the following season he put me on the bench for the trip to Auxerre. I wasn't fit. I was still coming back from injury but just being involved was a great pick-me-up and I think that had been part of his thinking to include me in that squad. It was another mark of his great man-management.'

Smith went out to further bolster his team and again the pedigree of his captures was there for all to see. German midfielder Jorg Albertz came in from Hamburg and Swedish international Joachim Bjorklund arrived from Vicenza to cover for McLaren.

Albertz still remembers being shocked by his Ibrox introduction and how he feared that Rangers' hopes of nine-in-a-row may have been left livin' on a prayer. Albertz said: 'From the first day I walked into Ibrox Walter Smith was like a father figure to me. Even when he wasn't there he would tell the rest of the boys to look after me. I know it is easier to settle into a team that is winning but I was made to feel part of things from that first day. I knew I had joined a top team and was being welcomed into a great dressing room although I wasn't quite sure what I had done that first afternoon.

'Walter told the players to take care of me and we were due to meet up that night at Ibrox because Bon Jovi were playing live. So after training I went out with the rest of the boys and we ended up in the pub. We all had a few beers and then when we got to the gig all the boys, including the manager, were singing and dancing to Bon Jovi in the middle of Ibrox. I thought to myself, "What have I done?" I thought I had joined a professional football team. This isn't how they do it back in Germany. I had been captain of Hamburg and we had just qualified for the UEFA Cup and it was a big decision to leave them. I also didn't know much about Scottish football although I was aware of Rangers and Celtic. In the end the lure of winning medals, playing in the Champions League and playing alongside top players like Brian Laudrup and Paul Gascoigne was too big an opportunity for me to turn down.'

Swede Joachim Bjorklund thought he was heading to European giant Juventus before Smith made his move.

Bjorklund revealed: 'I had played one season in Italy with Vicenza. I had done reasonably well in my first season in Serie A and it led to quite a few of the top Italians clubs expressing an interest in me. Juventus, in particular, were very keen and they even offered me terms. I had pretty much agreed terms with them but then they told me that they wanted me to see out my contract with Vicenza and then they would take me on a Bosman at the end of the next season. It just didn't feel right. Personally, it didn't feel like the right thing to do and morally I knew it was wrong on Vicenza. They had given me my chance in Italy and without them I would never have been in the position I was in. I felt that if I was going to move then they should be entitled to some sort of transfer fee and even if I had agreed to go to Juventus then who knows what would have happened in that next season? What would have happened if I had got injured? Would Juventus have still signed me or would I have been left in limbo?

'These were all questions that were going round in my head. My head was all over the place and I just didn't know what to do when I took a phone call from my agent telling me that Rangers were interested in signing me. He asked me if I was interested and right away I said definitely. I knew Scotland wasn't as good as the Italian league but I was well aware Rangers were one of the biggest teams in Europe. So I agreed to fly to Glasgow where I met with the chairman, David Murray, and the manager, Walter Smith. I was impressed with the stadium but the thing that swung things for me was the plans that Walter and the chairman had for the club. The club had done well domestically but they also had this ambitious plan, which they felt could help the club make a real impact in the Champions League. They had struggled at that level over the previous couple of years and they were both desperate to put that right. I also looked at the Rangers squad and they had a lot of top stars like Brian Laudrup and Paul Gascoigne, along with a number of quality Scottish players, including Ally McCoist, Andy Goram, Alan McLaren and Stuart McCall, who I had played against with the Swedish national team, so I knew how good they were. So basically I agreed to sign that day, having heard Walter and the chairman's very ambitious plans for the club.'

Jorg Albertz quickly started to live up to his nickname 'The Hammer' with some stunning early season strikes. 'I was lucky because I made an instant impact when I scored against Arsenal in Richard Gough's testimonial match,' the new boy revealed. 'It gave the Rangers team a small glimpse of what I was capable of. I played a lot that season at left back or in my preferred position of left midfield. It was easy for me coming into a team full of quality players. I knew that I had made the right decision in moving to Scotland.'

Rangers were also keen to continue their progression in the Champions League. They cruised past Russian side Alania Vladikavkaz. It was to be a big night for Derek McInnes who had now found his feet at Rangers after taking the step up from Morton.

McInnes admitted: 'My big game under the Gaffer was the match against Alania Vladikavkaz. I felt I had done well in the pre-season but the Gaffer decided to go with Ian Ferguson but he pulled up after twenty minutes and that gave me my chance. I came off the bench and scored and then set up Ally McCoist's goal in our 3–1 win in the Champions League. I walked off delighted and with the man of the match award. That was a big day for me because it showed I could play and mix it at the top level and I didn't look out of place in a squad who were regularly on the trophy trail and were awash with top players.'

The Russians were then thumped in the second leg and the reward was another assault on the Champions League group stages. This time the draw, on paper, looked a lot more favourable with Ajax, French outfit Auxerre and Switzerland's Grasshoppers making up the quartet.

It was a section where Rangers should have been looking to progress but their dismal campaign never got going. The theme was set in the opening game in Zurich, where Rangers were thrashed 3–0 by Grasshoppers. Swiss boss Christian Gross, who later went on to have a short and unsuccessful stop at Tottenham Hotspur, claimed the Rangers players had treated their trip to Switzerland like holidaymakers rather than as top European footballers. The embarrassment continued as Auxerre beat them at Ibrox and Ajax eased past them with a 4–1 win in Amsterdam. The Dutch giants backed that up with a 1–0 win at Ibrox and suddenly Smith's shell-shocked stars faced the prospect of finishing their European campaign without a single point. An Ally McCoist double against Grasshoppers finally gave the Scottish champions a long overdue win but things ended the way they had started with another nightmare away-day defeat, this time in Auxerre.

Joachim Bjorklund knows the team let themselves down badly on the European front. The straight-talking defender admitted: 'We never really made the impact that both Walter and the chairman hoped to make in my first season. It was a big disappointment, as were most of my European experiences at Rangers. I just wished the team and I had been able to give the club, the fans, the manager and the chairman the European success they craved. I have often wondered why we never had the same impact in Europe as we had in Scotland. Reflecting on things I think we were maybe a bit too naive when it came to the European games. There was a big difference in style between the Scottish league and the European competitions. It probably was quite a big step up and we tried to employ the same tactics as we did at home. We always felt that we had the quality to go out and score more goals than the opposition. We could do it in Scotland but couldn't do that in Europe. Maybe we thought we were better than we actually were.

'I think maybe we should have been a bit cleverer. Look at the Champions League draw we got that season. It was Ajax, Auxerre and Grasshoppers. It certainly wasn't a group that a club like Rangers should have been frightened of. Maybe that was the problem. Maybe we were over-confident and in the end that was our undoing. It was a major disappointment but I have to say that even without European success I never once regretted my move to Rangers. They are a great club and team and I look back with great pride on the fact that I managed to play for such a top team like Rangers. There aren't many clubs throughout Europe who get 50,000 fans for all their home games. There was also the fact we were going for nine titles in a row, so there was still plenty to play for over the course of that first season in Scotland.'

The confidence-stricken Rangers stars knew they had to get over their European disappointments quickly, especially as there was so much at stake on the domestic front. The Coca Cola Cup once again proved to be a worthwhile tournament. Rangers booked their place in the final with a six-goal thrashing of Dunfermline. For Charlie Miller it was a day he will never forget – for all the wrong reasons as he was left out of pocket and out of the team.

Miller joked: 'I could probably fill a book with all the rollockings I took off the Gaffer. The worst one was probably before we were due to play Dunfermline in the Coca Cola Cup semi-final at Parkhead. We were going to the hotel when I jumped into the bookies to put a line on. I had been given a tip on a horse and I had decided to back it. The horse was priced at 5–1 and I was just about to put £200 on it. I was just putting the money up on the counter when the man behind the desk told me that Archie Knox had just walked in. Archie screeched at me to get to the hotel because the Gaffer wanted to see me. He wouldn't even let me put the bet on. I went in to see the Gaffer and he told me to get my stuff and go home because I wasn't going to be involved against Dunfermline. It ended up being a sore lesson. The team won and it probably cost me a £6000 win bonus. To top it all off the horse I went to bet on also won and so I saw another potential £1000 disappear down the drain. It was an expensive lesson to learn but Walter obviously felt it was the only way I was going to learn. But to be fair the Gaffer was never one to hold grudges. That was shown because I also got back in the team and I also played in the cup final against Hearts.'

The final saw a repeat of the previous season's Scottish Cup final. This time the win wasn't to be as convincing as Hearts pushed Rangers all the way in a seven-goal thriller. But doubles from Ally McCoist and Paul Gascoigne ensured the trophy was bound for Ibrox again. Derek McInnes was dropped for that Celtic Park clash and admitted it was one of the real low points of his Rangers' career.

McInnes explained: 'The League Cup final was the one instance where I really felt hard done by under Walter Smith. I had played in every game in the run-up to the final and scored in the 6–1 semi-final win over Dunfermline. I was confident that I would at least be on the bench for the final. But when the Gaffer named his team I wasn't in it or even on the bench. I was left gutted and I couldn't fully understand why I wasn't involved. I felt really hard done by. I was delighted for the players that we had won the cup but my own celebrations that night were a bit muted because I was just so disappointed because I hadn't been a part of things. I just didn't see it coming and I just felt I had been denied my first real piece of silverware where I had really played a part in the team's success.

'The next day I went in to see Walter in his office and he gave me a medal and said to take it because I had earned it. He also said I would get the bonus because I had earned it. He sat me down and told me it had been a really tough call and the reason he hadn't spoken to me on the day was because he knew I would never have agreed with what he had said. He explained he had decided to put Theo Snelders on the bench because Andy Goram had been struggling with a calf problem, Peter van Vossen because he needed another striker and then Davie Robertson, who had only just come back from training. I couldn't understand that one but he said he named Davie out of loyalty to him because he had never let him down through the years. It is only now as a manager I understand that you have to make decisions, which aren't easy to make, but they have to be done for the sake of the team. I have to say I still joke with Walter about it but even today not being involved in that final still hurts and still doesn't sit right with me.'

Despite the occasional harsh decision, you can count on the one hand the players who had genuine grievance against the Rangers manager. Smith continued to do whatever he could to keep his squad happy – even if it meant gate-crashing their Christmas Day celebrations.

Joachim Bjorklund explained: 'I remember my first Christmas in Scotland. A couple of my uncles and some of my in-laws had come across from Sweden because it was our first Christmas. We were all sitting in the living room when the door bell went and when I answered the door I was really surprised to see the Gaffer standing there. It was the last person I expected to see on my doorstep. I knew he lived beside me in Helensburgh but he also had his own family, so it was a really nice gesture to leave them to come and see how one of his players was. He was fantastic. I thought he would just pop his head round the door but he stayed for a couple of hours, speaking to all our family and making them feel really welcome. It was a fantastic gesture and one that all my family still talk about.'

On 2 January the only place Smith was interested in first footing was Ibrox as championship rivals Celtic visited. He knew the importance of keeping all three points at home. He wasn't disappointed. Jorg Albertz's opener was cancelled out by Paulo Di Canio before a brace from Erik Bo Anderson made it a Happy New Year for the blue side of Glasgow.

Albertz recalled: 'To be fair to Walter we didn't lose many Old Firm games around that time. Walter just loved taking on Celtic. He always got the boys up and motivated. He always knew how to get an extra ten per cent out of us when it came to the Old Firm games. I was lucky enough to score in quite a few of those games and every time I did I always looked at it as a real career highlight. I scored my first goal against Celtic with a free kick which was something special and then I scored against them in two consecutive games in the league and cup within the space of a couple of weeks.'

Ian Ferguson also reckons that was the match where he saw Smith at his most animated. 'That day when we beat Celtic was special,' the midfielder claimed. 'But it wasn't until after I had watched the game back on television that I realised what it meant to Walter. I had never seen him celebrate on the touchline the way he did when Erik Bo Anderson scored his goals. The cameras panned on to him and he was running up and down the touchline like a mad man as he celebrated the goals. It was bizarre because it was really out of character for the Gaffer. He is normally so calm and controlled, especially in the dugout, but that just showed the importance of that win. It was a massive win because it was so close at the top of the table between Celtic and ourselves.'

It was clear that it was going to be straight slug-out between Smith and Tommy Burns's Celtic, who had dived ahead going into the final run-in.

Ferguson admitted: 'Tommy's Celtic were a great side. Tommy deserved enormous credit for that Celtic team he put together. He had some top players like Jorge Cadete, Pierre van Hooijdonk,

Paul McStay and John Collins. They had some wonderful players and had one of their most successful seasons ever. They hardly lost a game that season, outside of the Old Firm games, and still finished second. That must have been absolutely soul-destroying for him and every Celtic player in his dressing room, but it just showed how good and consistent that Rangers side were under Walter. I don't think there is any doubt if Celtic had racked that points total up in any other season then they would have finished as champions, but we were just so determined to keep our run of titles going. We were so close to nine-in-a-row and we had this feeling that we just weren't going to let anybody stop us.'

Smith delved into the transfer market again to sign Chile international Sebastian Rozental for £4 million but a horrific early injury meant Rangers fans, like Daniel Prodan before, never saw the best of him.

The final Old Firm game of the season at Celtic Park was going to go a long way to deciding the destination of the title. Celtic knew if they won it they would pull even further ahead while Rangers needed a win to get destiny back in their own hands.

Brian Laudrup recalled: 'I remember there was such a pressure in the build-up throughout that season. I had only been part of the team for the previous three seasons but I remember the closer we got the more crazy the pressure became. That season was particularly taxing physically and mentally. We had so many injuries that a lot of the time I had to play up front myself.'

Since Rangers were struggling with injuries, Smith decided to hand Mark Hateley a shock return from QPR. A delighted Hateley said: 'It was a massive gamble for me coming back to Rangers. I had won six previous titles with Rangers but I knew if we failed to make it nine-in-a-row then I would have been remembered for that failure rather than what I had achieved first time around. I remember I took the call from my agent to say that Walter Smith had been on and he wanted me to come back to Rangers. It took a whole nanosecond for me to make up my mind. It was the easiest decision of my entire footballing career. Going back to the club where I had so many great years was a no-brainer. I had always said previously that I had wanted to finish my top-flight career at Rangers and suddenly I was getting this unlikely chance again.'

The Celtic game proved to be an ill-tempered clash that was settled by Laudrup's goal. The Danish superstar even back then knew his goal could be massive. Laudrup explained: 'That game and my goal were two big highlights from my time at Rangers. The Old Firm games were always crazy but that one was even worse because Celtic were two points clear in the title race. It was just such a mad game. It had everything, Pierre van Hooijdonk and Paul Gascoigne missed penalties, red cards and in the end my goal managed to give us the points we were so desperate for. That win allowed us to regain the initiative in the title race and from then we never really looked back.'

Joachim Bjorklund had been used to derby games in Italy and Sweden but he is first to admit they were nothing like the Rangers v Celtic game. 'I have to say my best Rangers memories were probably the Old Firm games,' Bjorklund insisted. 'They were special games with the big rivalry between the fans and all the media interest. It used to fill pages and pages days before the game. The atmosphere in those games was so intense and was like nothing I had experienced before in my time in Sweden or in Italy. The Celtic game that really stands out for me was the last one at Parkhead in the nine-in-a-row season. Every Old Firm game was massive but that one was even bigger. Celtic were really going for it and if they had won that game it would have given them the chance to really pull away. It was even more special because it meant we hadn't lost to Celtic in all four league games and it was the first time one side of the Old Firm had done that for a good few years.

'It was a big win in terms of the title race and also allowed us to gain our own revenge because Celtic had knocked us out of the Scottish Cup ten days or so earlier. That was a big anti-climax and we knew we couldn't afford to let them have the league as well, so that was why we were so determined to go out and win that game. We went on to win the league and make it a great first season for me in Scotland. There is no doubt that taking twelve points from those Old Firm games was massive. If we hadn't won those games then we wouldn't have won the league. That is how important those victories were to us that season.'

Rangers then, unexpectedly, stalled again as they lost to Kilmarnock and Motherwell, although wins over Raith Rovers and Dunfermline were enough to keep them ahead of Celtic. The day of destiny arrived on 7 May 1997 when the Light Blues made the long trip to Tannadice. They knew a win there would be enough to help them claim their own piece of Scottish football history.

Brian Laudrup revealed: 'Before the game Walter Smith sat us down and said: "You can all become heroes of a lifetime or be known as nearly men stuck on eight-in-a-row. It is up to you to decide what you want to happen."'

The game wasn't a classic but Rangers got what they wanted as Laudrup's header was enough to seal the win and finally let Smith and Knox get their hands on that ninth title in a row.

Laudrup was delighted. He said: 'That nine-in-a-row championship was just so special. I still have a fantastic feeling when I think back to that day. It is also rather bizarre that we won the goal with a headed goal from myself. I never scored many headers in my career so to score such an important goal was unbelievable. I just had this tremendous mix of joy and relief that we had finally made it and equalled Celtic's record. The dressing room was just chaos. With everybody shouting and screaming and champagne and drink being thrown everywhere. We all knew what it meant to the club and to people like Walter Smith who had been there from the start. If we hadn't won the league and we had ended up finishing with eight-in-a-row then it would have been one of the biggest disappointments in Rangers' proud history. It would have taken the team and the club a lot of time to get over it, so I was just relief that we didn't have to try and get over that potential heartache. Even now I know how massive that league win was for Rangers because whenever I go back to Scotland people always talk about that season and my goal. As I said, that day and that season, like my time at Rangers, will stay with me forever.'

Once again big decisions had had to be made by Smith in that Tannadice clash. Jorg Albertz, who had played well for most of the campaign, was, rather surprisingly, left on the bench.

Albertz explained: 'The only disappointing thing for me that season was that I was dropped for the Dundee United game that won us the title. Walter didn't think I had been at my best in the run-up to that game and he decided to leave me on the bench and go with Charlie Miller because he thought Charlie had been playing well and deserved his chance. It was hard to take but it proved to be the right decision because Rangers won the league. It was more important that the team got results than trying to keep one player happy. I was probably angry with Walter for a whole two minutes and then when the final whistle went I couldn't wait to party and celebrate with the rest of the boys.'

But it proved to be an inspired decision as it was Miller who turned creator for Laudrup's all-important goal. 'That nine-in-a-row game at Tannadice was probably my most memorable game at Rangers,' Miller explained. 'I crossed the ball for Brian Laudrup's winner and it was a special night for everyone concerned. I remember sitting next to Derek McInnes in the dressing room and we both said this is great. It didn't really dawn on us at the time just what the team had achieved that night. We were still relatively young and carefree but I can only imagine the pressure the likes of the Gaffer and the senior players were under to deliver the title, especially as they had been on the verge of something that is never likely to be seen again in Scottish football. I was just pleased to play in the game because that season I had found myself in and out of the team.

'I also hadn't been involved the week before. We were due to play Motherwell and we were due to meet up at the hotel the night before but I ended up bumping my car on the way there. I ended up being late, although I phoned the Gaffer to let him know what had happened. I thought my weekend couldn't get any worse until he named the team and I wasn't even named amongst the substitutes. That was why I was probably happier than anybody when the team lost to Motherwell. I didn't want the team to lose but from a personal point of view I just longed to be involved in the game that made it nine-in-a-row.'

Alan McLaren captained the side in the absence of captain Richard Gough and he could see what it meant to all the club's long-serving stars. McLaren said: 'The nine-in-a-row season was the one that stands out for me. Winning it was great but I could see it meant even more to the likes of Walter, Ally McCoist, Archie Knox, Ian Durrant and Ian Ferguson, who had been there for the majority of the seasons. They had won all nine and that final title was absolutely huge for them. I was captain for the game at Dundee United where we clinched it. I was skipper because we had been absolutely devastated by injury. Gough had played along-side me in the defeat against Motherwell but missed the trip to Tannadice while David Robertson and myself had both been struggling but we knew we had to play. In the end Brian got the goal and helped us to get the win we needed. It was a massive relief because we didn't want it going to the final game away to Hearts. I knew how difficult a venue Tynecastle was to go to and it was just good that we didn't have to go to the capital to get the win we needed.'

Defender McLaren was also perfectly happy to step aside and let Gough lift aloft that ninth title. McLaren explained: 'I remember we went back into the dressing room and the Gaffer came up to me and asked it if was okay if Richard Gough went up to lift the trophy. I looked at him and I thought: "Is he having a laugh?" Richard Gough had been the captain for the majority of the titles and quite rightly he should have been the one going up to collect the trophy. I knew what it meant to Richard and there was no way I was ever going to deny him that moment of glory. The Gaffer didn't even have to ask me but the fact he did showed that he wanted to keep everybody happy. You could see what it meant to the older boys like Richard and Coisty. These guys were in tears because it had been such a massive thing to make it nine-in-a-row. It was down to a mix of things, winning the title, finally getting the monkey of Celtic's nine-in-a-row off their backs and probably the sheer physical and mental drain of making it nine-in-a-row. I knew how I felt so it must have been even more draining for them.'

Gough was just delighted that after all the blood, sweat and toil the main goal had finally been achieved. He was also able to bow out on a high ready for his next challenge of playing Stateside for Kansas City Wiz. The defender said: 'Nine-in-a-row for obvious reasons was the big one for me. I think that everybody saw that from my reaction when I lifted the trophy. I think we all knew if we had failed that season then it would have been an absolute disaster for Rangers FC.

'We all realised the pressure we were under and there were spells over those final few weeks where I thought we were going to throw it all away. To be fair, Walter and Archie Knox handled the situation really well and helped to keep a lot of it off the players. So to finally reach that milestone was just really special. That night's celebrations were something special. It had been a long and challenging road but we had finally got there. The fact it has only been achieved twice in Scottish football tells you how rare an achievement it actually was. Teams have waves of success but it is very unlikely they will have spells as long as nine seasons again.'

Mark Hateley was just glad his return had turned out the way he had hoped. He admitted: 'Nine-in-a-row was special and was the reason why I came back to Rangers. There was no doubt that title was massive but so were the other eight that helped the team get to that point. It was some achievement to get a team to maintain a winning way for nine consecutive seasons. I didn't actually get a medal because I hadn't played enough games that season but that didn't matter to me. To have helped Rangers achieve nine-in-a-row and just to be part of it was more than enough for me.'

Ian Ferguson, who has the second most Scottish titles behind Celtic's Bobby Lennox, believes that day has guaranteed Smith legendary status within Scottish football.

Ferguson said: 'Every title I won was special but that day when we got over the line at Dundee United, knowing we had achieved nine-in-a-row was probably the most special. As a Rangers fan I knew what it meant because I always remember the Celtic fans saying it would never be achieved. I could also see what it meant to Walter Smith. The joy and delight on his face was there for everyone to see and quite rightly so. He had ensured that Rangers were guaranteed their place in the history books. Now when people talk about Rangers and our nine-in-a-row teams they will automatically think of Walter. He had a hand in every title and was in charge for most of them. It has now given him legendary status in Scottish football and quite rightly so. Like the Celtic fans, I certainly don't think we will ever see another Scottish team win nine titles in a row. If you look at his teams will you ever see a Scottish team that would be able to boast such names as Mark Hateley, Paul Gascoigne or Brian Laudrup? In fact I would be surprised if any other manager after Walter Smith goes on to have more success than he did, especially at Rangers.'

Ally McCoist was equally delighted to have stepped out of the shadows of Celtic and knows nine-in-a-row may never be seen again. The Ibrox legend admitted: 'Without a doubt the big high-light for me under Walter Smith was winning nine-in-a-row. That management team and players had a very special bond. It was something that I don't think I will ever see again but hopefully I am wrong and many Rangers teams of the future will have it.'

Every Rangers player that day has their own personal memories. Derek McInnes said: 'That nine-in-a-row season was when I played my most games for Rangers. I had a lot of injuries but that campaign was probably my best. I did, however, have to go in for a double hernia operation in the final run-in. We lost to Motherwell in the second last game and it meant we had to go to Tannadice to win it. I had only come back from training and I didn't expect to be part of things but he told me I would be travelling with the squad. Then when Walter named the team, this time, I was amongst the substitutes, and I was lucky enough to get on and be involved in one of the biggest matches in Rangers' history. It was unbelievable. I was delighted but I was probably more delighted for everybody else, especially those players who had won quite a few titles in a row and also for the fans, because I was also one of them.'

For Alex Cleland and Gordan Petric it was rather ironic that their big day had come at their old stomping ground Tannadice. Cleland admitted: 'It was good to clinch the title at Tannadice because it was a place where I had started my career and had so many happy memories. It didn't matter where we were going to win it because once we got to eight-in-a-row I was always confident that we would get to nine. I felt we were destined to do it. I knew we had good enough players and a top coaching staff so there was no reason why we couldn't do it. The only thing was maybe the pressure but we had big characters in that team and on the sidelines. They had broad shoulders and they showed they had what it took to produce when it really mattered.'

Petric added: 'It was good to win the league at Tannadice that day but it was quickly forgotten. The one thing about Walter and his team was that as soon as something was won it was immediately put to one side and everyone started looking to the next challenge. That comes with playing at a big club because you can't afford to rest on your laurels. It was good to get nine-in-a-row but it was even bigger for the Rangers supporters. They had been forced to listen to the Celtic fans boast about their own success and this gave them the chance to get their own back.'

Smith is first to admit that finally sealing that ninth title in a row was one of his finest achievements because his team had been pushed all the way by a very good Celtic side. The Rangers boss knew his team produced something special because any other season it would have been Tommy Burns and Celtic who would have been left holding the trophy.

Smith admitted: 'Celtic's nine-in-a-row was a proud record for them, but I don't think anyone could have handled the Celtic manager's job any better at that time than Tommy Burns. His team did everything it could – you couldn't have asked for any more of a manager in one season. Celtic hardly lost a game in that 1996–97 season but still couldn't win the championship. There was something going on then that none of us had a great deal of control over, but Tommy handled all that with a great deal of dignity. He was unfortunate in his management spell at Celtic. He faced a Rangers side which was on a mission, if you like, to try to equal Celtic's record.'

Burns's hard work may have left him empty-handed on that occasion but it certainly didn't go unnoticed. It was to lead to him hooking up with Smith in an unlikely alliance later in his coaching career.

12

WALTER TRIES TO PULL OFF
HIS OWN ITALIAN JOB

(1997–98)

THE CELEBRATORY champagne hadn't even gone flat when the next big question was being asked of Walter Smith and his men. Could this Rangers squad make Scottish football history and become the first team to win the title for a tenth consecutive season? So for that, the 1997–98 campaign was always going to be one of the biggest in recent history. The Rangers fans dreamed of it, going one better than Celtic's legendary nine-in-a-row side, while the Hoops supporters were even more desperate to bring an end to one of the darkest periods in their history and to ensure Jock Stein's own achievements remained up there, unsurpassed.

The Rangers manager clearly felt many of his long-serving stalwarts, that had served him so admirably, were coming to the end of the road and he needed to seriously revamp his squad for the new season and for the longer-term future of the club. Smith decided to introduce more of an Italian influence, as he turned to Serie A for new blood. Italian international Sergio Porrini came in from Juventus, Marco Negri and Rino Gattuso checked in from Perugia, Swedish international Jonas Thern swapped Roma for Ibrox and Lorenzo Amoruso knocked back one of the biggest clubs in world football to leave Florence for Glasgow. Smith was determined to land central defender Amoruso, in particular, after

Chelsea had stolen the legendary Italian striker Gianluca Vialli from his grasp the previous season.

Amoruso said: 'It was Walter and the chairman Sir David Murray who persuaded me to sign for Rangers. I had never been to Scotland before I met them at Cameron House Hotel on the banks of Loch Lomond. The scenery was spectacular and I was even more impressed with Walter and the chairman's plans for Rangers. They were both clearly ambitious and wanted to make Rangers stronger in Scotland and on the European scene. The chance to play in the Champions League was also a big thing for me. It was at the time where only one or two teams from each country qualified for the competition so it was going to be very difficult for me to get that chance if I had stayed in Italy. I always wanted to play at the highest level possible and for me that was the Champions League. I also have to admit Rangers made me a really good financial offer, which was also very appealing. They really pushed the boat out to take me to Glasgow. Manchester United were also keen to sign me. Also the previous season Rangers thought they had signed Gianluca Vialli and lost out at the last minute. I think Gianluca had even been up in Glasgow but then Chelsea came in at the last minute to take him to England. I think the chairman and Walter were determined that wasn't going to happen again. They knew my agent was talking to the Manchester United chief executive Martin Edwards when they offered me a contract. In the end I discussed things with my agent and my family and decided that I wanted to go to Rangers and a big part of that was my discussions with Walter and the chairman at Loch Lomond.'

Italian international Sergio Porrini had even more experience than Amoruso, having started off at AC Milan, but it was with fellow Serie A big-hitters Juventus where he really made his name. The hard-nosed defender had lifted the Italian title league and the Champions League, seeing off Rangers en route, during his time with the Old Lady of Turin and his signing was seen as a major coup. Porrini wanted a new challenge and even more silverware. He also revealed Smith was a major influence on his decision to swap Serie A for the Scottish Premier.

'Walter Smith was a big part of my reason to join Rangers,' Porrini claimed. 'When I first arrived in Scotland for talks and to look around he was there to meet me and to introduce himself. I immediately saw he was a great person. He could have quite easily left it for somebody else to try and sell the club to me but he didn't. He knew how difficult it was for me, as a foreign player, to take the decision to move to another country. I had won everything in Italy and in the European club competitions and I decided I wanted a fresh challenge. That was when Rangers came in for me and I already had first-hand experience of playing at Ibrox in the Champions League with Juventus a few years earlier. It was a great stadium and I remember the atmosphere was electric. So I knew how big Rangers were but then when I met Walter that sealed the deal for me. I knew moving to Scotland he would do whatever he could, away from the pitch, to help me to settle in. He couldn't have been more helpful. He realised it was difficult being so far away from our families and he would quite often allow some of the foreign boys an extra day off here and there so we could go back home and catch up with everyone. That was important and was a big factor in helping us to settle in Scotland. It would have been a lot more difficult if Walter hadn't been so understanding.'

Young midfielder Rino Gattuso was seen as one more for the future, although back then nobody could have predicted, even Smith, how far this gutsy Italian would go in the game – lifting the World Cup with Italy and the Champions League with AC Milan. Back then Gattuso was still looking to make his way in the game and his fellow Perugia team mate Marco Negri was seen as the star attraction. The striker had scored an impressive fifteen goals in Serie A and although it wasn't enough to keep his side up it had brought him to the attention of Smith, who was still actively searching for a long-term replacement for the legendary Ally McCoist. Napoli tried to keep Negri in Italy but Smith eventually got his man for a fee in the region of £3.75 million. Negri was in no doubt he was making the right decision but for young Gattuso he had to think long and hard about leaving home to try his luck in Scotland.

'I have my father to thank for persuading me to move to Scotland,' Gattuso admitted. 'I was still at Perugia when I first heard of Rangers' interest and I wasn't really too sure. I knew they were a great club with many top Italian players but I was still very young and I was very close to my family so it was a big decision for me. I discussed things with my family and it was my dad who really encouraged me to join Rangers. Rangers had made me a very good financial offer and he said I would be mad to turn my back on such a good opportunity. I had been offered 250,000 euros, basic per month while he had to try and get by on 500 euros a month. So from that viewpoint it made it an easier decision to make.'

Sergio Porrini had seen it all and done it at the top level of European football but even he admitted he was shocked by the ten-in-a-row frenzy that greeted him when he first set foot in Scotland. The twice-capped Italian said: 'I remember from the first time I stepped off the plane in Glasgow the only thing I was asked about was ten-in-a-row and could I help Rangers to do it? It was the only thing on everybody's lips when they talked about Scottish football. Of course it wasn't just the press but the fans as well. I quickly realised the importance of winning this title. Of course that was also one of the reasons why I had joined Rangers, to try and help them achieve that goal.'

The summer recruits joined up with Smith's squad but for one of the new boys it was quite some considerable time before the Ibrox faithful were to see him in action. Lorenzo Amoruso had been troubled with an Achilles problem from his time back in Florence that was to end up curtailing him for most of that debut season.

The £4 million signing admitted his frustrations over those early months and how important Smith and his back-room staff were in helping him through it. Amoruso explained: 'Walter paid a lot of money for me and I was desperate to repay him for the faith that Walter and Rangers showed in me. Walter took me to Scotland and my biggest regret at Rangers was that I never really got the opportunity to give him much back – only four or five games after I had been out injured for ten months. But, right away, I could see what kind of man he was. When I signed I had the injury and I ended up needing a couple of operations to get things sorted out. Rangers initially wanted me to see their specialist in London, which I did, but eventually I asked to go back and see my own surgeon and Walter agreed. He could see I was really low as I just couldn't get fit and so Walter allowed me to go back to Florence to spend some time with my family. He also sent Archie Knox out to see me and to make sure my rehabilitation programme was okay. I was really grateful to Walter for that. He could have quite easily kept me in Glasgow because I was a big-money signing but he is the sort of man of who will do anything for his players. I don't think anyone could speak badly of Walter. I really thought of him as like a dad who has faith in his son to let him play the way he wants. That's the way he was with the guys in the team. He would tell them to go out and enjoy them-selves and express themselves as players. Of course, there was a professional approach as well but it was all about the atmosphere he created. There are lots of coaches who can train players in terms of athleticism and so on, but the mental well-being of the team is crucial. Motivation can so often be the difference between a win or a loss. It's Walter's character as a man that makes him stand out. He has a way of talking to his players. He has calm dialogue with them and it works. Everyone knows how well Gazza played for a couple of years. Everything he did during that period was thanks to Walter. He had to take him by the hand all the time. Everyone remembers Walter taking Gazza in for

Christmas dinner but there were so many more incidents. But Walter is good at that – you can talk to him about everything and anything. I know he was like a real father figure to Rino Gattuso but he was like that for so many of us. He is just a great, great man.'

The Italian contingent was also helped to settle in by Brian Laudrup and Paul Gascoigne. The pair had also had spells in Italy with Fiorentina and Lazio respectively, and were able to get over those initial language barriers. However, even the new boys quickly found out, first hand, the madness of the Geordie genius.

Rino Gattuso admitted that Gazza and quite a few of his team mates led him a merry dance in those early months – especially as he had no idea who Queen Elizabeth II was!

The future Italian international explained: 'Thankfully I took the decision to move to Glasgow. It was hard moving to a foreign country and new surroundings but everybody at Rangers was really good and really went out of their way to help me settle. I met and played with so many great people. Walter Smith and Paul Gascoigne, in particular, were a big influence on me. Paul had been in Italy at Lazio and so spoke Italian and he took me under his wing and as a fellow midfielder I would also play beside him. Gazza and Walter were two great mentors and they really helped me settle on and off the pitch. I was also on the end of some of their dressing-room wind-ups. The players seemed to think it was funny that when I first arrived that I didn't know who the picture of the lady hanging up in our changing room was. I was from Italy, I didn't know that it was Queen Elizabeth II but the players thought it was funny and used to make fun of me.'

Marco Negri made an instant impact in the SPL – netting twice on his league debut in a 3–1 win over Hearts and then bagging all the goals in a 5–1 win over Dundee United. However, although ten-in-a-row was massive, the Rangers support and hierarchy were also looking for more of an impact in the Champions League. Yet that failed to materialise as they eased past Faroes minnows GI Gotu and then crashed out of the Champions League to Swedish side IFK Gothenburg. The pressure increased further on Smith when Rangers also flopped out of the UEFA Cup to lowly French side Strasbourg. Suddenly questions started to be asked about the manager's long-term future after another campaign of European embarrassment.

The flak was flying and some of Smith's blood-stained stars knew they had to roll their sleeves up and dig themselves and their manager out of a major hole. Stuart McCall admitted it was hard because there had been such a changing of the guard and some of the British bulldog spirit within the Ibrox dressing room had been swapped for a more cosmopolitan feel. It had taken some of the foreign players more time to learn just exactly what it meant to pull on that light blue jersey.

McCall admitted that led to one of his few fallings out with Smith, when he left him on the bench for the trip to Easter Road. McCall explained: 'Walter was great and I think I only had one or two arguments in all our time together. The one that stands out was in the season where we were going for ten-in-a-row. I had been out for a long spell with a knee injury and had come back and played in a few games. I remember we had dropped a few points and we were struggling. We really needed to try and win our next match away at Hibs. Gordon Durie and I were trying to get it drummed into the foreign players the importance of getting the win. We didn't have the Richard Goughs and John Browns, etc, and Ally McCoist was injured so it was left to us, as two of the longer-serving players, to get the message across. Then in the morning of the game Walter named his team and I was on the bench. I was distraught because I was so pumped up for the game. I remember I walked out of the room and as I did the wind caught the door and it slammed shut. By the time I got to the bottom of the stairs Walter was standing there waiting for me. He had a face like thunder because he thought I had slammed the door in anger. He said to me: "Do you not want to be on the bench?" I said: "No, I don't because I am desperate to play!" He told me that I had been out for a long time and I just needed to recharge the batteries because I had played a lot of games in a short space of time. We agreed to disagree and I took my place on the bench. We were down 2–1 at half-time when the manager sent me on and within thirty seconds of the restart we were 3–1 down. I thought, "Oh no!" But we battled back thanks to goals from Gazza and Jorg Albertz. I then set up Marco Negri for his second and we ended up winning the match 4–3. I was delighted because I knew it could have been a big win. I remember I then went to the Gaffer on the Monday to ask him for an extra day off. I came in and the Gaffer was in the gym. I went across to him when he was lifting weights and asked if I could have a word. He said: "Yes, but can you wait until I stand up?" I don't know if he thought I was going to have a go at him but I just wanted to ask him for a day off.'

The Rangers players were also unaware that Smith had already held discussions with chairman Murray over his own long-term future. The strain of more than a decade on the Rangers management team and the demands of constant success were beginning to take its toll on the Ibrox boss. A combination of another premature European exit and stuttering league performances saw Smith offer his resignation with immediate effect but that notion was dismissed out of hand. Instead the chairman managed to persuade him to remain on and attempt to make it ten-in-a-row before he stepped down at the end of the season. It was announced at the end of October that Smith would relinquish his post at the end of the campaign but in the meantime would also be helping the club to find his successor – someone who could help Rangers make their mark in the Champions League again. To many people inside and outside of Ibrox it wasn't really a surprise but for many of the team they knew it was the beginning of the end.

Ian Ferguson recalled: 'When the news came out that Walter was to step down it really was an emotional day. It did have an effect on a lot of the players, if not all of us. There were a lot of the guys, like myself, who had been involved in quite a few of the nine-in-a-row titles, and had worked every day side by side with Walter. To many of us he was a friend as well as our manager so it was always going to have a major impact on the majority of us.'

13

NO WAY FOR A LEGEND TO LEAVE!

THE EMOTIONAL announcement that the manager was to step down was meant to end months of speculation and allow Walter Smith and his Rangers players to get on with making history. That, however, was never going to be the case because Smith had other problems and issues he had to address behind the scenes. Star player Brian Laudrup was out of contract at the end of the season and was looking for a fresh challenge while Paul Gascoigne also looked set to join him, as he eyed up a return to England.

Laudrup explained: 'I knew in the last season I was going to be leaving Rangers. Ajax made a move for me in the final year of my contract. I told Rangers and they didn't want to sell, which was great, and they said they wanted me to see my contract out. I then saw out the final season and when I knew Walter was leaving I also knew I would be moving on. There was a lot of interest but I just concentrated on my football. Chelsea came in for me in the January and everything was agreed but I never signed until the May, until the season in Scotland had finished. I thought it would have been disrespectful to Rangers and Walter to sign a pre-contract. Every player is different but that, for me, was the right way to do things.'

On top of that, long-serving Ibrox gladiators like Andy Goram, Ally McCoist and Stuart McCall also all had frustrating spells on the sidelines through injury, which, despite their aging limbs, took something away from the Rangers team.

Midfield war horse Ian Ferguson acknowledged: 'Brian Laudrup and Paul Gascoigne were also going to be leaving at the end of that season, so there was a lot going on in the background. I think those things all had an effect on our performances and even our form.'

Also some of the new recruits were struggling to come to terms with the speed and physical demands of the Scottish game. As everyone will vouch, the Scottish top-flight is definitely not Serie A!

Serbian defender Gordan Petric might have been one of the Ibrox foreign legion but, at least, he had managed to get some Scottish Premier Division football under his belt, with Dundee United, before he moved to Rangers. He also had the advantage of having played the previous season at Ibrox and had that experience the likes of Sergio Porrini, Jonas Thern and Rino Gattuso were still coming to terms with.

Petric admitted: 'We tried hard to win ten-in-a-row. It didn't come down to a lack of effort from the players because we gave everything but it wasn't enough. We had a lot of players who had been at the club for a long time and many of them were maybe a bit tired and maybe couldn't hit the levels they had done so successfully in previous seasons. Also we brought in a lot more foreign players. I know I was a foreign player but I had at least played in Scotland before I moved to Scotland but for many of the new boys this was their first experience and maybe it was a bit of a culture shock to them.'

Top scorer Marco Negri looked to have adapted the best out of all Smith's summer signings. He had netted thirty-two goals in his first five months of the season but a freak eye injury, allegedly playing squash, kept him out for the remainder of the campaign. The loss of Negri's goals had a damaging affect on the team. That; in the end, also proved to be the beginning of the end for Negri's

Ibrox career, as mood swings and problems behind the scenes meant Rangers fans never saw him get anywhere near that sort of level again. Swedish international Joachim Bjorklund is in no doubt that if the Italian striker had stayed fit then Rangers would have won the league.

Bjorklund said: 'There were also a number of other issues with the manager and a lot of the team's longer-serving players were also due to leave at the end of the season. All these things had an impact although they shouldn't be used as excuses. There were a number of other factors. Marco Negri scored thirty-odd goals before Christmas but he hardly featured in the second half of the season after he hurt his eye playing squash with Sergio Porrini. I think if Marco had stayed fit and played like he had in the first part of the season then we would have won the league. I have no doubts about that. I know a lot of people blamed some of the Italian players that arrived at the start of that season but that is wrong and extremely unfair. They were all quality players and all put in big performances that season. Every single one of those Italian players was a quality player and that is shown by the careers that every single one of them had. It would be unfair to blame one player for our failure to win the league. We won and lost as a team and that is the way it should be.'

Porrini enjoyed his time at Rangers and admitted the games that really stood out for him were the big European matches and the Old Firm showdowns. Maybe after playing in the Champions League with Juventus taking on the likes of Dunfermline or Kilmarnock on a wet and wild Wednesday night didn't hold the same appeal. Porrini's first couple of experiences of the Old Firm saw a win and a draw before Celtic took their revenge on New Year's Day at Parkhead, as the league title race continued to frantically see-saw from one side of Glasgow to the other.

'The Old Firm games were amazing,' the Italian recalled. 'The New Year derby that season was just something else. I have never experienced an atmosphere like it. In Italy the supporters come to the stadiums to shout at the opposition but in the Old Firm games both the Celtic and Rangers supporters got right behind their teams. It was a really hostile environment. When you took to the field you were not only playing for a great team but also a wonderful, passionate support. It was always tough in the Scottish league when you played teams away from home although it always seemed a bit easier at Ibrox, but there was no doubt that the highlights of the season were the European games and the Celtic matches. They were the ones that were that bit extra special, especially when you had 50,000 Rangers fans packed inside Ibrox cheering us on.'

That Celtic defeat was a set-back but the Light Blues were still very much in title contention and Smith was doing everything in his power to drive his team on. He might have been serving his notice but there was no way he was just going to see out time. Smith had taken the team to the verge of something previously unthinkable and was determined to bow out on a high. He might have been tired and emotionally drained but it didn't dilute his desire and determination to deliver, as Joachim Bjorklund found out to his cost after a shoddy performance cost the title hopefuls even more points at Kilmarnock in late February. Smith knew at that stage of the season every point had to be a prisoner, especially with Rangers and Celtic neck and neck.

'The manager always expected a lot from his players and quite rightly so because we were playing for a big club and were being paid accordingly,' Bjorklund accepted. 'If you didn't perform at the standard he expected then he wouldn't be slow in telling you. There was a game where I was pretty poor down at Kilmarnock. I had a nightmare of a first half and I was that bad that the manager substituted me at half-time. He sent on Tony Vidmar for me. He slaughtered me and I deserved it because I didn't play well at all. He was absolutely fuming with me and the rest of the team. He really was angry and there was no way I was going to say anything back to him. I knew better. After he gave me both barrels in the dressing room he turned round and kicked this big metal trunk that we kept all the kit in. You could see he had hurt his foot. I am surprised he didn't break his foot because he didn't hold back, but that just showed how much winning with Rangers meant to him. I suppose there was also the added pressure that we were going for ten-in-a-row.'

Rino Gattuso admitted that first campaign was a big learning curve for him and playing in the pressure-cooker of that title-chasing season gave him a real footballing education. He also believes his time at Ibrox went a long way to helping him to achieve the top-level success he had with Italy and AC Milan.

'The big thing at Rangers for me was the way they taught me to combine aggression with loyalty,' Gattuso explained. 'I was never blessed with the individual talents of a Gazza, Brian Laudrup or an Andrea Pirlo. I am not the star player. I am more of a team player who gives every ounce of energy to the team. That was something that was installed in me by Walter Smith at Rangers. It was also a big thing for me that the Rangers fans, who were wonderful to me, took to me right away. I think they appreciated the job I did. It wasn't glamour but I did everything I could to battle, run or win the ball back. I tried to drive the team on. The hairs still stand up on the back of my neck when I think of the Rangers fans chanting my name. It really was a special time I had at Rangers. I think my team mates appreciated the job I did because they nicknamed me Braveheart after that famous Scottish legend William Wallace. Looking back I know going to Rangers was a very big move in my career. They are a big club and gave me tremendous responsibility in an important team. All these years on there was no way I would ever have dreamt of having played in a World Cup final with Italy or in two Champions League finals with AC Milan. But it goes back to what I was taught by Walter at Rangers. The harder you work the more chance you have of achieving the objectives you must always set yourself.'

While Gattuso was getting his fair share of first-team exposure more home-grown talents were becoming increasingly frustrated by their sporadic outings. None more so than future captain Barry Ferguson.

His brother and former Rangers star Derek Ferguson explained: 'I recall at the start Barry was really frustrated with Walter. He would come in for a game and then be out for a few and Barry was getting a bit annoyed with the situation. At that point Walter tended to go for the more tried and trusted experienced players rather than blooding youngsters through the ranks. I had to sit Barry, like the big brother, down and tell him to just be patient and his time would come. I had been in a similar situation myself when I had come through the ranks at Rangers and that is just part and parcel of football when you come through the ranks on either side of the Old Firm. The bottom line is that Walter is experienced. Barry might not have thought it at the time but Walter did know best and I think time has proved that to be the case.'

Rangers and Celtic kept hammering away at each other and a Scottish Cup and league Old Firm double within the space of a week in the April looked like it could go a long way to defining the season of these two great rivals.

Rangers took first blood in the Scottish Cup with a 2–1 win to ensure their manager's last day would be a final back at Celtic Park against Hearts. The win came courtesy of goals from Ally McCoist and Jorg Albertz but it was an even bigger match for Italian defender Lorenzo Amoruso, who made his long over-due debut as a second half substitute.

'I still remember making my debut against Celtic,' Amoruso recalled. 'The week before I was training but didn't feel anywhere near ready, but then after a few days I started to feel a lot better and Walter asked me if I felt I could be involved. I was a little bit surprised but I thought why not? I knew I couldn't play ninety minutes but I still felt I could make some sort of impact. Gordan Petric ended up getting injured and Walter just turned to me and said: "Go out and do what you can do!" I went on and we won the game. I also played reasonably well and that was probably my highlight of what was a terrible season for me.'

That gave Smith's leg-weary troops the belief and confidence going into that all-important top of the table clash at Ibrox. It was to be the manager's last Old Firm experience and he and his players were determined he was going to go out on a high. Rangers did precisely that as goals from Jonas Thern and Jorg Albertz helped to humble the Hoops. That much-needed victory saw the teams draw level on sixty-six points each, although Rangers had a much superior goal difference.

However, that slender advantage quickly disappeared as a 1–0 defeat at Aberdeen the following week put Wim Jansen's Celtic back in pole position. Smith knew his team still had to keep the pressure on and they thrashed cup final opponents Hearts 3–0 but more mistakes down at Kilmarnock left the title in the hands of Celtic.

Smith's men travelled to Tannadice, which had been home to many a Rangers title celebration, on the final day and although they got the win, Celtic's victory over St Johnstone meant that a season that everybody at Rangers hoped would be ten-in-a-row ended in absolute heartbreak.

Jorg Albertz dejectedly recalled: 'That was a great Old Firm win and got us right back into the title race but then we dropped points up at Aberdeen which in the end cost us. I don't know why we didn't win the title. We tried our best but at the end it just wasn't good enough. I was disappointed but I felt it more for the likes of Walter who was about to leave the club.'

Even now Smith finds it hard to talk about how his first Ibrox spell ended. He joked: 'I try to obliterate that season from my memory. We won the Old Firm game and then threw it away. When we got to the stage where we had won nine-in-a-row, the games took on even more serious connotations than the previous ones.'

Sergio Porrini and the rest of the new arrivals had come in for an enormous amount of stick that season and he admitted he felt a huge share of guilt that Rangers failed to deliver that elusive tenth title.

He said: 'That final day when Celtic won the match to clinch the title was one of the worst in my career. I felt awful. The manager had brought in quite a few Italian players, like Marco, Lorenzo, Rino and myself to try and help the team win the title and we failed to do it. It was awful. It was even more disappointing because I believe we should have won the league. We had the better team but injuries to Lorenzo, Brian Laudrup and Paul Gascoigne proved very costly in the end. I think if they had been fit we would have made it ten-in-a-row. It was just so disappointing to go so close. People say the foreign players didn't realise what it meant the same as the British players but that wasn't the case. I felt personally responsible that we hadn't won the league. Then heading back to Ibrox after the game and seeing the devastation and tears amongst the Rangers support really was awful. But the person I felt for most was Walter. You could see the hurt and devastation in him. Also due to the fact he had announced earlier in the season that he was going to be stepping down. This was a man who had been so used to winning and suddenly he was bowing out of Rangers without the title. It was a terrible way for him to leave after everything he had done for the club. I am just glad he got the chance to return to Ibrox and lead the club to even more success in his second spell.'

Swedish star Joachim Bjorklund reckons the pain of that season is even harder to take because he believes that Rangers had a better squad of players than Celtic.

Bjorklund said: 'We went for ten-in-a-row and I still believe we should have made it but we didn't. Our problems started when we failed to qualify for the Champions League. That was a major set-back to everybody at the club. There were also a few changes in the squad over that season and quite a few more foreign players came in. They were all quality players and we had a good squad, so it hard to explain why we didn't do better in every competition that season. We also lost the Scottish Cup final and finished second in the league. For a lot of top teams that would still be seen as a successful season but for Rangers I knew that second best was never enough. It was a real blow, especially not making it to ten-in-a-row, because even going into the final couple of months we still felt confident we could win the title. We had a 2–2 draw at Aberdeen and that was probably the big result that cost us the title. It was a game we knew we should have won and walking off the pitch I think we all knew the damage that those dropped points could do to our title hopes.'

Long-serving goalkeeper Andy Goram was more philosophical about his team's shortcoming. He reckons the real achievement was equalling Celtic's nine-in-a-row run although he also acknowledged it would have been nice to have passed it. However, 'The Goalie' held his hands up and admitted Rangers that season just weren't good enough.

Goram explained: 'Everyone says it was a major disappointment not to make it ten-in-a-row. It was a blow but we still got what we set out to achieve – to equal and cancel out Celtic's nine titles in a row. That was history in itself and the tenth one would have been a bonus but it wasn't the be all and end all. The pressure was all on us making it to nine and all the players who were involved in those title wins can be proud of their achievements. Unfortunately when it came to ten-in-a-row we had run out of gas and we just weren't good enough. It was maybe just a season too far for many of us.'

Richard Gough, who had been persuaded to return from America to aid Smith one final time, reckons that title was thrown away.

'As far as I am concerned we had the tenth title in our grasp and we contrived to muck it up,' the Scottish international insisted. 'A lot of people think we failed because Walter had announced he was to retire at the end of the season but that had nothing to do with it. We could have and should have still won the league. We were ahead but dropped points against Aberdeen and Kilmarnock cost us that title. If we had won those games we would have won the league. It had absolutely nothing to do with Walter leaving.'

There was still one final task for Smith to take charge of, the Scottish Cup final. It was at least a way of trying to erase some of the pain caused by their late title loss. But the physical and mental drain of losing the championship was too much of a handicap to overcome and Hearts, managed by Jim Jefferies, came out on top 2–1.

Ian Ferguson, who had been there from the start of nine-in-a-row, admitted it was a terrible way for their manager to bow out. He said: 'It was a very emotional day. That day we lost the Scottish Cup final to Hearts, knowing we had lost the cup final and also missed out on ten-in-a-row the previous week. That season still sticks in my throat today. I won ten titles with Rangers and won thirteen cups but that season was definitely the worst one I had in all my time at Rangers. We had gone into the season hoping to break the record but it just wasn't to be. There were just so many different factors that in the end meant we weren't able to achieve that goal. It was just a sad way for the manager to go. He had been so successful and to leave the way he did felt wrong. It wasn't just him, it was also the same for guys like McCoist, Durrant, McCall and Goram. These were people I had grown up with and so to see them also leave like that was disappointing. There were tears everywhere that night and it was a sad, sad occasion. I suppose, looking back, players and managers come and go from clubs and I was lucky and privileged to play alongside so many great players and under such a top manager.'

Lorenzo Amoruso had only come in for the tail end of the season and admitted even in those difficult times he realised what a special person Smith was and what a great club he had signed up for.

'It was a sad day that Walter's last game in his first spell at Rangers ended in the disappointment of losing the Scottish Cup final to Hearts,' Amoruso accepted. 'It was bad enough that we had lost the league but it meant such a great successful manager was leaving Ibrox empty-handed. That was wrong and I also felt a sense of guilt. Walter had shown a lot of faith in me and paid a lot of money but I had hardly kicked a ball because of injury. I believe if I and other top players had been fit then I am in no doubt we would have won the league but it wasn't to be. That night we all had a meal and it was hard for the first couple of hours but then the boys started to come out of their shells and starting to smile, laugh and joke. I found it strange but they said: "Lorenzo, I know we are losing the Gaffer but he has been here for many years and done so many great things for this club that we can't let him leave on a low. He has done too much for this club." In the end, it ended up with Coisty and Walter taking the microphone and giving us a song or two. It was unbelievable and I had never seen anything like it before but it was then I realised what a special club Rangers really is.'

14

GAZZA – THE FLUTE TO THE SUIT

PAUL GASCOIGNE himself admitted some of his best footballing moments came during his three years at Ibrox. His move to Ibrox certainly allowed him to defy the critics who claimed that he was done and past his best – a catastrophic run of injuries had finally taken their toll on this particular national icon. There certainly weren't many people, outside of Ibrox at least, claiming he could get back to the sort of top level that saw him light up Italia 90. The World Cup in Italy had become a distant memory and now Gascoigne had to prove he still had the mental strength and, more important, the physical capability to cut it at the very top level.

Walter Smith, after learning of Gazza's availability, knew that with his natural ability he could be a major asset to his Rangers' squad in their quest to take them to eight titles and beyond. He also knew a fully fit Gascoigne could also provide the key to the Champions League. The real questions were on other fronts. Could he keep himself fit and, more importantly, out of trouble? And could Walter Smith manage him successfully where others had struggled?

After meeting with Gazza, Smith felt he could keep him on the straight and narrow and get everyone talking about the England international's football rather than the sideshow that comes with his headline-hogging off-the-field activities.

The Geordie's slate was wiped clean and it was now up to him to perform, because past reputations and transfer fees counted for nothing under Smith. From day one he made sure that even somebody with the A-list pull of Gazza wouldn't be getting any special treatment. The Rangers manager sent John Brown to make an early mark on his new boy.

Brown admitted: 'Gazza was an absolute genius on the pitch and one of the most generous guys you will ever meet. Unfortunately he just had too many hangers on but he could put a smile on anybody's face and was as daft as a brush. Thankfully I was never on the end of any of his pranks because I think he knew I wasn't going to stand for any of his nonsense. That came from our first training session where I marked Gazza. Walter told me not to hold back on him. Gazza started to try and basically take the piss with the ball. He then tried it again and I absolutely smashed him. After that I think he knew where he stood, but what a great guy and what an exceptional player to have in your team. I was certainly glad I was playing with him rather than against him every week.'

Midfielder Derek McInnes watched Smith take the Geordie under his wing and there is no doubt he responded with his performances on the pitch. McInnes reckoned that if their Rangers boss hadn't been able to turn Gazza's career round then nobody could.

McInnes admitted: 'Man-management is a huge part of modern-day football management and Walter is a master at it. When you are dealing with players like Paul Gascoigne there is no set manual as how to deal with different individuals. The bottom line is that when it came to 3pm on a Saturday every single player in that Rangers team would go out and give their all for the manager. It didn't matter if your name was Gascoigne or McInnes. That says a lot and was a major part in the trophy haul he amassed at Rangers. He had that drive because he knew, like everybody else, that if he wasn't delivering trophies then he would have been seen as a failure.'

The Rangers boss was also long enough in the tooth to know

while 'Gazza' brought some undoubted magic there would be times when the mayhem wouldn't be too far behind. The likeable midfielder was never far away from the edge and that was shown the day he sent Scottish football into uproar, when he controversially pretended to play the flute in front of the Celtic support as he warmed up. Not surprisingly, the Celtic fans exploded into uproar and there were also suggestions that days later the Englishman received death threats. Bizarrely, it was the second time Gazza had done it, but the first time had been during pre-season and that hadn't attracted the same publicity. This time Smith couldn't support him. He had to hit him hard because if he didn't then the Scottish Football Association would. Team mate Ian Ferguson held his hands up and admitted he was the man responsible for Gazza's infamous wind-up.

Ferguson explained: 'Gazza was good in the dressing room but it was me who probably got him in the best wind-up. Looking back it was utter madness on my behalf. I could have ended up getting him killed, it was that bad. One day we were sitting and I said to Paul: "You should run in front of the Celtic fans and kid on you are playing the flute. They will take it as a bit of a laugh and they will really appreciate it." Gazza took me at my word and sure enough the next thing I saw he was up in front of the Celtic support pretending he was playing an imaginary flute.

'Needless to say the Celtic fans went absolutely mental and I am surprised some of them didn't run on to the pitch and lynch him there and then. It wasn't until after he did it he realised what a mistake he had made. He came into the dressing room after the game and gave me what for. He was raging and rightly so. It caused a real furore and at one point he even received a death threat from the IRA. I have to say I now regret ever suggesting it because Gazza got into a lot of trouble over it and I think he might also have been hit with a couple of weeks' wages of a fine over it.'

Smith certainly knew how to handle him. Whether it be to

The Rangers dream team – Graeme Souness with his No. 2, Walter Smith

Walter Smith and Archie Knox flank David Murray as they are appointed the new Rangers management team

Walter's new-look Rangers side claim the 1991-92 title in his first first full season in the Ibrox hotseat

© PA IMAGES

© DAILY EXPRESS

© DAILY EXPRESS

Walter and his
Rangers team
who made it
seven-in-a-row

TENNENTS SCOTT
WINNERS 1

A blood-stained Richard
Gough lifts aloft the
eighth title in a row

Rangers celebrate their
1996 Scottish Cup
victory

Walter Smith lifts the 1996
Coca Cola Cup flanked by Brian
Laudrup and Jorg Albertz

Brian Laudrup scores his landmark goal against Dundee United that clinches nine-in-a-row

Walter and Archie stun British football with their shock capture of Paul Gascoigne

Walter Smith joins Ally McCoist, Andy Goram and Brian Laudrup in saying an emotional farewell to Ibrox

The Rangers team celebrate clinching nine-in-a-row

The Rangers nine-in-a-row team

© WILLIE VASS

90 MINS
SCOTLAND   1
FRANCE   0

Walter Smith and his
Scotland assistant
manager Tommy Burns

Seeing is believing -
Scotland 1 France 0

Smith's Scotland – carrying
the hopes of a nation

Gary Caldwell scores the
goal that sinks France

© WILLIE VASS

Sir David Murray and Walter Smith as the manager's second coming is announced

© WILLIE VASS

Walter Smith joins penalty hero Nacho Novo to celebrate their UEFA Cup semi-final penalty shoot-out win over Fiorentina

The delighted Rangers team celebrate their win over Fiorentina

© WILLIE VASS

Rangers
UEFA Cup
final team

A dejected Walter Smith
shows his appreciation to
the Rangers support after
the UEFA Cup final loss

Walter's other team – Walter, Ally McCoist,
Kenny McDowall and Ian Durrant show off the
2008-9 title trophy after the Dundee United win

Captain Davie Weir and
Walter Smith celebrate
being named Clydesdale
Bank player and manager
of the year 2009/10

Matchwinner Kenny Miller lifts the 2009-10 Co-operative Insurance Cup above his head after nine-man Rangers see off St Mirren

Walter raises the 2009-10 SPL trophy

Walter Smith about to spring a Champions League surprise on his old Manchester United boss Sir Alex Ferguson

Walter Smith joins his team as they clinch the 2009-10 SPL title at Easter Road

A final Hampden hurrah as Walter lifts
the 2010-11 Co-operative Insurance Cup

The end of Walter's
reign – as he takes his
final Ibrox bow

A champion to the end
as Walter helps captain
Davie Weir to lift the
2010-11 SPL title

Walter's Rangers –
a family affair

shout and scream, give him a public dressing down or to admin-
ister the ultimate punishment – stop him from playing football.
That happened one weekend after Gazza had stepped out of line
on the Friday. Smith sent him home and told him he wouldn't
be involved with the first team. There were also incidents where
Smith even threatened to put him on the transfer list to try and
get him back to his best on the pitch. That proved to be a more
severe penalty to the Geordie than any monetary loss or fine
could ever bring. Gascoigne was one of the bigger earners at Ibrox
but ask any of his team mates and they will tell you that was
very much secondary to his football.

Serbian Gordan Petric, who signed on at Ibrox the same summer,
explained: 'Gazza signed the week before me and he went to great
lengths to help me settle in. He also knew my good friend Alen
Boksic, who he played with at Lazio, so that helped us break the
ice. He is a wonderful person and one of the nicest people I have
met in my life. I remember when the team started talking about
contracts. Nobody would discuss what they were getting but Gazza
just turned around and showed me his wage slip. It was fair to say
he was earning a lot more than me! But he deserved it because he
was a true entertainer and under pressure and the media spotlight
twenty-four hours a day. People wanted a piece of Gazza and he
was never out of the limelight. Even when he went for the occasional drink he was followed and, to be fair, I never really saw him
as a big drinker. He was under enormous pressure all the time, but
Walter Smith still managed to get Gazza to produce some brilliant
moments of magic. Walter was a great manager for Gazza and for
every single one of the Rangers squad who played for him.'

With Gazza around there weren't many quiet moments in the
inner sanctum of Smith's dressing room. Not surprisingly the
playmaker was at the centre of a lot of the antics and his Rangers
team mates knew they had to watch their backs.

There was the infamous fishy tale that spelt the end for Gordon
Durie's car. Former St Mirren star Ian Ferguson explained: 'Gazza

decided to stick a couple of fish in Gordon Durie's car. He left one under the seat so Gordon would see it and take it out. But he was clever because he also hid a second one under the wheel arch, so nobody could see it. Gordon just laughed things off when he found the first fish and threw it out. Then a couple of days later the second fish started to really stink up his car. He searched high and low to find where the terrible stench was coming from but he just couldn't get to the bottom of it. The smell got that bad that "Jukebox" had to end up getting rid of the car and that was all down to Gazza.'

Defender Alex Cleland also remembers the day he was stitched up by some Gazza high jinks. He explained: 'I had come in to training with a new suit because we were due to head off to the Moat House the night before the game. I hung it up on my peg but when I returned it was nowhere to be seen. It had been replaced by one of Gazza's suits and it was absolutely stinking. He would wear the same clothes for three or four days at a time and right away I thought I am going to kill him. I couldn't even wear his suit because it was just a mess. So I headed off down to Jimmy Bell's room to borrow a tracksuit and I raced over to the Moat House. I was fizzing but as soon as I walked in I saw Gazza sitting with the suit on. I just started laughing. It was far too short for him and I don't know how he got it on. He looked a right state but that was Gazza. He would do anything for a laugh. Thankfully I got my suit back but I don't think it ever fitted me right again.'

There are also numerous accounts where the firebrand Rangers star harangued the life out of the McCoist family. Living close by, Gazza would think nothing of throwing stones at Ally McCoist's bedroom window – any time of day or night. Although that was normally a last resort because the Englishman would try opening the windows and doors first. It wouldn't have been the first time that McCoist came down with a baseball bat in his hand only to be met with a smiling Gazza who had been making full use of his kitchen and all its contents.

Rino Gattuso could also have ended up challenging Gazza as Public Enemy No. 1 if another of his Old Firm pranks he had cooked up hadn't been extinguished by Brian Laudrup. Andy Goram recalled: 'Paul Gascoigne was a great, great guy but he was also absolutely mad. When Rino Gattuso first came across he always went over to Gazza because he had been across in Italy with Lazio and knew a bit of Italian. Wee Rino would follow Gazza about everywhere. The wee man had just broken into the team and was making a real name for himself. I remember he was set to play against Celtic for the first time and I saw Gazza talking away to Rino. I could see the wee man was really pumped up and I went over and pulled Brian Laudrup, who could also speak Italian from his own time out there. Brian went across and spoke to Rino and then just started shaking his head and walked back across to us. I said, "What is it?" He said that Gazza had told him that if he scored a goal he should run in front of the Celtic fans and cross himself. If Brian hadn't have got a hold of him then the wee man would have been lucky to get out of the ground alive. That was just Gazza. He didn't think of the consequences. He just saw it as a wee laugh and a bit of fun.'

Jorg Albertz revealed how the old rivalry between Gazza and him also came to the fore over their old England v Germany backgrounds. Albertz explained: 'Gazza was a great guy and always great value in the dressing room. He was always full of life and pranks. You had to watch him like a hawk. Thankfully he only turned his attentions to me once but I think he obviously thought better about things. He used to joke that I looked like a boxer and maybe that was enough to put him off. The only real time I got it from Gazza was on one of our Christmas nights out. We all used to have to dress up in fancy dress and it got to the stage of the night where we all had to sing our national anthems as part of the mayhem. It took a while because there were quite a few nationalities in the squad at that point. Of course Gazza sang "God Save the Queen" and then when it came to my turn you could only imagine what he got up to. He started calling me Adolf Hitler and started doing all these Nazi salutes. It was all done in Gazza's typical, good nature although you knew he would be far worse if he had a couple of drinks in him. The point was that he wasn't really a big drinker.'

But it didn't matter what he did because Gazza was loved by everyone inside Ibrox and absolutely adored by the Rangers support. That was down to his undoubted ability and displays like in the championship decider against Aberdeen, his Old Firm heroics or the delightful goal he scored against Steaua Bucharest. Then there were the other incidents where he pretended to caution referee Dougie Smith after he had dropped his yellow card. In the end, it was the Rangers star who ended up in the book. There was no doubt that Rangers ended up getting value for money and a lot of that was down to the manager, who took a lot of the outside pressures off his shoulders and gave him the platform to go out and play. He responded. Rangers won titles and cups. For Smith, it was certainly worth setting another seat at the Christmas Day dinner table and upsetting the family routine if Gazza continued to gift-wrap further success for the Light Blues. But that wasn't the only time the England international got his teeth into things at Rangers.

David Robertson recalled: 'Gazza came in one day and he had just had his teeth done. The problem was that they were probably an inch too long and when he came in the likes of Coisty absolutely slaughtered him. Gazza took things pretty badly and you could see he was really hurting. I think the Gaffer saw that as well and told him to forget about training and just to go and get his teeth fixed.'

Certainly in his three years at Ibrox the talented Mr Gascoigne gave everyone in Scottish football, including Smith, plenty to smile about – until the day he followed the manager out the door. The England international was quite rightly inducted into the Ibrox hall of fame in 2006 and takes his place proudly alongside Smith.

15

IBROX BRAVEHEARTS

WALTER SMITH had decided that after nine titles in a row he had achieved all he could at Ibrox. He had stayed on, with a little gentle persuasion, to try and claim a Scottish record by trying to make it ten but it wasn't to be. It was clear that the pressure and expectations were beginning to have an effect on Smith. He wasn't getting the same buzz or excitement. He realised he was becoming stale and both he and Rangers needed something different to re-ignite that old spark.

Rangers turned to experienced Dutchman Dick Advocaat while Smith was hardly short of offers after his glory days at Ibrox. After much deliberation and consideration, his next port of call was to see him swap the light blue for a different shade of blue at English top-flight side Everton. He was convinced by the Goodison Park board to head to Merseyside rather than to take on the job at Sheffield Wednesday. Unfortunately, the tools Smith had been promised for the job never came to fruition and he became more of an accountant, trying to sell players and balance the books, rather than a football manager looking to add titles and cups to the already impressive haul he had amassed at Ibrox.

Smith explained, 'When I look back at my time at Everton I enjoyed every day. There is no bitterness whatsoever. It was a great honour to manage that club. I blame myself really for my own assessment of where the club was when I accepted the job. I should have maybe been a wee bit more patient and dug into the background of the club more before joining. Peter Johnson [then the Everton owner] told me he was going to spend some money on the team and he did. But in doing so he put the club in a perilous financial position. He left and a lot of the players I bought [including World Cup winner Marco Materazzi and Olivier Dacourt] had to be sold straight away again. We had something like eighty-six transfers in and out of the club during my time and there was never any stability.'

In the end, four years of survival and fire fighting came to an end and Smith, for the first time in his managerial career, had been sacked. But he was barely out of the game before he accepted a short-term invitation to become Sir Alex Ferguson's assistant manager at Manchester United. After that it wasn't long before his country sent out an SOS for him, via the chiefs at the head of the Scottish Football Association. The gamble to appoint a foreign coach, in German Berti Vogts, had badly backfired. Instead of being big tournament regulars, like Scotland had been under Andy Roxburgh and Craig Brown, the country had suddenly found itself deep in the doldrums. Scotland was becoming a laughing stock. The team had crashed to an embarrassing eighty-eighth in the FIFA rankings, behind the likes of Syria, Burkina Faso and the United Arab Emirates. In the end, results and poor performances forced Vogts to fall on his sword and on 2 December 2004 Smith was charged with the job of trying to help Scotland rise and become a footballing nation again.

Smith, on the day of his appointment, admitted: 'I'm fortunate enough in that I didn't need the job but I love football. If you have fear of criticism or not doing well then you should not be taking the job in the first place. I would like to think we are better than 77th [ranking had risen slightly from the all-time low of 88th] in the world. We have young players coming through whose expectation levels as far as the fans were concerned were probably too high and I won't be capping as many players as Berti did. Over the next few months, I want to gather a good group of twenty-four players together who I feel are the best men for the job.'

Smith knew he had to raise spirits and the appointment of his back-room staff was going to be vital. He knew, no matter what he did, that he would be accused in some quarters of bias towards Rangers and that was why he knew he needed somebody with a Celtic connection to try and balance things up a little more. The man he went for was Tommy Burns, who had already proved himself as a top manager, who had pushed Smith all the way when he had been in the Celtic Park hotseat.

Then Smith, perhaps, pulled off one of his biggest masterstrokes when he persuaded his legendary Rangers striker Ally McCoist to dip his foot into coaching for the first time following his retirement from playing in 2001. McCoist had already made a name for himself on television, mainly with *A Question of Sport*, and Smith felt his bubbly personality, his passion and his will to win could help get the famous Hampden roar back behind Scotland.

McCoist explained: 'It was unbelievable how I got involved with Walter. He just called one day and asked if I would meet him for lunch in Glasgow. Walter sat me down and asked me if I would like to be involved with him in the Scotland set-up. I was thrilled and honoured. I just couldn't believe it. I didn't need to be asked twice. I was delighted the great man had seen something in me which he felt could help him and Scotland. I honestly thought he was going to ask me to take one of the Scotland teams at under-17 or under-18 level but no, he said he wanted me to work under him with the full squad. I will never forget the moment he asked me. I just couldn't believe it. I was chuffed to bits and I can honestly say I never saw it coming. It came straight from left field but, for me, it was a no-brainer.

'Walter told me to go away and think about things, but right away I said, "I don't need to think about things. I will do it."

Walter said, "That is your first mistake. I have told you to go away and think about things, so go away and think about things. Now you've learned your first lesson." He said there was no point in knee-jerk reactions. So I took my time and went away and thought about things, although I still came back with the same answer. By that point, Walter was more than happy to welcome me onto his back-room team. I have to say it is a decision I have never once regretted.'

Smith was also able to use his contacts and his powers of persuasion to bring back the likes of Davie Weir who had called time on his international career after being far from impressed with Vogts' nightmare spell.

Weir admitted: 'It was Walter who opened that door that enabled me to return. He brought me back into the national set-up and allowed me to wipe away the bad memories I had when I left the Scotland set-up first time around. I honestly thought at that stage an international return had passed me by but Walter believed I could still offer something and brought me back into the Scotland set-up and this is something I will be eternally grateful to him for.'

Striker Kenny Miller also felt Smith brought more stability to the team, both personally and collectively. He said: 'When Walter Smith took over he was taking over a team that was struggling. It was a really bad time for the Scottish national team. Our performances and results simply weren't good enough. There was a lot of negativity surrounding the team and everybody wanted to jump on the bandwagon and give us a kicking. But the Gaffer came in and immediately lifted the team and the whole country. It was still pretty much the same group of players but within weeks Walter and his management team had totally changed the mindset. There was no doubt the manager was the catalyst for turning Scotland's fortunes around.'

Experienced defender Weir knew it was a time when Smith and Scotland needed all hands to the pump. 'After Berti Vogts there is no doubt that the national team was on the slide,' Weir acknowledged. 'There, maybe, wasn't the same pride in the Scotland team and that is not a criticism of Berti Vogts. We hadn't qualified for a major final for a few years but then suddenly Walter came in and got us back in a position where we had a chance of qualifying for World Cup and European Championships again. There is no doubt that was down to Walter. As a coach he is the best I have worked with. The way he analyses and changes things in games takes a real talent. It is something special. He is a top manager and you can learn so much from working with him.'

Scotland were already well on their way through their World Cup 2006 qualifying campaign although a nightmare start under Vogts had all but killed qualification hopes. Draws with Slovenia and Moldova and a defeat to Norway left Smith with a mountain to climb. It was more about salvaging pride then qualification. The new man was handed a baptism of fire as his first competitive game in a World Cup qualifier in Italy. He admitted before a ball was even kicked that the performance was more important than the result. It certainly proved to be the case as Scotland lost 2–0 in Bari. Lee McCulloch, who was given his first start that night, admitted that night was the first step on the road to recovery for our battered nation.

McCulloch said: 'The one thing that struck me when the Gaffer took charge of Scotland was the camaraderie he instilled in the squad. The dressing room was unbelievable. Normally when players are dropped they hate the manager and slaughter him behind his back, but I can honestly say I never saw that when the Gaffer was in charge of Scotland. He, somehow, knew how to keep everybody happy, whether they were playing or not. The players who weren't playing would just walk away and say, "Well I just need to try harder to make sure I get in his squad next time." That went a long way to raising the standards and levels within the Scotland set-up. Also I would say that bringing Ally

McCoist in alongside him helped. Coisty was his best signing – I don't think anybody can argue with that.'

A Hampden win over Moldova was followed by a goalless stalemate in Minsk against Belarus and a 1–1 home draw with Italy. That unbeaten run culminated in an away win in Norway. Top-scorer Kenny Miller was at the heart of that run, netting three goals in the games against the Italians and Norwegians. He said: 'Before Walter Smith came in I didn't know where I really stood. I would start a game, under Berti Vogts, do well, and then in the next match I would go expecting to play and then I'd be told I wouldn't be in the starting eleven. It was hard to get any continuity in terms of form. Walter came in, showed faith in me and pretty much played me from the start. It didn't help that in the first few games I didn't score although I had quite a few chances. I remember we were out in Austria for a friendly and Walter pulled me aside. He knew that not scoring was starting to weigh on my shoulders but he assured me that he would continue to stick by me, if I continued to give everything for the team. Walter's talk filled me full of confidence and I actually walked away from it feeling ten feet tall. Maybe it was coincidence, I don't know, but I went out and scored against Austria, then against Italy and got a couple out in our win in Norway. Walter laid down the blueprint for Scotland and then allowed Alex McLeish to come in and build on it.'

Suddenly Scotland had a chance of qualifying from Group Five but the World Cup dream was quickly crushed by Belarus's shock Hampden win and Norway's win over Moldova. Smith's team signed off their rollercoaster campaign with an impressive away win in Slovenia.

The World Cup had gone but it at least gave the Scottish public hope that they could make Euro 2008. Not that the draw did Smith many favours as it lined them up against World champions Italy, France, Ukraine, Lithuania, Georgia and the Faroe Isles.

The campaign, however, was opened up without fear after a 6–0 demolition of the Faroe Isles and a 2–1 win away in Lithuania. The next challenge was to come in the shape of the French. The majority of the players who were involved that day, when Gary Caldwell scored his famous winning goal, put the win down to Smith's inspirational half-time team talk.

Former Rangers defender Steven Pressley admitted: 'I had obviously played under Walter at Rangers and then I played for him again for Scotland. I knew he was a great man-manager and that was there for all to see in the national squad. Players had come from all these different clubs and every single one of the squad had total respect for Walter. It was actually during our time together with Scotland that I witnessed Walter giving one of the most inspirational half-time team talks I have ever heard. It was during the Euro qualifying win over France at Hampden. He just hit the nail on the head with everything he said. He talked a lot about our experiences of playing for Scotland and used that to our advantage. His tactics on how to play when we didn't have the ball were also spot on. Basically it covered tactics, motivated the players but at the same time brought a calmness to the team, along with the right instructions to see out such a famous win. The Scotland players take a lot of credit for that but nobody can underestimate the part Walter played that day and in the entire qualifying campaign.'

Christian Dailly confirmed that Smith had stirred the passions within the home dressing room at Hampden that day in a way even Braveheart William Wallace would have been proud of. Dailly said: 'I have to say Walter's team talk in that France game also sticks with me. He just basically spelt out what it was like to play for Scotland. There were boys in the dressing room who were frustrated that they weren't getting the ball enough but he said you have to accept that when you play top teams. You just have to make sure that when you get the ball you make the most of it and do something with it.

'With Walter whatever he says goes. Basically Walter also told us and predicted how the second half would pan out and he was spot on. That is another big asset that Walter has. He has an uncanny ability to read how a game is going to unfold. That is a unique characteristic that I have never really come across before. Walter is also a man who knows how to dish it out if you aren't pulling your weight. I am sure that came from working under Jim McLean for so long at Dundee United. But to be fair if he blasted somebody then you knew it was for the right reasons. He would never do it just for the sake of it.'

The 100 per cent record was lost a few days later in the Ukraine but suddenly Scotland were back in the ball game when it came to automatic qualification. Lee McCulloch recalled: 'The Gaffer had us up in the top twenty of the FIFA rankings. We had been at our lowest under Berti Vogts and now with the Gaffer in charge we were suddenly in one of our highest ever positions. He had instilled a great team spirit within the squad. He also got the whole country booming again and we were suddenly a team that everybody could be proud of.'

Just as Scotland looked on the verge of doing something, a desperate SOS arrived from somewhere closer to Smith's heart. Paul Le Guen had decided to bring an end to his shambolic Ibrox stay and Rangers chairman Sir David Murray had only one man's name on his list – even though it was bad news for the rest of the nation. It was Smith's first love and he knew he had the chance to re-write history after the way his first spell at Ibrox disappointedly finished. It also gave him the opportunity to get back into day-to-day management and away from the boredom of continual committee meetings at Hampden.

Wigan star McCulloch feared Smith's departure would see all his previous good work fall apart. 'I remember when I heard the rumours that Walter Smith could be going back to Rangers,' McCulloch admitted. 'I remember thinking if he does go then it will be a real blow to the team, the nation and myself. We had been doing so well under him and I had also been a regular in all his squads. I hadn't featured all the time under Berti Vogts but that certainly changed under Walter Smith. Then when Walter left I was thinking what if the new manager doesn't fancy me? Also, on the Scotland front, who would finish the job that Walter had started?'

In the end he was replaced by Alex McLeish and Scotland narrowly missed out on Euro 2008 although Christian Dailly reckoned they would have got there if Smith had seen out the campaign. Dailly explained: 'I have to say I was really disappointed when Walter left for Rangers. Not only were we losing a great manager but I felt under him we had a real chance of qualifying for the European Championships.

'There were quite a few Scotland highlights for me under Walter. The big ones were beating France at Hampden and scoring for him in our win out in Lithuania. I honestly believe that if Walter has seen out the campaign we would have qualified. I truly believe that. He just has something about him that seems to get that wee bit extra out of his players. I think that in itself could have taken us over the finishing line, but Rangers came in for him and he obviously felt it was too good an opportunity to turn down.'

Smith was criticised by the SFA for his decision to walk out on his country, forcing the former national coach to defend his honour. He said: 'Statements were made that I have left Scotland at a critical time. I went to Scotland at a diabolical time and this is the way they act at the end of it. It irks me a wee bit. They are trying to make me look like a baddie. I will always be grateful to the people there that gave me the opportunity to manage the national team, but who helped raise Scotland's stock? It annoys me that they couldn't have allowed me to go with a bit of goodwill because I have given them two years where the pressure has been taken off them. It was a difficult decision for me to leave Scotland, I accept the responsibility and I have a lot of regrets. This is the only job I would have left Scotland for.'

16

WHO SAYS YOU SHOULD NEVER GO BACK?

(2007)

WALTER SMITH returned to Ibrox knowing it was a far different place from the one he had left behind almost a decade earlier. The Ibrox war chest he had been so used to during his nine-in-a-row years was very much a thing of the past. Those days had long since gone, since Dick Advocaat's lavish spending days, splashing the cash on top stars like Giovanni van Bronckhorst, Arthur Numan and Fernando Ricksen. The one he will also be remembered for was his club record signing of Norwegian flop Tore Andre Flo for £12 million from Chelsea.

After that the harsh reality hit the Rangers hierarchy. They could no longer keep spending outwith their means and Sir David Murray could no longer afford to self-fund the club at the same extravagant level. The reins were very much pulled in. And that has pretty much been the case ever since. Alex McLeish was asked to win titles and make progress in the Champions League by raiding the bargain bins of Europe and the SPL or by generating funds through the sale of his own stars. It was the same for ex-Lyon manager Paul Le Guen, who had turned to his homeland of France to try and make full use of his limited financial resources. But, unlike McLeish before him, Le Guen didn't have the knowledge to fully comprehend the demands of the Scottish game and to realise that second best, behind Celtic, just wasn't an option.

That was something Smith was more aware of than most as he had coped with that constant pressure on an almost daily basis on his way to nine consecutive titles. He had also shown at Everton and with Scotland that he didn't need a bulging chequebook to get the best out of players – a charge that had been continually levelled at him during his first managerial spell at Rangers. Smith also, like every other Rangers fan, was left hurting by the club's sudden demise.

Rangers legend Ian Ferguson truly believes the Rangers management position was the only one that could have prised Smith away from Scotland: 'The one thing about Walter is that he always wears his heart on his sleeve. He is a Rangers man and the club means everything to him. That is why he will have felt he had to answer the chairman's call, when he needed somebody to steady the ship. A lot of people say you shouldn't go back to a club, especially if you have been successful first time around. But the Gaffer took on the challenge because he felt the club needed him and he felt he could help them out of a difficult situation. As a Rangers supporter, there was no way Walter could have said no. It left him in a difficult position to walk out on Scotland for Rangers but I don't think he would have left that position for anywhere else but the Rangers job.'

Smith knew what he was going back into and was well aware it was going to be a long-term job – hence the three-year contract. His first task wasn't even to slug it out with Celtic for the title. The SPL was already out of sight by the time he took charge in January 2007. Gordon Strachan's Hoops were already way out in front, proving too strong for Le Guen, who previously had a glittering managerial CV with Lyon. The Frenchman had struggled to come to terms with the Scottish game and more worryingly had started to lose elements of the dressing room. His final stance came in the win over Motherwell where he dropped captain Barry Ferguson, while he had also had issues with top-scorer Kris Boyd over his attitude and on-the-field work rate.

Smith started to work on his own back-room staff before he had even got the job and used some of his insider knowledge to get an early assessment from Ian Durrant, who was put in temporary charge until the appointment was finalised. Smith decided, once again, to bring in Ally McCoist as his assistant – knowing it would be a masterstroke with the Rangers support and could also offer the club a long-term successor. He also raided rivals Celtic for their highly-rated coach Kenny McDowall. McDowall was named first-team coach along with Durrant, who had been promoted from the reserve team.

'Walter called me up around the time when it looked like Paul Le Guen would be leaving Rangers,' McCoist revealed. 'He asked me if I would be interested in going to Rangers as his No. 2. Once again, for me, it was a no-brainer. It was the club I had supported and played for and there really wasn't a decision to be made. But Walter told me I should give it some thought because I would be giving up a lot with my television commitments, especially my work with *A Question of Sport*. I didn't agree with him because although I miss working with the people I have met in television the chance to come back to my club was just too good to turn down. I honestly believe that if I hadn't taken the Rangers job I wouldn't have been able to live with myself. Thankfully I did take it and I am honoured that we have managed to enjoy some wonderful times again second time round.'

Former Rangers star Gary Stevens admitted he is surprised that McCoist and Durrant took the step into coaching. Stevens explained: 'I played alongside both of them and back then I wouldn't have backed them as managerial material, although they have more than proved they are up to the job. Walter has shown to be the perfect mentor. What I would say is that as long as Ally and Ian are going about then I am sure the dressing room will be full of banter and laughs. To be fair to Ally he has a rapier-like wit and intelligence while Durrant always used to dish out stick as well but nobody could ever understand him.'

The short-term goal for Smith was simple – guarantee second spot and a possible crack at the Champions League. The SPL title was already gone while the Scottish Cup had also been lost after the shock defeat at Dunfermline just days before he stepped into the job. There was, however, still the UEFA Cup and before that he had to try and unite the fractured dressing room again.

At his Murray Park unveiling he admitted: 'The emphasis has got to be on the creation of a team. There has to be a togetherness more on the pitch than anywhere else. We have to set out to achieve the formation of a team with everyone working together and Rangers maybe haven't shown that consistently this season. There has been a split on the pitch as well because they have lost more points to bottom-of-the-league teams than top-of-the-league ones.'

Smith immediately pinpointed the fact that the Rangers defence needed to be strengthened. He went and raided the bargain basements to bring in long-serving general Davie Weir and former Aston Villa defender Ugo Ehiogu. That gave him two solid centre halves. Smith also named Allan McGregor as his main goalkeeper, ahead of the Frenchman Lionel Letizi, while midfielder Kevin Thomson arrived from Hibs.

The likes of Filip Sebo, Libor Sionko and Karl Svensson, all who had been signed by Le Guen, all found themselves on the Ibrox fringes. Smith went for a more British approach as he went back to basics and made Rangers, first and foremost, hard to beat. Central defender Sasa Papac also feared he was on borrowed time under the new man.

Papac admitted: 'When Walter came in I was a bit unsure about what would happen. Paul Le Guen had signed about a dozen players and one by one they left Rangers in January. I wondered when it would be my time to go, too. I just assumed I would have to leave because everyone else was leaving. Not that I wanted to leave but I just thought maybe it was inevitable because a new manager had come in. But I decided not to think about it too much. I just decided to concentrate on training and see what Walter would do. I just wanted to show what I could do and I learnt quickly to adapt to this new way of playing football. I think Walter saw I was giving everything in training and getting better day by day. He didn't speak too much with me about the future but he put me on the bench a few times and when there were some injuries he just said to me, "You will play tomorrow." There was a game against Aberdeen that we won 3–0. It was my first start for Walter and I played well. After that there was no problem and I played a lot more regularly.'

Papac's saving grace was his adaptability. Smith asked him to fill in at left back despite the fact it wasn't his natural position. The Bosnian didn't grumble, he got his head down and got on with it and, in the process, won over Smith and made the full-back slot his own.

'I think maybe Walter felt I wasn't physically strong enough to play central defence like he would want,' Papac admitted. 'Maybe I wasn't strong enough for Scottish football but he saw I was technically solid and good enough to play at left back. He put me there in a couple of games and it worked out okay. I can say now I am not a central defender but a left back. This is my position now and I enjoy it.'

The defence was shored up while recalled skipper Ferguson and a young Charlie Adam provided the creativity in the middle of the park while Boyd produced the goals. It certainly worked as Smith made an impressive bow in a 5–0 thrashing of Dundee United.

The feel-good factor continued together as Rangers continued their unbeaten domestic run and brushed past Hapoel Tel Aviv in the UEFA Cup. The Light Blues continued to eat away at Celtic's massive points deficit. They were never going to catch them but, at least, Smith's side were starting to regain a bit of respectability. The team continued with a 1–1 draw with Spanish side Osasuna before Smith returned to the Old Firm cauldron. This was his first real test and he didn't disappoint as new boy Ehiogu scored the only goal of the game. There was then disappointment in Europe as they lost out in Spain to Osasuna and bowed out of the UEFA Cup. The team continued to look impressive on the domestic front and that was down to Smith.

Papac explained: 'I didn't know Walter before he came back to the club for a second time but Stefan Klos used to speak about him a lot, and told us all the things the other players who played with him the first time had to say. I was a young boy in Bosnia when Walter had his first spell as manager at Rangers so I didn't experience first hand what he was achieving but when I moved into football then of course I knew of his name and his reputation.'

Smith managed to piece together a thirteen-match unbeaten SPL run before they were finally beaten by Kilmarnock in the second last game of the season. A crack at the Champions League had been assured. The team finished twelve points behind Celtic but there was hope amongst the Ibrox legions that there was a wind of change about to sweep through Scottish football.

Striker Nacho Novo, who had been an Alex McLeish signing back in 2004, added: 'Walter inherited a club that was in a dire financial situation. It required a minor miracle to turn things around and I think Walter more than produced that. It is a lot easier to come into a job when the team are doing well but it is a lot more of a challenge when the team is struggling, like we were at the time after Paul Le Guen left. He instilled confidence and belief in us and turned us into a very different team. I think if Walter had been in charge at the start of the season then we could well have won the title.'

17

THE UEFA CUP ADVENTURE

(2007–08)

THE FACT that Rangers had qualified for the Champions League caused Smith another major headache that summer. The cash-strapped Light Blues needed the finance from Europe's top club competition but at the same time it meant Rangers would need to kick off their qualifiers before the Scottish Premier League season had even sparked into life.

It was a worry as Smith had made several changes to his squad and he hoped the turmoil wouldn't disrupt his team. French striker Jean-Claude Darcheville came in from Bordeaux, Kirk Broadfoot from St Mirren and Alan Gow from Falkirk, although that deal had already been put in place by Paul Le Guen. Smith was also given limited funds and he used them to buy US international DaMarcus Beasley from PSV Eindhoven, Scotland star Lee McCulloch from Wigan Athletic, Daniel Cousin from Lens and central defender Carlos Cuellar, who had impressed in the previous season's UEFA Cup win over Rangers with Osasuna. Smith had sent out former Rangers star John Brown to scout Cuellar, who cost around £2 million. Brown came back with a glowing reference and business was done.

The Light Blues were drawn against Montenegro outfit FK Zeta in their first Champions League qualifiers. The good thing was that the first game was at Ibrox and despite an unimpressive performance and Alan Hutton's red card they managed to pull out a 2–0 win thanks to goals from Davie Weir and Lee McCulloch.

The tie was seen off by summer signing Beasley who scored the only goal out in Montenegro to fire Rangers into the next qualifying round.

Defender Kirk Broadfoot said: 'I actually made my debut in the Champions League qualifiers against Zeta. We weren't great over the two legs. It was still the start of the season and we were still trying to blend in together but we managed to do enough to get through, although I admit those games weren't pretty.'

The next game brought the former European force Red Star Belgrade to the fore. Those two ties proved to be nerve-jangling. A last-minute goal from substitute Nacho Novo gave Rangers an Ibrox win, while a 0–0 draw out in Serbia sneaked them through. It gave Rangers a much needed financial boost from the group stages of the Champions League. They were drawn once more in a so-called 'Group of Death' against the mighty Barcelona, Germans Stuttgart and French heavyweights Lyon.

Broadfoot added: 'When we managed to squeeze past Red Star Belgrade to make it into the group stages the draw caused a big buzz around the club.'

Things couldn't have started better, with a 2–1 home win over Stuttgart, thanks to a goal from Charlie Adam and Jean-Claude Darcheville's penalty. Then came one of the biggest results of the campaign as Rangers went out to France and produced a classic away performance – thumping Lyon 3–0 with goals from McCulloch, Cousin and Beasley.

McCulloch admitted: 'We played really well that night and that was one of our top European performances. I think we surprised a lot of people that night, including Lyon. They were still a top team who had a real Champions League pedigree so to go there and win was just massive. It wasn't just the win. It was the manner of the win. We ended up coming out convincing winners and that result made a lot of people stand up and take notice.'

Six points out of six was beyond even the wildest dreams of even the most ardent of Rangers fans, but they knew that the biggest test was still to come when Barcelona arrived at Ibrox. But even the precocious talents of Lionel Messi, Ronaldinho and Eidur Gudjohnsen were unable to break the Light Blues down as they held out for a goalless draw. A clearly frustrated Messi blasted Smith and his Rangers team after the game, claiming they were 'anti-football' with their ultra-defensive tactics.

Suddenly Rangers had a genuine belief they could progress but goals from Messi and Thierry Henry allowed Barcelona to gain their revenge in the Nou Camp. It looked good when Rangers went 2–1 up in Stuttgart before the Germans came back and won 3–2. Rangers' Champions League qualification came down to the final game at home to Lyon. This time it was the French side's turn for revenge as they overturned their earlier defeat with a 3–0 win at Ibrox. It was a bitter blow to Smith that left Rangers with nothing but the consolation of a UEFA Cup slot.

Looking back Davie Weir admitted: 'If you look at that Champions League draw, we were in very decent company and we were very unlucky not to go through into the knockout stages of that tournament, never mind the UEFA Cup. We weren't far away and we got some decent results beating Stuttgart and Lyon over there while we also got a draw with Barcelona at Ibrox. I know Lionel Messi criticised us after the Barcelona game at Ibrox for taking an anti-football approach. What did he expect us to do when you look at Rangers' resources compared to the players Barcelona have at their disposal? I think the Gaffer should have been praised for his tactics because there aren't many teams who can hold a team of the quality of Barcelona. If you look at teams in Europe now they are now adopting the same type of tactics that Walter employed that season. So in many ways he has started the trend. Everyone could see how successful it could be, if employed in the right way. I definitely think we could have gone through to the knockout stages of the Champions League with a bit more luck.'

The January transfer window saw Scotland star Alan Hutton sold to Tottenham for £9 million and that allowed Smith to sign Stevie Naismith from Kilmarnock and bring Northern Ireland cap Steven Davis in on loan from Fulham.

Rangers were paired with Greek side Panathinaikos in the last thirty-two of the UEFA Cup. A goalless draw at Ibrox left Rangers with it all to do but they managed to scramble through on away goals thanks to Nacho Novo's goal in the 1–1 away draw.

New signing Christian Dailly was delighted he was able to make an early impression in his Rangers career. Dailly recalled: 'I think a big thing for Walter was that he knew me and he knew I could provide cover in a number of positions. Wherever I was put in he knew he could trust me to give everything. I ended up making my debut in the UEFA Cup away to Panathinaikos. I came off the bench for Charlie Adam and that was a good night as Nacho Novo scored late on to get us a point. So that was a good start to my Rangers career.'

The UEFA Cup run also brought a European return for Kirk Broadfoot who had been omitted from the Champions League action. Broadfoot admitted: 'My big disappointment was that I didn't actually feature in any of the Champions League games. I didn't actually come back in until we dropped out of the competition and into the UEFA. I then played in every game until the final.'

German big-hitters Werder Bremen were tipped to end Smith's European run but goals from Daniel Cousin and Steven Davis gave Rangers a 2–0 first-leg lead. The trip to Germany proved a far different encounter as the SPL outfit had to hold on, losing 1–0, to go through 2–1 on aggregate.

'We went on to have some really good nights in that European run,' Dailly acknowledged. 'We went over to Sporting Lisbon and won over there and the night we lost in Werder Bremen was also a big night. We lost 1–0 that night and looking back I still don't know how we managed to keep it down to the one and go through 2–1 on aggregate.'

The next round it was to be another away day to remember that put Rangers through against Sporting Lisbon. A 0–0 Ibrox stalemate meant Rangers had to at least get a scoring draw away in Portugal to make the semi-finals. They did more than that as goals from Darcheville and Steven Whittaker, who had also come in from Hibs, sparked some wild celebrations.

Broadfoot said: 'We were really excellent that night. Sporting were a good team but we managed to put on a really solid defensive display and they just couldn't find a way past us. We then scored through Jean-Claude Darcheville while Steven Whittaker capped off a brilliant night with a great solo effort.'

Teams from Greece, Germany and Portugal had fallen by the wayside and next up was Serie A giants Fiorentina, who boasted top players, like disgraced Chelsea star Adrian Mutu and former Italian striker Christian Vieri.

The Viola may have had an abundance of attacking talents but over the two games the deadlock couldn't be broken. Rangers' play wasn't pretty but it was effective. McCulloch admitted: 'The Gaffer just managed to get us to go out and churn out results. We might not have played the greatest football but our tactics worked. If you ask any fan what would they prefer, pretty football or a European final, I know what most people would take. You can play good football any week of the season but how often do you get to a European final?'

It eventually went to the drama of a penalty shoot-out in Florence's Artemio Franchi Stadium. Things didn't look good when captain Barry Ferguson missed his kick but keeper Neil Alexander bailed him out as he stopped from Fabio Liverani. Rangers midfielder Brahim Hemdani then scored to put the pressure on Vieri, who buckled, as he fired over to give Rangers the advantage.

Alexander, who had stepped in for the injured Allan McGregor, recalled: 'It was a fantastic achievement and something I'll always look back on with fond memories. When I was at Cardiff I didn't have the best penalty record, but when I went to Ipswich I saved three in five in the space of six months and when I went up to Rangers I just kept it going. I just tried to look confident and make the penalty taker's job a little bit harder because penalty takers should always score as the advantage is always with them. Against Vieri I tried to put him off by taking my time and trying to con the referee by checking to see if the ball was on the spot. That might have played a part in him firing over the bar.'

It was all down to one kick and the responsibility fell on the shoulders of gutsy Spaniard Novo. He was already a fans' hero but if he netted it then he knew he would be guaranteed legendary status. He coolly slotted home his right-foot penalty, sending Sebastien Frey the wrong way as he fired Rangers into the UEFA Cup final.

Novo, who joked he would have jumped off the Kingston Bridge if he had missed, still gets goosebumps when he thinks back to that night. The striker said: 'My penalty winner against Fiorentina was probably the biggest moment of my Rangers career. Just to score the penalty was amazing because we could see what getting to the UEFA Cup final meant to everyone. It was amazing. It just doesn't get much better than scoring a penalty in a European semi-final. I still can't believe it. I could feel the eyes of everyone in the stadium on me as I stepped up to take the penalty. There was a great goalkeeper in front of me, but I knew I had to score for Rangers. You look to the fans there and see that they have travelled from all over the world to be here supporting us. They are the best. I just tried to keep as calm as I could and score. It went in and that's all that mattered. I cannot describe the feeling I had when I saw the ball go in.'

It was a night that left Ibrox legend Lorenzo Amoruso with a bittersweet taste. He was delighted to see Rangers book their place at the City of Manchester Stadium but it was at the expense of his old team Fiorentina.

'I joked when the draw was made that I couldn't lose,' Amoruso laughed. 'It didn't matter if it was going to be Fiorentina or Rangers because I told everyone that I would be going to the final regardless. On paper I felt that Fiorentina were the stronger team. Rangers had a lot of injuries and selection problems so I thought they would find it tough, although I warned the Fiorentina players that you could never write off any of Walter Smith's teams. That was shown by the fact they had got to the semi-finals of the UEFA Cup. It was even more remarkable because they employed a game plan which allowed the players to really play to their strengths. It went to penalties but it was a really great performance from Rangers to go and beat an Italian team on their own soil. I know it surprised a lot of people in Italy, especially the media. They expected Fiorentina to win and it was a bit of a shock to lose to a team from Scotland but you have to give Walter and that squad of players credit for getting through that tie. Also you don't get all the way to a European final on luck alone. Rangers were well organised and also had a squad of players who gave absolutely everything to keep that great run going.'

Suddenly there were dreams of a repeat of the 1972 European Cup Winners Cup campaign and a possible second European trophy. Rangers were to meet big-spending Russians Zenit St Petersburg. A bit of spice was added to the occasion as they were managed by ex-Rangers boss Dick Advocaat and also had former Ibrox star Fernando Ricksen in their ranks. The good thing was it was almost like a home game for Rangers. A simple trip across the border meant thousands of Ibrox legions were going to head for Manchester.

Kirk Broadfoot explained: 'We went down to Manchester a couple of days before the final. The atmosphere in the dressing room was really buzzing and we were all really looking forward to the final. The fans were all up for it and although we knew Zenit St Petersburg were a good team, we still felt that if we played well then we could beat them. It was just amazing to be part of a Rangers team that had reached a European final. It was just brilliant from the penalty shoot-out win in Florence all the way to Manchester. I remember walking out on to the pitch in Manchester. To see all the Rangers fans was just sensational. There were thousands and they made it a really brilliant atmosphere. It was walking out and seeing the fireworks go off when the nerves really kicked in.'

The spark, however, was lacking from Rangers' play. The marathon season left Rangers toiling and second-half goals from Igor Denisov and Konstantin Zyryanov killed their hopes. The dream was in tatters but the team and his players had done Smith proud – even if some of that achievement was slightly tarnished by the troubles in the city centre later that night.

A dejected Broadfoot admitted: 'Unfortunately we never really got going and they got their goals and probably deserved to win. It was a massive disappointment. I was absolutely gutted at the final whistle. I think we all knew it was a once in a lifetime opportunity. We had done brilliantly to get to the final but we just couldn't get over that last hurdle. We were all disappointed it didn't happen and nobody more so than the Gaffer. To be fair to him he was great and he came out after the game and told us to get our heads up because we had done the club proud and he thanked us for our efforts.'

Boyhood Rangers fan Lee McCulloch really felt for the Ibrox support that day. McCulloch said: 'One of my biggest highlights was getting to the UEFA Cup final but, at the same time, it was also my biggest disappointment because of the result. It was a fantastic day and it was just great to get all the way to a European final. Seeing all the fans we had in Manchester and just not being able to do it for them over the ninety minutes was a real disappointment. Our fans are amongst the best in the world and they certainly deserved another European trophy.'

Smith was criticised for being over-cautious in that final but Sasa Papac reckons he couldn't have approached things any other way. 'My best memory of playing for Walter is the UEFA Cup final,' Papac insisted. 'With this team, and not a very big budget, it was a really amazing achievement. We beat teams that were better than us who had much bigger budgets. It was a special sensation to get all the way to the final. We didn't look too far ahead, just round by round. Walter was always encouraging us and telling us not to be intimidated by the other teams, that we could beat them. The football we played that year wasn't great but it was very effective. We had a quality and played to our strengths. If Walter had sent us out to be more attacking we might have lost the first game. The tactic was to have six or seven players who played very defensively but it worked. It was a shame we could not win the final but the run to get there was very special.'

The remarkable European run which had kicked off in the Champions League helped to put Scottish football back at the top table and defender Davie Weir reckons it is something that Smith and every single one of his squad can look back on with great pride. 'The UEFA Cup run was special,' Weir admitted. 'It was a big disappointment that we didn't go on and win it but it was still a tremendous achievement to get all the way to a European final. We beat some top sides on the way to Manchester. To get past teams like Werder Bremen, Sporting Lisbon, Fiorentina and Panathinaikos really took some doing. It showed what a good side and spirit we had. I think we can all look back on that campaign with great pride. It was still a real achievement despite the fact it didn't end the way we all had hoped.'

The one big question that is always likely to gnaw away at the back of Smith's head is – could he have done anything differently that might have got the team that final result? The bottom line is that nobody at the start of their European campaign, albeit in the Champions League, would have ever thought or dreamed it was going to end with Rangers getting to a major final. It was an achievement in itself just to guide a Scottish club to the UEFA Cup final, especially when you look more closely at the meagre resources Smith had available to him. Smith and his team gave absolutely everything in that campaign, both domestically and in Europe. His limited squad was pushed to the maximum and every single one of his players gave every last ounce of sweat and blood for the cause. That was seen at the final whistle of the UEFA Cup. Players just slumped to the City of Manchester Stadium turf, heartbroken and totally dejected but also physically and mentally exhausted. Zenit St Petersburg was just a bridge too far.

'We never thought this season would lead to a European final and we have to give the credit to the players for what they have achieved in nineteen games in Europe,' Smith proudly claimed. 'I'd never have imagined we'd get to the UEFA Cup final. It was a terrific achievement with the group we had. The players thoroughly enjoyed it and I did also. We had a really solid team last season. That was evident in the final. We weren't fresh going into the game but Zenit won it because they had a few players with an outstanding level of ability. Our teamwork got us through very difficult games and we can take pride in that.'

Rangers fans, like supporters of every big club, always crave European success, whether it be in the Champions League or Europa League. It is the holy grail of football. But, as we have seen in recent Scottish football history, it is almost impossible to try and juggle the domestic and European demands and still be successful. The volume of games and the lack of resources have made it incredibly difficult. You only have to look back to Smith's old team, Dundee United, back in the 1986–87 season. Under his former manager, Jim McLean, he led them on their marathon run to the UEFA Cup but, like Rangers all these years on, they just ran out of gas in the final straight, as they lost to IFK Gothenburg over a two-legged final and were shocked by St Mirren in the Scottish Cup final. It was also the same for Sir Alex Ferguson as he led his Aberdeen team to the 1983 European Cup Winners Cup but they came up short in the domestic title race.

Parallels can certainly be drawn from the recent European campaigns of Rangers, Aberdeen and Dundee United. It is a theme that runs hand in hand with Scottish teams when they are successful in Europe: limited resources and a back-breaking schedule, which in the end are always going to take their toll – as Smith and his players found out at the end of that 2007–08 campaign. The good thing was that, despite the disappointment and the pain that UEFA Cup run, Smith certainly helped to put Rangers back on the European map.

18

RUNNING ON EMPTY LEAVES
RANGERS WITH A CUP DOUBLE

(2007–08)

THERE was a clear and common theme to the majority of Walter Smith's summer signing policy. Kirk Broadfoot, Alan Gow and Stevie Naismith were all Rangers fans and knew what it meant to play in the light blue, aided mainly by British based-players who knew how to cope with the demands of the Scottish game. They were all desperate to move to Ibrox and that was a massive shift from Paul Le Guen's foreign legion. Smith had tried to sign Scotland cap Lee McCulloch when he first arrived but had been given short shrift from the then Wigan boss Paul Jewell – even though the player had pleaded with him to be allowed to return home.

McCulloch revealed: 'The move dragged on for a bit and I didn't know if it was going to happen or not. Rangers made an offer for me in the January of the previous season, but Wigan turned it down. I was keen to get up the road for family reasons and to join the team I supported as a boy. It was an opportunity that I didn't want to let pass me by. I basically had to go in and kick off with Wigan to try and get the deal to happen, but they stood firm and refused to sell me. I was gutted but I had got word, via a third party, that the Gaffer still wanted to sign me and was determined to push the deal through in the summer. I was told to sit tight and not to worry because Walter was a man of his word and he would make it happen. It proved to be the case as he came back in for me and eventually the deal was pushed through.'

A lot of people thought McCulloch was mad to walk out of the English Premier League for Rangers but, for the player, it was the easiest decision of his career. 'I knew I had taken a step forward. I had joined a massive club who were challenging for trophies and playing in the Champions League,' McCulloch insisted. 'People were wrong to criticise me for leaving the English Premier League for Rangers. People in England don't realise how big Rangers and Celtic are. They have a pop at the SPL but they don't know the tradition or the size of these clubs. Being Scottish, I knew what it meant to support a club like Rangers. My dad used to take me to Ibrox when I was a younger and I loved it. I remember Richard Gough, Ally McCoist, Ray Wilkins, Mark Walters and Mark Hateley. I knew I wanted the chance to follow in their footsteps to play for such a massive club.'

Versatile defender Kirk Broadfoot had been a stand-out as St Mirren had re-established themselves in the SPL and was brought to Smith's attention by Ally McCoist, who had kept himself fit by training at Love Street. Smith was convinced to sign Broadfoot on a pre-contract.

Broadfoot recalled: 'I remember Gus MacPherson and Andy Millen [the manager and assistant manager of St Mirren] told me that Ally had been really impressed with me in those training sessions. I don't know if he recommended me to Walter Smith as well. Rangers had tried to sign me in the January but it never came off. Obviously, I was disappointed but then I got a call from my agent to tell me that Rangers were prepared to sign me on a pre-contract. I went up to Murray Park to hold talks with Walter Smith and my agent thrashed things out with [chief executive] Martin Bain.

'To be honest, the financial aspect of things didn't really bother me too much. I was going to be earning more than I was on at

St Mirren, but the big thing for me was getting the chance to sign for Rangers. I had been a Rangers supporter as a boy. I had sat in the stands and cheered them on and it really was a dream come true. The day I did my medical and signed was just amazing. My dad had watched Rangers week-in and week-out and Walter Smith was an absolute legend to both him and me. The Gaffer, to be fair, was absolutely brilliant that day. He spent most of the time talking to my dad. I don't think my dad could believe that this legendary Rangers manager, who he had supported, was suddenly taking time to speak to him and to make it feel like it was also his big day – which it was. My dad got his photograph taken with Walter and I know how much that meant to him. That is the thing about Walter Smith, he is such a great guy. He has got time for everybody from the players to the families, staff and the supporters. He gives everyone respect and, as a result, he gets it back ten-fold. The Gaffer really appreciates that when it comes to Rangers it is a real team effort. I remember the Gaffer told me to come in and give it my all. That is what he asks of all his players.'

Stevie Naismith was Smith's final signing of the August window. Celtic had tried to push the price up by declaring their interest in the Kilmarnock star, but there was no way he was even going to entertain such a move.

The striker admitted: 'There was a time when I was a bit worried that my deal wasn't going to happen. The transfer dragged on. Kilmarnock and Rangers were struggling to strike a deal. But, fortunately, I knew Ally McCoist and Ian Durrant from their own time at Kilmarnock and they assured me the deal would happen. Thankfully it did and the day I finally signed for Rangers was the best moment of my football career – so far. The first couple of times I met the Gaffer I realised what an aura and presence he had, although he was also a guy who was really easy to talk to. That is one of the reasons why he is so respected and why everybody is willing to fight tooth and nail for him. Even around the training ground he has created a great atmosphere and most of the time he is the one in the middle cracking the jokes. But, at the same time, when you know he is mad, he doesn't have to say anything.'

Naismith was very much viewed as one for the future. He found it hard going from being a big fish in a small pond to a little fish in a big pond at Ibrox. He acknowledged it took him time to adjust.

'When I first arrived at the club I didn't really realise what it was like to play for Rangers,' Naismith openly admitted. 'The Gaffer, though, was brand new. He made it clear from the start that I wouldn't be playing every week. He saw me more as a player for his longer-term project. He told me not to be too down and just to keep going. The one thing about the Gaffer is he has a knack of making you feel wanted even when you aren't involved in the first team. It allowed me time to see what playing for Rangers was all about. It was part of my transition from a smaller club to a bigger one. At Kilmarnock we would go to places where we would be more than happy to come back with a draw, but at Rangers a draw anywhere is a bad result. You need to try and win every game.'

Those signings along with Daniel Cousin and Jean-Claude Darcheville made Rangers a much tougher nut to crack. Celtic manager Gordon Strachan knew his team was going to be given a run for their money. That was shown as Rangers took first blood with an impressive 3–0 win over Celtic, thanks to Nacho Novo's double and another from Barry Ferguson, in the first Old Firm meeting of the new campaign.

Another of Smith's former Scotland stars, Christian Dailly, was persuaded to come in during the January window, replacing Ugo Ehiogu who returned to England. Every player in the Rangers squad was going to have to play their part as they fought it out for the CIS, Scottish and UEFA Cups and the league.

Dailly revealed the reasons behind his move. He said: 'The

deal the manager came up with was probably pretty innovative at that time. He phoned me up and asked if I would come up a do a short-term job for him. He felt my experience could help his team and bring a bit of cover to his squad. He told me I wouldn't play every week. I would be there as cover, but the team had a lot of games coming up and I would definitely play my part. I said, "That sounds good but I don't really want to uproot my family. They are settled down in the London area and I can't really see myself moving back to Scotland." I thought that might bring an end to things, but he said, "I've had a think about that as well. Would it work if you only came up and trained a couple of days a week and I left you to do your own training down the road?" Suddenly there were no more barriers and I agreed to move to Rangers on a six-month contract. I ended up staying at Rangers for eighteen months. Every time I left London for Glasgow I had to plan my journey with military precision. It was hard work but moving to Rangers turned out to be a great move for me, especially at that time in my career.'

Suddenly everybody was talking about a possible quadruple. Could it be done? With such demands came a gruelling fixture programme and the February pretty much saw Rangers playing every four days. Smith knew his team was close to breaking point and even he snapped after a touchline set-to with Hibs boss Mixu Paatelainen that saw him sent to the stands following Nacho Novo's controversial red card.

East Fife, Motherwell and Hearts were all disposed of before they met Dundee United in the CIS Cup final. Kris Boyd's late equaliser cancelled out Noel Hunt's goal. United's Mark de Vries scored again in extra time before Boyd levelled again to take the game to penalties – with the Ibrox side holding their nerve to lift the cup.

Kirk Broadfoot was delighted to pick up his first trophy as a Rangers player. He admitted: 'The one thing I found when I made the switch from St Mirren and working with Walter, Ally McCoist and Kenny McDowall was the winning mentality they instilled in you. It was different from St Mirren. Every week we wanted to win but at Rangers you have to win. I came in and played in the early European games. I was delighted to come in and get my chance to play in the team right away. The big game in that first part of my Rangers career was the CIS Cup final against Dundee United. It came just days after we had played out at Werder Bremen. United made us work all the way and it went to penalties before we finally pulled through. It was my first final with Rangers and to come away with a winner's medal and to lift the cup was just absolutely mind-blowing, knowing most of my family and friends were all in the stands to cheer me on.'

It was also a big day for Christian Dailly who won the cup against his former side. Ironically, he had been part of the Dundee United team that robbed Smith and Rangers of the Scottish Cup and a back-to-back treble in the 1993–94 season.

Dailly said: 'I played in the CIS Cup final against Dundee United. That was a special moment playing in a final against my old team. I know I have Walter to thank for that. I had won the Scottish Cup with Dundee United and suddenly I was back at Hampden, but this time I was helping Rangers to get one over on Dundee United in the League Cup final. It was all a bit surreal.'

The first leg of the possible quadruple was complete and now it was a case of going flat out in every other competition. March became just as manic – with eight games crammed in. Kevin Thomson scored the only goal in the Old Firm derby to put Rangers six points clear with a game in hand. The run to the UEFA Cup final brought fierce debate that the domestic season should be extended. That was something that was quickly opposed by Celtic, as they desperately tried in vain to hold on to their crown.

That led to a two-barreled response from Smith as he aimed his sights clearly at Celtic chief executive Peter Lawwell, who had been publicly defending Celtic's cause. Smith said: 'We have the sporting integrity side of things, which actually gave me a good laugh, in the sense that Peter Lawwell seems to be the person who is at the head of the sporting integrity committee of the SPL – chairman and chief spokesperson. Peter would be better coming out and saying he wants Rangers to play four games in a week because it suits his team and helps their quest to retain the championship. If it was the other way about, I would also be hoping that Celtic would have to play four games in seven days. He is as well coming out and being honest about it rather than trying to hide behind what he calls sporting integrity. At the end of the day, it is sport and we have to try and win. He is only trying to do what is best, or what he feels is best, for his club by saying the season shouldn't be extended. He is doing it for his own reasons, not for sporting integrity or the league.'

While the league fight rumbled on, both off and on the park, Rangers booked their place in the Scottish Cup final after a hard-fought penalty shoot-out win over St Johnstone, which came at a cost. Stevie Naismith suffered serious cruciate ligament damage. He admitted: 'I was feeling really low and I wasn't really around Murray Park when I started trying to get back to full fitness. But every now and then the Gaffer would pop his head round the door and have a chat and ask how I was getting on. It was good because it showed the manager hadn't forgotten about me and I was still in his thinking. It gave me a wee lift and made me push that wee bit further to try and get back to full fitness.'

The fixture list was hardly kind, as Rangers were asked to play Old Firm games on either side of their UEFA Cup semi-final against Fiorentina. That helped Celtic to drag themselves back into the title race. Jan Vennegoor of Hesselink hit a last-minute winner at Parkhead. The Hoops then landed an even more damaging blow when they beat Rangers 3–2 – after they had been 2–0 behind. Rangers had their eyes elsewhere as they knocked Fiorentina out of the UEFA Cup to book their place in the final.

Proud captain Davie Weir said: 'Come the end of that season we had the chance to become the most successful team in Rangers' history. We were still going for a domestic treble and, of course, we had the UEFA Cup final as well. We could have been one of the most successful sides Scottish football had ever seen. It was just disappointing that we couldn't pull it off after going so close on all four fronts. The ironic thing was that we achieved all that success in the face of fierce criticism that we weren't a good team. We took a lot of stick, but I think the way we played and performed that season was the perfect way for us to silence our critics and to make them eat their words.'

Two finals and the league run-in meant Smith's struggling stars were asked to play fifteen games in just thirty-six days. After losing the UEFA Cup final to Zenit St Petersburg, they were asked to play three games in five days.

Kirk Broadfoot is adamant the demands on Smith's squad were just too much in the end. He said: 'I think the European run ended up tripping us up. We were playing Wednesday, Saturday, Monday and Wednesday at one stage. It caught up on us at the end. I don't think anybody would have given up the run to the UEFA Cup final but I am in no doubt that if we hadn't had the European games then we would have won the league.'

Points dropped against Motherwell gave Celtic the advantage although a 3–0 win over St Mirren brought both Old Firm rivals level – although the Hoops had a better goal difference. It came down to the last day with Rangers hoping to get a better result at Aberdeen than Celtic got at Tannadice. It wasn't to be. Celtic got the win they needed while Rangers crashed in the Granite City.

That was to be Smith's biggest disappointment. He insisted it was an even more damaging blow than losing the UEFA Cup final. He said: 'You have to handle winning and losing. We didn't achieve what I set out to achieve – to win the title. We weren't good enough to handle the overall situation and it led to a disappointing end to the season, given the highs we had in the previous few months. I don't think you can take an individual game as a highlight. The UEFA Cup campaign as a whole was a highlight, getting through those games, albeit luckily on some occasions. Getting to Manchester was a big thing but it doesn't take away the disappointment of losing.'

Christian Dailly admitted it was unbelievable the way Walter Smith turned Rangers around. But he also said: 'That European success ended up costing us. We had something mad like thirteen games in a twenty-three-day spell. There was no doubt having that amount of fixtures in such a short space of time had a massive bearing on us when it came to the end of the season. Every single one of the players were dead on our feet. It wasn't just the physical demands but also the mental pressure. We not only had to play games but we also had to win them and that, in the end, proved a bridge too far.

'I know the pressure is on you to win every match at Rangers, but that period definitely drained us and left us with absolutely nothing. I remember being in the dressing room after the Aberdeen game. The place was really quiet but everybody was just completely drained. We had been fighting in four competitions and that had taken its toll. Walter thanked us for our efforts that day. We were disappointed but I don't think we could have done much else. Every single one of us had our foot flat down on the pedal and gave absolutely everything. I think even though we had lost the league you could see that Walter was really starting to build something special at Rangers.'

The team bowed out on a high by beating First Division Queen of the South 3–2 in the Scottish Cup final – thanks to a Kris Boyd brace and another from DaMarcus Beasley. Lee McCulloch is adamant that Rangers weren't helped by the SPL and Scotland's footballing authorities. McCulloch said: 'I felt really hard done by at the end of that season. We were going for four trophies and everybody was telling us we weren't going to do it. We gave it a fair shot and we weren't too far away. I think maybe if we had been given a more even crack at it then we could well have pulled it off. We ended up having to finish with this mad rush of games. We had to play something like four games in eight days. It just became humanly impossible. Everyone at the club showed a good mentality and you didn't hear too many of us moaning about the fixtures. We gave it our all but, in the end, we came up short. It was hard to take but it was one we just had to take on the chin. We won the Scottish Cup by beating Queen of the South but even that felt like nothing more than a consolation after we had lost the UEFA Cup final and the league.'

19

THE TITLE THAT SAVED RANGERS?

(2008–09)

A SUMMER of heartache and pain only spurred Rangers on to try and set the record straight going into the 2008–09 campaign. There were only four weeks between the Scottish Cup final and the return to pre-season training. Walter Smith now had to drag his squad back off the beach and get them ready for the Champions League qualifier with Lithuanian outfit FBK Kaunas – who were heavily backed by Hearts' majority shareholder Vladimir Romanov.

It wasn't the toughest of draws but could also have been viewed as a potential banana skin. Smith was able to use what limited funds he had to bring in Northern Ireland star Kyle Lafferty from Burnley, ex-Hearts striker Andrius Velicka and former Celtic hitman Kenny Miller back for his second spell at Ibrox.

Miller was a player Smith felt could do a real job at Ibrox, although he would have to win over certain sections of the Rangers support – who hadn't forgotten his short spell with Gordon Strachan's Celtic. Smith had witnessed Miller's qualities at first hand with Scotland and knew he was strong enough to silence the boo boys. Miller admitted: 'I was a Scottish boy and knew the size of the club. That was one of the reasons why I joined Rangers in the first instance, although I don't think I would ever have got that second opportunity had it not been for the Gaffer and Ally McCoist. The fact I had also played for Celtic meant I don't think many other Rangers managers would have viewed me as a serious signing option. It took a lot of bottle for the Gaffer to take me back to Ibrox. He knew he would get it in the neck, and so would I, if it didn't work out. I remember I went and met the Gaffer before I signed for Rangers. He told me he didn't care what people said or thought about the move. He knew I could do a good job for him and felt I could be a big player for the team. I knew I would have his backing and those of the people within Ibrox and that was good enough for me. I just had to go out and do my best and try to win over the other doubters who weren't so sure.'

While there was new blood, Smith had to use all his powers of persuasion to keep the rest of his squad together. Lee McCulloch had failed to produce his old form and was considering his future, as Stoke City and several other clubs offered him a summer escape.

McCulloch explained: 'My first season didn't really go the way I had hoped. I had struggled with injuries, I had lost form and my confidence had also taken a hit. I just found it hard to be consistent and to play every week. It was a real test of my character. It was at a time when Stoke City and a couple of other clubs had enquired about me. I wasn't sure if I should leave or not. But I also had a determination to make the grade at Rangers. I didn't want to be viewed as a big-money flop. I went in to see the Gaffer and he was first class. He sat me down and said: "We will stick by you. We want you to stay and we will give you the time and support you need to get back to the way we know you can play." Hearing that was a big boost to my confidence. Thankfully I kicked on from there and my performances started to improve and I got some of my old confidence back.'

Smith also decided to make a simple adjustment to McCulloch's play. Rather than being a more offensive midfielder he saw something in him that he felt could see him transformed into a holding player. It was a switch that proved to be the making of McCulloch at Rangers.

'I had always been a midfielder but then one season under Billy Davies at Motherwell I was asked if I would play up front,' McCulloch explained. 'I scored a few goals and then got my move to Wigan. They signed me as a centre forward but I remember I went in to see the manager Paul Jewell there and told him I felt more comfortable back in the midfield. The next thing I knew he had me playing wide on the left, coming in to use my height from the flank. That was the position I came to Rangers as but then Walter asked me if I fancied playing as a defensive midfielder. I wasn't really sure because it hadn't been a position I had been used to. But the Gaffer asked me to give it a go. He gave me a few pointers and sent me off to do some work with Coisty. Since then that has been my position and I haven't really looked back. The Gaffer tells me that he deserves all the credit for the transformation. He is probably right.'

Rangers' preparations weren't helped as inspirational defender Carlos Cuellar missed the start of the season through injury. The Ibrox opener saw the Lithuanians hold out for a shock 0–0 draw, although Smith still had faith his ring-rusty stars could battle through in Kaunas. Things looked good when Kevin Thomson gave Rangers the lead but Kaunas fought back through Nerijus Radzius. Smith's men were still in the driving seat and would still go through on away goals until Linas Pilibaitis's late sickener dumped them out of Europe. It was a hard one to take – getting knocked out at the first stage just weeks after they had taken a bow at the UEFA Cup final.

Dailly admitted it was a real low point. He said: 'We had to cope with the disappointment of crashing out of the Champions League to Kaunas. After getting to the UEFA Cup final the previous season that was a major blow to the team and the club. It also left me with an unwanted problem. It meant we wouldn't have as many games so my role would be a lot more limited. It was tough but then that was the deal I had signed up to. Walter had made that clear from day one. I just had to be patient.'

The financial blow from that premature exit couldn't be under-estimated. Smith still had enough in the kitty to sign Algerian defender Madjid Bougherra from Charlton – although he probably knew what was going on behind the scenes as Aston Villa triggered Cuellar's £8 million release clause.

Bougherra, who had made his name with Crewe and Sheffield Wednesday, admitted: 'The first thing that struck me when I first met Walter Smith was his charisma. You could sense right away he was a big-club manager who had a proven record at the top level. Those early discussions were good for me because it gave me a good insight into the man I was about to play for. Walter has a really good understanding of the game. He is intelligent and lets everybody know what he expects and wants from his players and teams. He is a very level-headed man. He never gets too high when you are winning and never lets you get too down when things aren't going as well. He is a manager that inspires a lot of confidence in you and that is why his players want to really play for him.'

The sale of Cuellar allowed Smith to go out and add some much-needed creativity that would allow his team to open up more than they had the previous season. A deal was struck to sign Steven Davis on a permanent basis from Fulham, while Portuguese playmaker Pedro Mendes arrived from Portsmouth.

Mendes explained: 'I didn't really know Walter before Rangers made their move. Rangers were a big club and that was appealing in the first instance. My agent told me how good Walter was and he would be a good manager for me to work under. Harry Redknapp also told me how good a person and a manager Walter was. Then when I went to Rangers all the good things people told me about Walter were confirmed.'

The league campaign saw Kenny Miller make his mark with a double against Celtic. Mendes and Daniel Cousin also netted, as Rangers came away with a morale-boosting 4–2 Parkhead win. Portuguese international Mendes admitted it was the perfect introduction to the Old Firm game. 'I will never forget my first Old Firm derby. It was an extraordinary day not only for myself, but for all the players and the Rangers fans. I scored that day but the most important thing was to get the victory at Celtic Park.'

That turned out to be a wake-up call for Celtic. By the time the next Old Firm game came round the Hoops had moved four points clear and Scott McDonald's winner at Ibrox stretched that to seven.

Smith had his work cut out and pleaded for calm – although everybody above him knew Rangers were in deep financial trouble. The stories started to leak after Birmingham City tabled a £2.8 million bid for top scorer Kris Boyd. The Ibrox playing staff were then told that the club needed to sell at least one player to balance the books.

Assistant boss Ally McCoist feared what would have happened if Smith hadn't been there to keep everything together. 'I don't think there was anybody better equipped to guide us through the situation we were in than Walter,' McCoist acknowledged. 'It was always going to take somebody with great strength and a great knowledge of the club. Walter knows what Rangers is all about and, for me, he is the only man we could have had at the helm who could have guided us through such troubled times the way he did. We are not out of the woods yet but what Walter has achieved should never be forgotten. We were all lucky, and I include myself, that we had Walter in charge. I honestly believe that if anybody else would have been in charge then I think the club would have been in serious trouble. People should never underestimate what Walter has done for Rangers. A lot of what he has done for the club has been behind the scenes. That has been vital, but people will probably never find out about that.'

Smith knew he had to call on his experience to hold things together and urged his players to blank out the financial situation and get on with what they were paid to do – play football. They did precisely that and managed to cut the gap on Celtic ahead of the 0–0 Parkhead game. They continued to keep in touch and fancied their chances going into the CIS Cup final against Celtic. The match went the distance before extra-time goals from Darren O'Dea and Aiden McGeady handed the trophy to Gordon Strachan's side.

Kirk Broadfoot, who was red-carded late on at Hampden, admitted: 'Being sent off in the League Cup final was a real low. I had been struggling with injury but the manager asked me to play. I knew I couldn't let him down but looking back maybe I shouldn't have played. I ended up getting sent off and we also lost the game, so the day couldn't have got any worse for me.'

There was to be even more unwanted front-page attention. Smith had to deal with captain Barry Ferguson and Allan McGregor after they got involved in an all-night drinking session at the Scotland team hotel, Cameron House, after the qualifier in Holland. National boss George Burley punished them by leaving them on the bench for the Hampden qualifier with Iceland. They were then photographed giving the V-sign to watching photographers. The pair were banned indefinitely from the Scotland set-up before they had to face the wrath of their club boss. Smith made them issue a public apology, fined them and told them to stay away from Murray Park for two weeks. Their days at Rangers looked numbered as Ferguson was stripped of the armband. It was handed to Davie Weir.

Weir admitted: 'It was a great moment for me when the manager decided to give me the armband. It was a big enough thing for me to sign for Rangers because I was a Rangers fan as a boy but to be given the captain's armband was a real honour. It was great to be given the armband and the chance to go up and pick up trophies. It is the ultimate honour for me. It is something I am very proud of. Not many people get the opportunity to captain Rangers. When you see names like John Greig, Richard Gough and Barry Ferguson then it is nice to be mentioned in that sort of company. The only disappointing thing for me was the way in which I inherited the armband, with Barry leaving the club and all the nonsense that surrounded his departure.'

Ferguson and McGregor did get back into the team although the Rangers squad never looked back from Bevvygate. They went the rest of the season unbeaten. They saw off St Mirren to seal a Scottish Cup final appearance against Falkirk.

The 1–1 draw at Hibs allowed Celtic to go top of the table on goal difference, but it all changed again in the second last game of the SPL campaign. Rangers beat Aberdeen while it was Celtic's turn to slip up at Easter Road. Once again it went to the last game and Scotland was bracing itself for another 'Helicopter Sunday' finale.

Rangers had to go to Euro hopefuls Dundee United while Celtic took on Hearts – although that match was to quickly drift into insignificance. Smith's team took the Tannadice game by the scruff of the neck and despatched United quickly out of sight. Goals from Kyle Lafferty, Mendes and Boyd ensured the title was destined for Ibrox and Celtic's four-in-a-row charge was stopped in its tracks.

A delighted Davie Weir lifted the trophy. 'Every league is massive when you are at Rangers but that was my first one and I think we all knew how big it was for the club,' Weir admitted. 'Especially as we had gone so close the previous season and missing out on that left a bit of a bitter taste in the mouth. This time we didn't have the distraction of Europe and so with more of a level playing field in terms of games we proved over the season that we were the better team. It was just such a special day to lift the trophy and to see the helicopter coming in.'

Pedro Mendes said: 'The day we clinched the title on that memorable afternoon at Dundee made me very happy. It was the end of a very difficult year for us all, with all the problems at the club. The way we won it was just amazing. I can't really compare it to other titles I have won. Each one has a different story. But the way we came back from behind, against all the odds, and won it the way we did should make everyone at the club very, very proud. It was a fantastic achievement.'

The title success and guaranteed Champions League money from the direct entry to the group stages also went a long way to filling the sparse Ibrox coffers. Smith explained: 'My game plan was to win the championship this year because qualification for the Champions League would be really, really tough. The chairman [Sir David Murray] has been under a bit of pressure. Winning the title was so important, and will alleviate the pressure on the chairman as well. We are in Europe and now we do not have to play a qualifying round. That is a huge thing for the club because of the financial issues. When I came back, the challenge was to turn the team around and get us back into a challenging position and the Champions League. We closed the gap, won the league and reached several cup finals. That is an achievement for the whole group at Rangers.'

Nacho Novo more than agreed with his manager. He added: 'To be fair every league I won at Rangers was special but that one in particular stands out. It was just so important for everyone connected with the club. Everyone knows the financial problems that Rangers had and goodness knows what would have happened had we not won the title that season. I think it is fair to say that the Gaffer went a long way to saving the club by guiding us to that success. It guaranteed us the Champions League money and stopped Celtic widening the gap between the two clubs. It really was vital that we won that title. If we hadn't then I would hate to have seen what would have happened to Rangers. That is the thing about Walter. He cares passionately about Rangers. I don't think anyone realises just how passionate he is about the club. He loves the club and he has surrounded himself with great people who also have the same feelings for Rangers, guys like Ally McCoist and Kenny

McDowall. They are Rangers men and they want the best for their club, just like Walter.'

Kenny Miller, who had finally won over the Rangers support with his all-action displays, also knew that title was a big one for his own career. He explained: 'I came back to help Rangers win the league and I knew if we hadn't won it then a lot of fingers would have been pointed at me. I had read and heard it all in the newspapers and radio phone-ins. So, to actually win the league that season was massive. It stopped Celtic making it four-in-a-row and I felt I had made a decent contribution to our success. It was a relief because there had been various points throughout the season where Celtic had looked strong favourites to win the league. They then let us in by slipping up against Hibs and we went up to Dundee United knowing that a win would guarantee us the title. Thankfully we got that result and, as they say, the rest is now history.'

Kirk Broadfoot reckons days like that were the real reason why Smith returned to the Ibrox hotseat. 'Winning that first league title was a big thing for us all,' the defender admitted. 'We had lost out the previous season and that had been a big disappointment – missing out at the death. At Rangers you need to win every game, but I think missing out the previous season made us even more determined that title was going to be ours. It would also have been four-in-a-row if Celtic had won it. Every title is important for Rangers but this one was probably one of the biggest. Financially the club were struggling and goodness knows what would have happened if we hadn't won the league and claimed the Champions League money. A lot of people say it was the title that saved Rangers. We will never know if it actually did but it certainly was a big title in the history of the club. I am sure the manager would have enjoyed it as well because it was his first title since nine-in-a-row. I am sure that trying to regain the title was one of the reasons why he left the Scotland job to return to Rangers. In doing that he had achieved what he had set out to do.'

Christian Dailly is in no doubt that title triumph was inspired by Smith. He explained: 'I was lucky enough to get back in the team in the final run-in. I played a good run of games and helped the team along the way. I also played enough games to get a medal which was good, but the most important thing was trying to win the title back for Rangers. The fact we had come so close the previous season had made us even more determined we weren't going to be second-best the next season. I have played in a lot of dressing rooms and different players have different mentalities. But that Rangers team all wanted to win. They had a mentality that they had to win every game. I think a lot of that came from Walter Smith. That was important to me because I have the same mentality but, as I have said, I have played along-side guys in teams who didn't take that same approach.'

Lee McCulloch reckons the championship ended up with the best side that season. 'I don't think anyone can argue that we didn't deserve to win that title,' McCulloch claimed. 'I think a lot of us were fired up to make sure we got it after what had happened the previous season. That had left us hurting and we were determined this was going to be our time. I was delighted because it was my first title as a Rangers player. I had been a supporter so it was an amazing experience for me to go out and lift that trophy. I had seen so many great players do it and suddenly I was out there lifting the trophy.'

Madjid Bougherra, in particular, had played a big part in Rangers' success and he knew he owed it to Smith, who had rescued him from Charlton Athletic's second string.

The Algerian said: 'It was the first major medal I had won in Scotland and I was very proud to have played my part in helping Rangers to the title. I remember after the game Walter was so happy. He came up to me and thanked me personally because he felt I had done really well for him all the season. I said, "No, it is me who should be thanking you – you are the one that has helped me and given me this opportunity." But that is typical of the manager. He always looks out for his players before himself.'

Stevie Naismith also came back from injury to play his part in getting the team over the line. The striker admitted: 'It was a dream when we won that title. At the time I didn't realise what I had been part of. The longer time goes on you realise how big that title was. It was my first for Rangers but it was also so important for everything else that was going on round about it. We knew we had to win it because of all the financial problems surrounding the club. The Gaffer managed the situation brilliantly. He would only tell us the bits and bobs that we needed to know and the rest of the time he would keep the rest of things away from us. That allowed us to get on with the football rather than worrying about other things we couldn't really influence. To be fair, the situation probably worked in our favour. A lot of the time the manager used it as a motivational tool to really get us going. You have to give the Gaffer enormous credit for getting so much out of such limited resources. What we achieved, in his own words, was absolutely remarkable.'

There was to be one more game left and it was the Scottish Cup final. Novo lived up to his super-sub billing as within a minute of coming on he netted the only goal of the game to sink Falkirk.

'Coming off the bench and scoring the Scottish Cup winner against Falkirk was the biggest highlight of that season,' the Spaniard admitted. 'I replaced Kris Boyd at half-time. The ball went out for a throw in and it just fell to me. I was about forty yards out and I thought I'm having a go here. I hit it sweetly and I knew as soon as I connected that it was going to end up in the net. It proved to be the only goal of the game – and what an important one. It meant we finished the season with a league and Scottish Cup double. It had been a draining season and all the players had given their all. We couldn't have given any more and so to end the season with two trophies made it all that bit more worthwhile. We had come out on top and I don't think anybody could argue that we didn't deserve to come out on top that season.'

It was the ideal way for fellow sub Christian Dailly to say his Ibrox farewells. He appreciated the gesture from Smith in letting him bow out on a high.

Dailly said: 'I came off the bench for the last couple of minutes. It was like back to the old days because Walter sent me on up front for Kyle Lafferty for the last couple of minutes. Walter just said just go out there and play on the centre-half's shoulder and try and get in behind him. I had spent most of the season playing in midfield or defence but he knew that even playing up front I would try to cover every blade of grass for him. I actually managed to do that but I just couldn't cap things off with a goal. It still was a good way for me to say my goodbyes. I left Rangers with a League Cup, Scottish Cup and an SPL winner's medal. Not bad for somebody who was only coming up for six months to help Walter out.'

20

WALTER HELPS RANGERS TO BANK EVEN MORE SUCCESS

(2009–10)

THE FULL extent of the Rangers' financial plight was there for all to see in the summer of 2009. Barry Ferguson and Charlie Adam were sold while Brahim Hemdani, Christian Dailly and Alan Gow were released. There might have been Champions League football but there was no money to spend. In fact the only signing Walter Smith could scrape enough money together for was the loan arrival of the French winger Jerome Rothen from Paris St Germain.

Smith's situation was magnified by the fact that Gordon Strachan had stepped down at Celtic and their Old Firm rivals were spending big to help new manager Tony Mowbray grab the title back. Smith also had to juggle the domestic and European games with an even more limited squad. The Champions League draw looked to have smiled on them favourably when they were placed with Seville, Stuttgart and new boys Unirea Urziceni from Romania.

It was the old head of Smith who took the early initiative in the SPL, as his team pieced together a decent unbeaten run. That included a 2–0 Old Firm win, thanks to two goals from Kenny Miller, and a 1–1 draw in the Champions League away to Stuttgart. Madjid Bougherra was the hero that night. He admitted: 'A big goal for me was in the Champions League qualifier against

Stuttgart. It was my first goal in Europe for Rangers and also got us a good result out in Germany. The one thing about the manager is he lets you go out and play your own game. He will say one or two things but will never try to overcomplicate things. He trusts you to go out and play your game. He doesn't put you under pressure. He allows you to go out and express yourself. I am a defender but I also like to get forward, when possible. He has never really had a go at me or told me not to attack. I appreciate that because I think it would take quite a lot out of my game if I wasn't allowed to get forward.'

Rangers continued to keep well clear of Mowbray's stuttering Celtic although results in the Champions League weren't as positive. They were thrashed at home by Seville and Unirea. There was the chance for revenge in Bucharest but they could only muster a draw, although young Danny Wilson was starting to make a real impression in the heart of the Rangers defence.

It was just as well that some of the Murray Park protégés were breaking through because a clearly frustrated Smith came out and confirmed that the bank was calling the shots. The money men had taken control of the club. He explained: 'It was eighteen months ago now that everybody was put up for sale. And for six months before that, we had the situation boiling away in the background. So we've had to deal with it for a couple of years now. But we've had a really good group of players, that's the one thing. They are great lads, terrific boys to work with. You could see on the pitch that, no matter how much they wanted the championship and how prepared they were to go for it, the brightness and bit of edge had been taken off them. That's simply because of the amount of hard work they've been prepared to do. I don't think people appreciate just how much it takes out of a player in an Old Firm team, to go and win every week.'

Smith, Kenny McDowall and Ally McCoist were all set to come out of contract and there was no sign of extensions being offered – although the trio initially indicated they were prepared to continue on a non-contract basis. A home defeat to Stuttgart and an away loss in Seville added to Rangers' problems as they crashed straight out of Europe, even missing out on the safety net of a Europa League place.

McCoist admitted it was a really bad period and it was left to Smith to show his true colours again. 'Walter's record isn't all about nine-in-a-row,' his No. 2 insisted. 'He has also shown he can manage in troubled times as well. There is no doubt it is easier when things are going well and everybody is smiling. The true test comes in times like these. I honestly believe we were extremely lucky to have Walter during these difficult times. I have already praised the manager's part in what he has done but every single one of the players has to be praised as well. Against all odds, they have delivered titles and trophies. You also have to remember it was against a back-drop where not only have they been put up for sale but so had the club. The manager still managed to maintain an environment where it was easy to work hard and also enjoy your football. The players definitely responded to that.'

Further fuel was added to the fire when Rangers legends Richard Gough and Mark Hateley criticised Smith's squad. That saw the Rangers manager angrily jump to the defence of his players. Smith said: 'Richard Gough and Mark Hateley are two who have made comments in newspapers and I get a wee bit disappointed by that. At times I get a wee bit fed up with every one of them coming out with these comments. It's as if they had the perfect answer to everything in football. And while they might be looking at the Rangers team just now and being critical, the team at the present moment has been successful. Okay, we maybe don't have a Gascoigne, Laudrup or a McCoist from the early days – guys to pull us out of problems, so it's more difficult for the players now than it was in the time when they played.'

Former captain Gough, from his own personal experience, wasn't surprised that Smith had come out and rounded on him and the rest of the critics. Gough admitted: 'Walter is very loyal to his players. He will protect them as much as he can and if somebody criticises them then he will be there to defend them. You find that because of that loyalty it makes the players even more determined to do well for him. His man-management has always been absolutely superb. If you ever had a problem with him you could always go and see him. He was also a bit different to Graeme Souness. He was a bit more mature because with Graeme it was his way or the highway. The fact that Walter is still managing a title-winning team well into his sixties tells you how good a man-manager he is.'

Sasa Papac has admitted that Smith's support of his players, in times of need or adversity, just makes them even more determined to go out and give every last ounce of energy to help their manager bring even more success to Rangers. The left back insisted: 'Everyone at Rangers over the last few years has always wanted to give everything for him. He gives you that drive to want to push harder and do better. He makes all his players want to improve and show they can give even more, even if they are tired or not playing well. I don't know how he does that but players never want to let him down. Sometimes you lose the game, that can happen, but no one ever comes off not having given 100 per cent. He's not the kind of coach that will come over to you every day wanting to talk about different things. You can have a joke with him and chat about things. Before a game, though, we have a meeting and he tells you his vision about the team, about the opposition, and about how he wants you to play. It is different to any other coach I worked with before.'

Rangers hit form in the run-up to Christmas with six straight league wins, including a 7–1 win over Dundee United – where Kris Boyd netted an impressive five goals. 'The 7–1 win over Dundee United is probably my favourite game playing under the Gaffer,' Madjid Bougherra revealed. 'Kris Boyd scored five goals and I also got one. We just played really well and everything just fell into place.'

By the time Lee McCulloch rescued an Old Firm point at the turn of the year, the Light Blues were already in total command. The January transfer window again didn't work in Smith's favour, as Pedro Mendes was sold to Sporting Lisbon while Celtic played their trump card getting Robbie Keane up on loan from Tottenham Hotspur.

Mendes admitted it was a big decision to leave Rangers in the financial situation they were in. He explained: 'All the problems that were in the club made it very difficult. Everybody was talking about the financial problems, the issues with the bank and the club being put up for sale. There were things the players were all aware of, but in Walter, we had someone that had the ability to make us keep digging for results. He kept the team together and made us successful.'

It was Rangers who remained in front and February proved a fruitful month as they saw off St Johnstone in the Co-operative Insurance Cup semi-final and beat Celtic 1–0 at Ibrox, thanks to Maurice Edu's goal, to go ten points clear at the top.

The Co-operative Insurance Cup final saw them paired with Gus MacPherson's St Mirren. Rangers were installed as heavy favourites but that appeared to go out the window as Kevin Thomson and Danny Wilson were sent off. But instead of giving up, the Rangers team managed to grab a dramatic later winner from Kenny Miller to sicken St Mirren and lift the cup.

Miller admitted a rollicking from Smith had spurred him and the team on to glory. He revealed: 'Scoring the cup final goal against St Mirren was another big day for me. That result will go down in history because I don't think there will be too many teams who will go down to nine men and still go on and lift a trophy. I scored near the end and it was just an amazing feeling. I had come in at half-time and started to have a go at some of my team mates about not doing enough. The Gaffer put me straight in no uncertain terms and also told me that I could have also have been doing an awful lot more. It certainly fired me up and hopefully my goal and second-half performance showed that. I was just delighted to have scored when we did because I don't think we would have held out in extra time. We were all running on empty and I hate to think what would have happened had we not scored when we did.'

Stevie Naismith came off the bench and helped to turn the game Rangers' way. He admitted: 'My cup final highlight was the one against St Mirren. I was a substitute against St Mirren but the Gaffer sent me on. He knew what I could do and told me to go out and play my normal game and just to get the ball and run at defenders. It was just such a strange cup final to play in. We were down to nine men and we still went on to win it. I managed to swing in the cross for Kenny Miller to score so that is a day I will always be proud of.'

Ally McCoist reckons that Smith's Hampden celebrations at the goal and the final whistle just showed what it meant to him to be manager of the Glasgow giants. He admitted: 'The one memory of Walter Smith, as manager of Rangers, that stands out for me was his reaction and celebration when Kenny Miller scored our Co-operative Insurance Cup final winner against St Mirren. We were down to nine men but we still managed to get the goal and win the game, against all odds. The way he celebrated was just amazing. It sums up, for me, just how much he wants to win. He might be over sixty but his determination and hunger for success still burn as bright as the day he started out in management. I think that day people really saw the Gaffer's true emotions. He gave people a glimpse of the real Walter Smith and it is not something a lot of people on the outside see. We all knew he was a winner but the way he celebrated that goal just sums Walter up for me. I still have the photographs of Walter when we scored the goal and again at the final whistle.'

McCoist also believes that the team spirit shown that day and that season was as good as he has seen in all his years at Ibrox. 'From a team point of view and the circumstances from which we lifted the cup, it will probably go down as one of the greatest cup final performances in Rangers history,' McCoist added. 'The players deserve enormous credit for digging that result out. We were against the ropes and despite having two men sent off we still managed to dig out a goal and to win the game. It really was a truly amazing team performance from the lads. It sums up what we had in that dressing room.'

Celtic were unable to live with Rangers and eventually Mowbray paid the price and was replaced by coach and former captain Neil Lennon. He might have improved results but the title was always destined for Ibrox.

A blistering run after a hefty defeat away to St Johnstone eventually saw the title wrapped up at Easter Road. Kyle Lafferty, who had struggled to live up to his big-money price tag, scored the only goal of the game at Easter Road to make it two-in-a-row. It was a league championship that more than took its toll on Smith and his first-team squad. Smith proudly said: 'That's what maybe separates this title from some of the other championships that I've been fortunate enough to win. This time we've done it with a small group and against the odds – especially this season. We're delighted for the group of players. We've had to ask a lot from them – even today they've lost the brightness they once had. They have come back on a regular basis and have been fantastic. For that and the consistency they deserve a lot of credit. Like a lot of things – when we've been under pressure they've come through. They are a resilient bunch and a difficult bunch to beat.'

Kenny Miller reckoned it was a good end to a season that had caused more than a few scary moments. He recalled: 'There was a stage where we were still on for the treble. We won the Co-operative Insurance Cup and were ahead in the league but Dundee United ended up putting us out of the Scottish Cup. We still managed to walk away with a double, which any season, is still a more than decent return.'

Lee McCulloch admitted his feelings on winning the title were slightly different from the previous year. He explained: 'After the first league win it became more of a relief the second time around. We were now expected to win the league. Also, because you have won something, then if you don't retain it then it becomes an even bigger disappointment. You really have to deliver but that comes with being a Rangers player.'

Madjid Bougherra reckons his manager's desire also rubbed off on to his players. 'Walter has won so many cups and titles at Rangers but it doesn't make any difference to him,' Bougherra admitted. 'He celebrates every success the same. You can see what being at Rangers and winning trophies at Ibrox means to him. He has never lost that hunger and that is a big thing at the top level of football.'

That is maybe due to the fact that he is still very much a fan at heart. 'The one thing about Walter is that he loves the club,' Ally McCoist explained. 'That goes back to the days when he used to jump on the Carmyle supporters' bus to go and watch Rangers. Nobody should ever underestimate his love for Rangers. The good thing about Walter is he never lets his feelings for the club get in the way of doing what is right for the club. That is another one of his great talents.'

21

ONE FINAL HAMPDEN HOORAY

(2010–11)

WALTER SMITH had just toasted his second consecutive title when he announced he would have one final season in the Ibrox hotseat. He also confirmed his hope that his No. 2, Ally McCoist, would be given the chance to succeed him. That was one of the reasons why Smith decided he would step down because he felt McCoist was due his chance after serving such a long apprenticeship.

Rangers star Stevie Naismith admitted he and the rest of the Rangers squad were delighted that Smith signed up for another season. Naismith said: 'We won back-to-back titles and that is something the Gaffer has to take a lot of credit for. His influence was massive in guiding us through everything that was going on. I remember the championship party for our second title. It was a great night. As it went on, all the coaches and players were getting drunker and drunker. The drinks were really flowing and then all the players started to go up to him and tell him he had to stay. We couldn't afford to lose him. We were even going up to Walter's wife and begging her to let the Gaffer stay on! That, for me, shows you just what he has done for Rangers and what he means to everybody at Ibrox.'

There may be a bit of a generation gap between Smith and most of his players but it never stopped him from being one of the boys. Former Kilmarnock star Naismith explained: 'I remember our pre-season trip to Australia. After our first game we went out for dinner in a local Italian restaurant. All the boys and coaching staff were sitting around this big table. There were three or four of the boys on their phones, Tweeting etc. The Gaffer just looked around in total dismay and shook his head. He said, "If this is the twenty-first century then you can keep it. I'd rather just sit here and get drunk!" It was so funny and everybody started laughing. It is that personality and sense of humour that helps make him the great manager he is.'

No. 2 McCoist reckons Smith is the same manager and man he was during the history-equalling nine-in-a-row years.

McCoist said: 'I don't think Walter Smith has changed that much at all. I have played under him and also been one of his assistants and I don't think he has changed, although maybe Walter is the only person who can answer that. Maybe, just maybe, he has mellowed just a wee bit. He has also learned to take a wee step back and let guys like Ian Durrant, Kenny McDowall or myself get on with things, but he is still very much like Sir Alex Ferguson. Walter is old school. He just loves to win, especially with Rangers.'

It maybe was a bit of a surprise that Smith had decided to stay on, especially as Rangers were on their knees financially and the bank was ruling the roost. The Rangers boss said: 'We are delighted to be settled and getting ready for another season. We have decided to keep this unit intact but I can certainly say that it will be my last season. I feel that in the last two years Alistair and Kenny have been ready to take over to let us older chaps leave. We have worked well as a staff and things have been very successful over the last few seasons.'

Smith's position was also weakened as the club were unable to agree a new deal with SPL record-breaking scorer Kris Boyd. He left on freedom of contract to join Middlesbrough. Nacho Novo returned to Spain with Sporting Gijon while Kevin Thomson and Danny Wilson were sold to bring in funds. Steven Smith and DaMarcus Beasley were also released.

He was given funds to sign Croatian Nikica Jelavic from Rapid Vienna, James Beattie arrived on a free from Stoke City and Vladimir Weiss on-loan from Manchester City.

Weiss revealed that it was the chance to work with Smith that convinced him to stand Celtic boss Neil Lennon up at the last-minute. The Slovakian revealed: 'Initially I had been in talks with Neil Lennon because Celtic had been the first team to get in contact. I had spoken to Neil a few times and everything had been agreed when Rangers came forward and declared their interest. It gave me a lot to think about. Rangers had been champions the previous two seasons and after I looked at things I also felt they had a better squad than Celtic. I then spoke to Walter Smith and after I did that I knew 100 percent that I wanted to join Rangers. Rangers were also more direct with Manchester City and got the deal done within two to three days, whereas Celtic had still to agree that side of things. Lennon phoned me when he heard of Rangers' interest but at that point I told him I had only heard of Rangers through my agent. Things then developed and he tried to phone me as I was just about to complete my move to Rangers. I decided not to take his call. He was probably going to give me what for but I knew in my heart of hearts that I wanted to go to Rangers ahead of Celtic.'

Captain Davie Weir is in no doubt Smith worked wonders in the transfer market. He said: 'I don't think anyone can underestimate what Walter Smith has done. He has had success with a lot of money. He has also had success with very little funds and backing, basically with one hand tied behind his back. His management of Rangers has been incredible, especially when you look at the club's financial problems and the fact he had to sell or let some of his top players go.'

The demands remained the same for Smith – his Rangers team had to go for the title and try to make an impact in the Champions

League. The pressure was certainly on in Europe after they had flopped so dismally the previous season.

Manchester United, Valencia and Turkish champions Bursaspor were the teams that stood in their way. The first match saw Smith's team travel to Old Trafford to take on old foe Sir Alex Ferguson. Smith then produced a tactical surprise as his 5–4–1 formation ground out an excellent 0–0 draw.

Kirk Broadfoot, who shouldn't even have played that night, recalled that game. He said: 'The manager's tactics definitely had a big hand in getting that 0–0 draw at Old Trafford. I hurt my ankle a few weeks before it but it was a game I was determined to be involved in. I never like missing any games, but especially not one of that magnitude. It was a defensive performance but the manager got his tactics spot on. We defended for our lives, although, to be fair, Manchester United didn't really create too many chances. I even think Sir Alex Ferguson admitted the Gaffer had sprung a surprise on him. That shows you just how good and well respected the Gaffer is.'

Stevie Naismith reckons Smith has a unique ability to second-guess the opposition and that, more often than not, allows him and Rangers to get the upper hand. Naismith admitted: 'He has this ability to tell you how a game is going to pan out and tell you what is going to happen. It really is spooky because most of the time he gets it spot on. He has shown that throughout his time at Rangers although no more so than during the UEFA Cup final run. The club hadn't got close to a European final for years but suddenly with a squad that wasn't meant to be as talented as in previous years he took us all the way. His systems and the way he sets up his teams work brilliantly. You only have to look to this season's Champions League. He adopted a 5–4–1 formation that got us a surprise draw against Manchester United at Old Trafford. Those tactics really work.'

Rangers drew with Valencia at home and beat Bursaspor before defeat in Spain and at home to United ended their Champions

League qualifications hopes. However, they had still done enough to drop into the Europa League – as they signed off with a point in Turkey.

Davie Weir said: 'Everybody wrote us off going into the Champions League and every point we picked up was a bonus. To be as successful as we have been you have to give Walter Smith enormous credit for the way he set us up, got us organised and gave us a chance to get results. Whoever follows in his footsteps will know it is going to be very difficult. Even to get into the Champions League for Rangers is going to be a massive task.'

Smith signed off the Champions League with Rangers making their mark on the European stage and still fighting on all fronts domestically.

That was despite the fact that Jelavic, who was cup-tied for Europe, was left sidelined for three months after he injured his ankle in the Tynecastle win over Hearts. It left Smith without his star man at a crucial part of the season and Jelavic feeling like his entire world had collapsed.

The Croatian recalled: 'I made a good start to my Rangers' career. I had scored a few goals and I felt I had settled really well. I had adapted to my new surrounding and I was really enjoying life playing under Walter at Rangers when I suffered my injury at Hearts. I was gutted with the injury but I could also see the disappointment in Walter's face after it happened. But he knew how disappointed I was and he remained strong for me. He was always there to keep my chin up. He was very positive and assured me I would come back a lot stronger. Even when I went to Croatia to get my operation Walter phoned me a lot to ask how I was doing and to give me words of strength. It meant a lot because managers at top clubs have so many things to do but the fact he took the time out to regularly call me meant so much. He was always there with words of motivation to spur me on. It did because I worked hard to get back to fitness. I was determined to get fit and back into the team and to repay the manager for the faith he had shown in me during my time in need.'

Another of Smith's new recruits was finding it hard to shine in his new surroundings and it was left to him to get him back on the straight and narrow.

Vladimir Weiss explained: 'I was still a young player and I knew I was still learning my trade. I came on and did well on my debut. That raised expectation levels but after the first few games I started to struggle. My confidence was a wee bit down and things weren't really coming off. I wasn't happy with my performances and neither were the fans. I went and saw the manager and he was brand new. He sat me down, spoke to me and gave me a lot of decent advice. He also built up my confidence and in the next game against Motherwell I went out to have one of my best games in a Rangers shirt. Once again he showed his man-management qualities.'

Smith was doing his best to paper over the cracks but on 2 January they were really shown up when Rangers were outclassed and outplayed by Celtic at Ibrox, as a Georgios Samaras double did the damage and left serious question marks over Rangers' title ambitions. The sub-standard performance left Smith distinctly unimpressed and he and his coaching staff left their stunned players in no doubt that they had let themselves down badly. He warned such abject displays wouldn't be tolerated and he didn't want to see Celtic's stars lapping it up in front of the Rangers players again.

That chilling warning still sends a shiver down Weiss's spine now when he thinks back to Smith reading them all the riot act. He admitted: 'The manager was always one to keep standards high. I remember after the New Year Old Firm game when we lost to Celtic. At that point everybody was talking about Celtic doing the treble and the fact that we were finished. The Celtic players were celebrating on the pitch and in the tunnel in front of us after they won that match. It was a horrible feeling.

'Walter and Ally McCoist eventually got us all sitting down in the dressing room. They were furious and went mad at us. They had every right because we had been poor and hadn't performed. They told us they'd better not see Celtic players celebrating on our pitch again. They basically told us to go out and use the rest of the season to turn things around and to have the last laugh on the same Celtic players who had tried to rub our noses in it. For Walter it was always about giving your all. Anything less wasn't good enough and it can only be a good thing for any professional footballer to work in that environment. Davie Weir always told me to take as much as I could from working under the manager because it would make me a better player and person and he was absolutely right.'

Things remained as unstable off the pitch and the January transfer window saw Smith lose another one of his star assets, as the SPL's top scorer Kenny Miller was sold to Turkish side Bursaspor. He admitted it was a big decision to walk out on Smith and what had been the best two-and-a-half years of his career.

Miller explained: 'I had been in contract talks with the club and it became clear that we were not going to be able to agree an extension. I knew I would be leaving, whether it would be in the January or the end of the season window, I wasn't quite sure. I was pretty open-minded about things but then January came and suddenly I had quite a few attractive offers on the table. I knew at my age it was going to be my last big move. My concern was that those offers might not still have been there at the end of the campaign, especially if I had picked up an injury in the second half of the season. So, after I agreed terms in principle with Bursaspor, I went in to see the Gaffer before the Inverness game. I spoke to the Gaffer and told him the situation. He gave me his views and we both agreed it was best for me to try and make the move in the January window. I remember he shook my hand, thanked me and wished me all the best. I really appreciated it because Walter had done so much for my career. I then went round the dressing room and shook the hands of the players and all the coaching staff. I have to say it was hard. I had so many great times with them at Rangers, and I don't mind admitting that I actually started to choke up. They were not only part of the team but I also classed them, and still do, as friends. It was a hard decision to leave them because working with them every day, under Walter and Ally, was just amazing. It was a pleasure and the best period of my career. It was a wrench to leave Rangers although I knew that for the sake of myself, my career and my family that I had to make the move.'

The bankers continued to squeeze the Ibrox purse strings, but Smith was still able to bring in record Northern Irish goal-getter David Healy and young Kyle Bartley on loan from Arsenal.

Smith has always made headlines with his transfer dealing at Rangers, from Paul Gascoigne to Brian Laudrup, and he didn't disappoint with his final throw of the dice. Hours before the close of the January 2011 transfer window he swooped to sign the controversial El-Hadji Diouf on loan from Blackburn. The Senegal star had a history of trouble, on and off the pitch, but, like Paul Gascoigne, Smith believed he could harness him and let Rangers get the best of his unquestionable footballing abilities.

Sasa Papac reckons Smith deserves to take a well-earned rest for everything he has done for Rangers – over both spells. The Bosnian said: 'I am not all that surprised that Walter is leaving as sometimes as a player or a manager you just have to say, that's enough. This season he has been very motivated for the team and wants to do well, but maybe he felt he wanted a rest for a couple of years. Football is a hard job, especially for a coach. When you are in charge of a team like Rangers you are always under pressure. Every season only first place is good enough. Second means you are a loser.'

Madjid Bougherra hoped McCoist would get the Rangers manager's job, but knows that anyone who takes over from Smith has a thankless task to keep producing Ibrox miracles. The Algerian admitted: 'It is going to be very hard for anybody to replace

Walter Smith. What he has achieved at Rangers is going to be very hard to replicate. The good thing is Walter has worked closely with Ally McCoist and Kenny McDowall over the last four years. They have learned a lot from the manager. So if anybody is going to replace Walter then Ally and Kenny, for me, are the perfect choice although I don't know if there is really a coach out there who could step in and fill the great man's shoes.'

Rangers chief executive Martin Bain announced on 22 February 2011 that McCoist had agreed to do just that and, assisted by McDowell and Ian Durrant, would take over from Smith at the end of the 2010–11 campaign. McCoist, speaking at his unveiling, said: 'It's a bit like taking the microphone from Frank Sinatra, taking over from Walter, because he's a very difficult act to follow. In terms of success, I hope I don't differ much from Walter. Our personalities are different, we have different ideas on selections and tactics. But, if I'm half as successful as Walter Smith, I will be genuinely thrilled.'

The announcement gave the leg-weary Light Blues a real boost as they went out to Portugal and, thanks to Maurice Edu's late goal, managed to salvage a 2-2 draw against Sporting Lisbon to go through to the next round of the Europa League on away goals. It set up a last sixteen clash with Dutch league leaders PSV Eindhoven. That was to be Walter's final European farewell. A gutsy goal-less draw in Holland gave them a chance but Jeremain Lens' goal at Ibrox and some controversial refereeing decisions left a sense of disappointment around his final Euro bow.

Before those PSV clashes was the highly controversial Scottish Cup replay exit to Celtic at Parkhead. Rangers lost 1-0 but the match made the headlines for all the wrong reasons with Steven Whittaker and Madjid Bougherra red-carded, while El-Hadji Diouf suffered the same fate after the game. However, the big flash-point was the touchline shenanigans of Celtic manager Neil Lennon and Ally McCoist. At one point Smith even had to act as the peacemaker, pulling McCoist back into line before things blew up at the final whistle and the Celtic manager had to be hauled away. It led to a Holyrood summit on the Old Firm hosted by First Minister Alex Salmond.

But more of a concern for Smith was the way their great rivals had gained the upper hand. Celtic had won three of the last four Old Firm games and drawn in the other. The critics claimed Rangers had gone and Celtic were on course for the treble.

Smith didn't have to wait long to silence their doubters. The Co-operative Insurance Cup final allowed the Light Blues the chance to put Celtic back in their place. Steven Davis netted the opener before Joe Ledley levelled for Celtic to take the game into extra-time. It was there that big summer signing Nikica Jelavic came to the fore to net and ensure that Smith, in his final appearance at Hampden, was to walk away a winner.

Jelavic was pleased after his injury hell that he was able to repay some of the massive faith that Smith had shown in him. The Croat said: 'It was the first big trophy for me. I was also pleased to score the goal that won us the cup. But it wasn't about me. It was all about the team because we have such a good team. We are one big family and I think we showed our unity that day when most people outside of the team had written us off but we believed in ourselves and the manager believed in ourselves.

'We knew together what we could achieve and that all came from the manager. It was good to score because Walter had paid a lot of money to sign me and I know he had brought me to Scotland to score goals and to win trophies. It was a special day because it was my first trophy in Scotland.'

Weiss was another who was desperate to produce that day and even played through the pain barrier to help Smith's side grab the glory. Weiss explained: 'My build up to Hampden wasn't great. I went to see the manager because my foot was still causing me concern. I went to see Walter and I told him I didn't feel I could play in both the cup final and in the game against PSV

Eindhoven. I told him I would give it a chance in whatever game he felt was best for the team.

'In the end he decided to put me on the bench for the cup final. I came off the bench and helped to supply the pass for the winner so it turned out to be a gamble that paid off. That day gave me a lot of confidence because I not only played my part but I helped Rangers to show we were a team of winners. We put down our marker that day. Walter also praised me after the game. He told me I had gone on and made the difference between the two teams. It made me feel about a million miles high and it once again showed Walter's man-management skills. I was equally pleased for him because I also knew it was going to be his final appearance at Hampden. To see him lift the trophy meant so much to us all.'

Rangers had held on to the League Cup and Stevie Naismith was delighted for his manager. He said: 'I think all the boys thought it would be great for the manager to pick up the trophy in his last appearance at Hampden. [Smith] never mentioned it once. For him, it is all about the squad and wanting the team to do it. The manager told us it was a great result and he knew we could do it. It turned out a great day all round.'

Those thoughts were echoed by Madjid Bougherra. The Algerian said: 'It was the last one for the gaffer and we wanted to win this trophy for him because he deserved to go with something good. We are all happy for him.'

22

A CHAMPION UNTIL THE END

WALTER SMITH was delighted to have walked out of Hampden with the Co-operative Cup under his arm but there was still one more prize he craved – retaining the SPL title – before he ended his long-time love affair with Rangers.

The shock-win over Celtic in the Co-operative Insurance Cup final had put Celtic back in their place and had sent a warning to their rivals that they were also far from dead and buried in the title race. Celtic still had games in hand although Smith knew his team were now at a stage where there was next to no room for error if they didn't want to lose their crown.

But the League Cup final left an unwanted hangover on his team and they were left punch-drunk by a late fight-back from Dundee United at Ibrox. Rangers had gone 2-1 ahead but were left stunned when Johnny Russell levelled. Smith's side knew they needed the win and went for all three points, only for David Goodwillie to steal them all for the Taysiders in the final minute.

Striker Nikica Jelavic revealed that their manager laid it on the line to his players after that game. The Croatian explained: 'There was a big pressure on us. It was a massive pressure we had on us. Walter spoke to every one of us after we lost to Dundee United. We were all disappointed but it can happen in any game. Walter told us we couldn't afford any more slip-ups.

We would need to go the rest of the season unbeaten and hope Celtic would lose.'

Even Smith, at that stage, feared the title was gone. He said: 'After we lost to United I did say we would need to win something like 28 points out of our last 30. But I felt it was a tall order and, at the time, I didn't really believe we would manage to do it.'

The rattled Rangers players reacted the best way they could – by winning games. They saw off St Johnstone, Hamilton, Aberdeen and St Mirren and then took their revenge on Dundee United, who had three players sent off, by thrashing them 4-0 at Tannadice.

Away from the pitch though, Smith also had to deal with a number of issues that tested all his years of experience. Rangers may have exited from Europe but there was still some unwanted fall-out to come their way from their clashes with PSV. The independent body, Football Against Racism in Europe (FARE) submitted two separate reports to UEFA claiming elements of the Rangers support, over both legs, had been guilty of sectarian singing. That led to a case being put to UEFA's disciplinary committee and the club faced an anxious wait to see what action was going to be taken, especially as there had been a long list of previous charges against their name.

Rangers, to be fair, have done a lot in recent seasons to try and fight the deep-rooted problem of bigotry. Smith also knew how serious this issue could become now UEFA were involved. He warned Rangers fans that the bigotry had to stop or their team could end up being banned from Europe if they didn't clean up their act.

Smith spoke candidly and honestly about the fact he had previously, as a Rangers supporter, sung outlawed songs like 'The Billy Boys' but insisted there is no place for bigotry like that in twenty-first century Scotland. He said: 'I started going in my early teens and, when I sang the songs, I had no realisation of what they meant. That was regarded as part of the traditions, but it didn't mean anything to me at the time and it doesn't mean anything to me now. It's still an aspect a lot of supporters look upon as a traditional aspect of the club, but it's no longer acceptable.'

In the end, FIFA decided to fine Rangers around £36,000 and banned their fans from travelling to the away leg of their opening 2011-12 Champions League qualifier. They were also hit with a suspended ban and told that they could end up playing a home game behind closed doors if they stepped out of line again over the following three years.

That was just one of a series of off-the-field issues that grabbed unwanted headlines as the 2009-10 SPL title race came into the final straight. Celtic manager Neil Lennon was subjected to death threats, a terrifying letter-bomb campaign and was attacked by a fan while he stood in the dugout at Tynecastle. Smith admitted if he had found himself in Lennon's position then he would have walked away from the game. He said: 'If I had been subjected to any of that sort of stuff I would have been out the door. I wouldn't have stuck around.'

All these things helped to ramp up the pressure as Rangers and Celtic slugged it out for the title, after predictions of a possible title challenge from Hearts quickly faded away. Rangers had also announced that Ally McCoist was to be Smith's successor but there was still a lot of uncertainty surrounding the club. Self-made millionaire and Rangers fan Craig Whyte had stepped forward to try and buy the club and rescue it from control of the Lloyds Banking group. But some of the Ibrox hierarchy were unhappy with his offer and tried to put forward a counter-proposal which delayed the possible takeover and continued to leave the club in limbo. That left Smith once again to steer the club through more troubled times and keep his team united on the pitch.

Weir explained: 'People have spoken a lot about our off-the-field problems but the manager never really let it affect us. That probably shows the brilliance of his management. Our working environment never really changed no matter what was going on in the background. He made Murray Park a great place to go and work and people enjoyed going in to do their job every day. We had nothing to complain about and had no excuses for not getting on with the job in hand. That was one of the real secrets of his management at Rangers.'

Five straight wins had given everyone hope but they knew, going into Walter's final Old Firm game, that they would need to win at Ibrox if they wanted to get things back into their grasp. The match, although not as ill-tempered as previous clashes, failed to see the Light Blues get the win they had hoped for, although things could have been far worse had Allan McGregor not saved Giorgios Samaras's second half penalty. Smith and his men had to make do with a goalless draw, which meant that if Celtic had won their game in hand it would be advantage to their city rivals.

Rangers knew they had to really turn the screw on Celtic and they put five past Motherwell. Their rivals then beat Dundee United before a former Ibrox captain handed his old team the chance to finally wrap up the title. Terry Butcher's Inverness side shocked Celtic 3-2 at the Caledonian Stadium. Smith and his players knew they had got off the hook and the title was now in full view. Celtic's slip seemed to lift a lot of the expectations off the shoulders of the Rangers players, as they started to display a freedom and flair which had only been seen fleetingly throughout the season. They were also boosted by the news that new owner Craig Whyte had completed his takeover of the Rangers club from Sir David Murray to give the club some much-needed financial security. The league leaders were, by now, full of confidence and followed that up with a four-goal rout of third-placed Hearts to take them to within two games of glory.

Vladimir Weiss, who missed the last few months with a broken foot, was always confident Celtic would crack under the title pressure. 'Celtic had chances to take the title but they never took them,' the Slovakian admitted. 'If Samaras had scored his penalty then Celtic would have won the title. I have no doubt about that but he didn't and Allan McGregor's save gave us all a big lift. Even after the game it was still advantage Celtic but I still felt that under Walter we could do it. I remember I did an interview around that time and I told the reporter that I thought Celtic would still drop points and thankfully that proved to be the case.'

Next was another Ibrox clash with Dundee United, the same side they had slipped up against, but this time there were no such problems as a 2-0 win ensured the league was going to go down to another Helicopter Sunday. This time it didn't matter what Celtic did against Motherwell as long as Rangers bettered their result down at Kilmarnock. If Smith and his team had been nervous they certainly didn't show any signs of it as they clinically blew away the Rugby Park side like cannon fodder. It took Kyle Lafferty just forty-five seconds to send them on their way. He then rattled in two more to claim his hat-trick, while Stevie Naismith and Nikica Jelavic also got in the act in the 5-1 win that was enough to see Rangers crowned champions for the 2010-11 season.

Nikica Jelavic admitted: 'Celtic lost at Inverness and suddenly we went into the final games knowing that if we won our games then we would be champions. The manager was brilliant over those final games. He told us we were good enough. We were the best team and we could do it. We went into the Kilmarnock game and won 5-1 to clinch the title, thanks to a hat-trick from Kyle Lafferty and goals from Stevie Naismith and Jelavic. I scored but the feeling at the end was one of the best I have ever had in football. I remember Walter congratulated us all on the pitch after the game. He shook hands with us all and you could see what it meant to him. He was celebrating like it was his first trophy. It was just so good to have won the title for him and all the Rangers fans.'

The SPL title was presented to Rangers on the Rugby Park pitch and captain Davie Weir insisted that his manager lift the trophy with him.

Weir admitted: 'I never really thought about it before the game.

I didn't really like to look that far ahead. Also, planning something like that, you never know how the Gaffer is going to react. I have known him long enough to know that he could quite easily have said no. Thankfully, after we had won the game, we managed to persuade him to go up with me. I think it was only right he came up and lifted the trophy with me because he has been a massive part of all our success. He also deserved to be at the heart of things. It has been a difficult season the way it has gone. There have been a lot of trials and tribulations and mud-slinging. The one thing about the Gaffer is that he has maintained his composure and dignity throughout. That shows the mark of the man. There aren't many managers who would have handled things the way he did.'

For Smith, it was the perfect way to sign off. It was his eleventh title although he always credits the first one to Graeme Souness. Smith said: 'I don't think you can pick and choose championship wins. If you've won a few, you're quite fortunate to be able to try to rate them, but each one is special.'

The title party continued back at Ibrox where Steven Whittaker, who Smith had bought from Hibernian back in 2007, admitted that every single Rangers player was determined to deliver for themselves, the fans and more importantly for their manager.

'It was Walter's last year and it was a great way for him to leave,' Whittaker said. 'He thoroughly deserved it. The manager was magnificent throughout the campaign and kept us determined throughout a very tough season. It was great to see him go away with another title. We wanted to win that title and we wanted to win it for Walter Smith. You have seen all the hard times we had to put up with throughout his last season. He was determined and that was passed on to the boys. We were all determined to give it our best shot, no matter what was put in front of us. In the end we managed to win the league and a cup.'

Big-money signing Kyle Lafferty had caused Smith a few headaches along the way but started to really fulfil his potential in the final weeks of the season. Lafferty admitted he and his side had been fired up by disrespectful comments from the Celtic camp and claims from their manager, Neil Lennon, that some of their other SPL rivals hadn't tried against them.

Lafferty said: 'Personally I think every single team wants to beat Rangers and Celtic so they can have a say in who wins the title. It is disrespectful to other teams to say they are not trying. I think we were the better team over the course of the season. Even when we didn't play well we still picked up points. That was the one thing Celtic couldn't do. When things got tough they failed. We had the heart and the desire in the team to win games even when we didn't play pretty football.'

Bosnian defender Sasa Papac reckons the 2010-11 double winning season had the Walter Smith effect written all over it. 'I honestly didn't believe we could win two trophies that season,' Papac openly admitted. 'But I also say that if you have Walter as manager anything is possible. For me he is the best manager I have had in my career. We have played in the final of the UEFA Cup, won three titles in a row and won a cup with nine men on the pitch.'

Even Smith knew he had built a special band of brothers that would give everything for the red, white and blue colours. He acknowledged it was going to be hard to walk away from them but for the sake of his long-serving No. 2 he had to make way. 'I'll always have a regret,' Smith emotionally claimed. 'I had a regret when I was arguing with myself about whether to do it or not. But I still think it was the right thing for myself and Rangers. The lads that have been working with me – Alastair, Kenny and Ian – have been patiently waiting for an opportunity to take over. They were due the opportunity, and that was part of my decision.'

Ironically Smith's last act as Rangers manager was to head off to Idaho to raise money for the club's charity through a whitewater rafting trip, along with the rest of his back room staff.

Certainly his survival instincts in his final few years at Ibrox would have stood him in good stead.

Smith now has to look to life outside of Rangers and is well aware that will be something of a culture shock. 'I suppose it will be quite odd not to be Rangers manager,' Smith admitted. 'But it's happened to me before! When you're sixty-three you've had more years when you're not the manager of Rangers than you have had being the manager of Rangers. It will be a strange circumstance.'

Walter Smith may now have left Rangers but what he has done for the club will never be forgotten. His legend and legacy will live on forever in the histories of Rangers and Scottish football.

The first page in a new chapter at Ibrox is ready to be written. The hope is that it will be just as successful as the Walter Smith era and that Ally McCoist and his team can build on the Gaffer's amazing record. Whatever happens, Walter Smith's achievements at Rangers will be hard, if not impossible, to eclipse. He leaves an astonishing legacy of success and a winning mentality to build on at Ibrox and takes with him the eternal gratitude and loyalty of Rangers fans everywhere.

23

A VIEW FROM THE DUGOUT

ALLY McCOIST (RANGERS ASSISTANT
MANAGER 2007–11 and MANAGER 2011–)

I know I am very fortunate that Walter Smith has taken me under his wing and given me my chance in management. I've learned just about everything from Walter. I know I couldn't have asked for a better teacher. I've picked up so much in terms of coaching and management and most of that has come from Walter. You are always learning as a player but I have learned even more working as a coach to Walter with Scotland and Rangers over the last five years. It has been an absolutely invaluable experience. I remember when I sat down with the late Tommy Burns when we were together at Scotland. He told me to soak up everything you can from top managers like Walter. I was more than happy to take that advice on board and it is something I have continued to do.

The great thing about Walter is how he handles situations. He has a temper but he knows how and when to say things. His big secret is that he never really flies off the handle. He thinks long and hard about everything he does. Very rarely will Walter do anything off the cuff.

He also gives Kenny McDowall, Ian Durrant and myself more of a hands-on approach when it came to the cup games with Rangers. But, to be fair to Walter, he always gives us our input.

The good thing about Walter is that although he lets us get on with things, when it comes to the cup games, he is always there and that is important, whether it be pre-match, half-time or in the dressing room after a game. We always sit round the table on a Friday, talk about the team and just generally chew the fat on things. Even when it comes to league games Walter will ask us our opinion and take our thoughts on board. At the end of the day, of course, the final decision is his and quite rightly so because he is the manager.

The first time I came across Walter was with the under-18 Scotland youth team. He worked alongside Andy Roxburgh when we made it to the European Championships in Germany and went out to play in competitions in Monaco, etc. So I have known Walter since I was seventeen. It has been a long time and I can say I have probably enjoyed every single minute working with him – maybe bar one or two!

IAN DURRANT (RANGERS FIRST-TEAM COACH)

I was speaking with Walter just before he took over at Rangers again. He wanted briefing on the squad and what I felt was needed to take the team forward. I was actually put in temporary charge until his appointment was finalised. I ended up taking the team for the Scottish Cup game at Dunfermline. It was a great experience just to manage Rangers for one day – even though I will probably go down as the worst manager in the club's history with a 100 per cent record for losing games! I had the job for a week and struggled so I don't know how the Gaffer has managed to do it for so long.

When Walter came in he handed me a job with the first team, which I was delighted about. I had done my apprenticeship with the youths and was delighted and really appreciated the chance to step up. Ally McCoist, Kenny McDowall and I have all been really lucky to work closely with the Gaffer over the last four years. It has given us all a great insight into top-level management. Walter also, to be fair, has delegated a lot of the jobs amongst us and given us more responsibility but we all know that when it comes to the crunch it is the Gaffer's call. But he is always there if we need to pick his brains or ask for advice.

I also have to say that working so closely with the Gaffer also has its pitfalls as well. I normally sit up in the stands with the Gaffer during games before he goes down to the dugout or sends me down with his instructions to Ally or Kenny. We played Celtic in the February game last season. The Gaffer was getting a bit frustrated with Nacho Novo. Wee Nacho was getting a bit excited and started getting pulled out of position as he tried to help the team get the win. I stood up and just as I passed Walter to head down the stairs something happened in the game and he jumped up and clipped me round the ear. But as he caught me I was on the step and it almost sent me flying. Later on, once things had calmed down, he said, 'Did I catch you when you were heading down the stairs?' I said yes and I was expecting a sorry but instead he said, 'You should know to keep out of my way! You know what I am like during a game!'

KENNY McDOWALL (RANGERS ASSISTANT MANAGER)

I had a fabulous four-and-a-half years working under Walter Smith. I didn't even know him at all before I started working for him. I remember when I was first approached, it was around the time when I was offered the manager's jobs at Inverness and Dundee. Somebody asked me if it was alright to pass my number on to Walter Smith. Walter was still the Scotland manager at the time so I didn't really know what he wanted to speak to me about. Then I got the call and we arranged to meet. It was there he told me he was going back to Rangers and wanted me to come in as first-team coach. It took me all of a millisecond to agree.

I might not have known him but the moment I started working with him things just went from strength to strength. He gave me a brilliant education into football management. Not only is he an incredible coach but he is also an unbelievable manager. He just knows how to handle players and all those skills have been an invaluable help to Ally McCoist, Ian Durrant and myself. Over our four-and-a-half years together we learned so much working under him.

Walter was also great because he appointed you to do a job and then he let you get on with it. He allowed us all our say and an input into things. We didn't always agree but Walter didn't want us all just to sit there and nod our heads. Even when he didn't agree he would give his reasons and that for us was an education as well, getting such an insight into a top coach. Our Friday tea and cake discussions were always interesting as we discussed the team and our tactics.

I would say winning the league in Walter's final season was the best ever. He taught us how to win, to get through a season and to win a league. It was amazing with everything that was thrown at us, the injuries and size of squad, that we still came out on top.

I still class him as our best friend. We are all sorry to see him go. He gave us all our chance and that is something we all have to be eternally grateful to him for. We now have to try and follow in his footsteps and we know that won't be an easy task.

TERRY BUTCHER (INVERNESS CALEY THISTLE MANAGER and RANGERS CAPTAIN 1986–90)

Walter is a very astute tactician. He is very quick to change things and when he sees a weakness in your team he is quick to jump on it. I mean you have to be a top coach if you are able to take a team, especially a Scottish one, all the way to a European final, like he did with Rangers in the UEFA Cup. He has a knack of knowing when to go for things or when to sit back and be a bit more cautious. That has been a major factor in him turning Rangers into such a formidable force.

I've had a few decent results against him, especially with Inverness, but to pull them off my team have had to be at the top of their game and the same time we needed Rangers to be a wee bit more off the pace. But even in defeat Walter is also extremely gracious. When Inverness beat Rangers at Ibrox he was extremely gracious and dignified even though you could see how disappointed he was. You know when you go into that coaches' room at Ibrox he will be there ready with a handshake for you although when Maurice Malpas comes in behind me he is normally given a cuff round the ear. I could sit in the manager's room at Ibrox for hours just listening to Walter and his coaching staff, Ally McCoist, Kenny McDowall, Jim Stewart and Ian Durrant. They are fantastic people and fantastic company.

DEREK McINNES (ST JOHNSTONE MANAGER and RANGERS PLAYER 1995–2000)

There was a game where Rangers beat us through a late winner from Sasa Papac. Walter and his coaching staff spent an hour in my office. I have a little fridge in there but it only holds so many so it was never going to last long with the Gaffer, Ally McCoist, Kenny McDowall, Jim Stewart and Ian Durrant there. But even when we beat them 4–1 later in that season the Gaffer still took the same time out to spend with Tony Docherty [St Johnstone assistant manager] and I. It would have been so easy to make his excuses and leave that day but he didn't and that just shows the mark of the man. I know it must have been difficult for him because I know how much of a winner he is. He just doesn't like getting beaten and that even used to extend to the head tennis in training where Archie Knox and Walter would team up against the players. I learned a lot from him and there are a number of traits I have tried to use in my own managerial career. Also Walter has such vast experience and I know if I ever need anything I can pick up the phone, knowing he will always call me back to give me advice or to help me out. It really is appreciated.

GUS MacPHERSON (ST MIRREN MANAGER 2003–10 and RANGERS PLAYER 1984–89)

I only really came across Walter Smith directly in management during his second spell back with Rangers. What I would say is that he is actually very, very quiet when you come up against him in the dugout (most of the time!). He is obviously a lot older and wiser and because of that he has been able to take a step back and seems to be able to look on from afar – that is why he spends long spells in the stands rather than on the touchline. He still makes all the major calls and decisions but, by all accounts, isn't maybe as animated as he was in his earlier days at Rangers.

Sometimes Walter is a man of few words but he is always gracious whether his team wins, loses or draws. I remember after the Co-operative Insurance Cup final he was absolutely brilliant with Andy Millen and me. He must have been delighted because his team had won the Cup with nine men but he also realised that we were probably at our lowest ebb. He told us to keep our chins up and just before he got on the bus he promised to phone me later that week and he kept his word. Even when we beat them at Love Street thanks to Stephen McGinn's goal, he came in after the game, had a cup of tea and congratulated us on our win, even though you could see he was hurting. That, for me, just shows the stature of the man.

The thing about Walter is that he always gives his players a lot of responsibility. He lets them go out and play. He has signed players like Lee McCulloch, Kenny Miller and Davie Weir. They are all players he trusts and knows will go out and do a job for him. I think that has been a regular theme throughout all his spells in management.

Walter is a man I have the utmost respect for. When he speaks then you listen. You know that he has such a wealth of experience and when he speaks, you, as a younger manager, can learn so much. I remember in my final season at St Mirren when we were struggling near the bottom of the table. He took the time to speak to Andy Millen (my assistant manager) and myself. He gave us advice on how to deal with relegation battles because he had been through something similar during his time at Everton. He is just such a top guy. I knew I could pick up the phone and call him any time even when he was Scotland manager. He would always get back to me and help me wherever he could.

The first time I actually came across Walter Smith was when he handed me my first professional contract at Rangers. I had just come off the ground staff at Ibrox and it was Walter and Campbell Ogilvie who dealt with my contract because Graeme Souness was away on a scouting trip. I wouldn't exactly say it was a negotiation. It was more a case of take it or leave it!

I remember when I was on the ground staff there was one day when Walter came in and he totally lost the plot with us all. He went mad because he didn't think we were doing some of our chores properly. Before Graeme and Walter came to the club it was a lot more laid back. We made sure the boots were all spotless but left a lot of the other jobs to the cleaning staff. That changed with Walter and Graeme and the young boys were all suddenly doing more and more. It was Walter and Graeme making more demands of us. They wanted us to work hard and do the best we could on and off the pitch. They were setting a standard and if you didn't meet it you would quickly be out on your ear. The tales of Walter when he was at Dundee United were legendary. He has always been a man who demanded the best. You only have to look at his own managerial record to see that when it comes to Scottish football greats he is right up there.

STEVEN PRESSLEY (FALKIRK MANAGER and RANGERS PLAYER 1990–94)

I never actually came up against Walter directly as manager. I was still assistant coach to Eddie May when we played them with Falkirk. I do, however, remember after our game at Ibrox Walter actually spent a lot of time with Eddie talking on a one-on-one basis. I know he gave Eddie a lot of advice and it was something Eddie was really appreciative of. There were a lot of people in the room but Walter still took time out to help a young manager on his way and that just shows the class of the man.

JIMMY NICHOLL (COWDENBEATH MANAGER and RANGERS PLAYER 1983–84 and 1986–89)

Walter Smith is a man who will contest every throw-in, free kick and foul because he has such a determination to win. I can tell you that when it comes to the touchline Walter can look after himself. He would go head to head with anybody. I never fell out with him and that is something I am pretty glad about. I have seen him in full flow and I certainly pity anybody who ends up on the receiving end of one of Walter's rants.

I remember the first time I got back into the Premier League with Raith Rovers in the 1993–94 season. We drew 1–1 at Ibrox. It was a real shock and even I couldn't believe it because it was only our third or fourth game back in the top flight. I went into Walter's office after the game and he was there along with Archie Knox, David Murray and a few others. I shook hands with them all and then the whole place went deadly silent. I actually thought, 'What have I done?' and I actually broke the silence by apologising for taking two points off Rangers. I told them they would get the points back the next week. It was only a wee blip and they would go on and win the league, which they eventually did.

Walter is a man who is humble in victory and gracious in defeat. I remember when I was No. 2 to Jimmy Calderwood at Aberdeen and we beat them at the end of the season to qualify for the UEFA Cup and, in the process, we cost Rangers the league. Walter, Ally McCoist and Kenny McDowall were all absolutely brilliant despite their obvious disappointments. They shook our hands, shared a few beers and congratulated us on getting into Europe. I know in the circumstances that must have taken some doing. But we have seen both sides because Jimmy and I were at Dunfermline on the final day when we lost to Rangers and Celtic's Chris Sutton accused us of lying down.

I know it sounds corny but I hang on pretty much every word Walter says. He is just such a top coach and somebody I have had the greatest respect for. I remember when I was taking my UEFA coaching badge and I went down to Everton to see him. Walter and Archie invited me to a training session and then came back to our hotel that night to give us a wee presentation and took a question and answer session after it. Every time I see him he is always there with advice and help whenever you need it and it really is appreciated.

KEVIN DRINKELL (STIRLING ALBION MANAGER 1994–98 and RANGERS PLAYER 1988–90)

I came across Walter again when he was in charge of Rangers and I was at Stirling Albion. Every time you meet him he is the perfect gent. We ran them close in the League Cup that night and he praised me for the team I had put together. Just to get recognition from somebody like that is something you really appreciate. But Walter has always handled himself well and is a great ambassador for Rangers.

TRIBUTES TO AN IBROX LEGEND

DAVE McPHERSON (RANGERS 1980–87 and 1992–94)

When you talk about good Scottish managers then Walter Smith is right up there. Sir Alex Ferguson is right at the top for what he has done at Manchester United but if you look at things domestically then Walter's record is certainly more than comparable. I enjoyed working with all the managers I had throughout my career but when it comes down to being successful and winning things then Walter stands alone.

I was lucky enough to work with Walter twice. The first time as assistant manager to Graeme Souness and then as a manager in his own right. I remember he would sit down and talk to the players about how we could improve our games. There was nothing major. The changes were maybe subtle but certainly helped your game. Certainly when he was Graeme's assistant he did a lot for me and I think he helped to make me a better player. I left Rangers to go to Hearts but I always hoped that one day I would get the chance to go back to Rangers and that proved to be the case.

DEREK FERGUSON (RANGERS 1983–90)

I have spent a lot of time in the company of Rangers greats like John Brown and Andy Goram. They can't speak highly enough about Walter Smith and that is a good enough reference for me. People use the word legend too much in modern-day football but it is probably the perfect way to describe Walter and what he has done for Rangers Football Club. What he achieved at Rangers second time around under the financial constraints he has had to operate under was nothing short of miraculous. Would any other manager have been able to do what he did in his second spell at Ibrox? I doubt it very much. For me, Walter Smith, quite rightly, stands up there as a Rangers great.

JIMMY NICHOLL (RANGERS 1983–84 and 1986–89)

Graeme Souness and Walter Smith gave me my first step onto the coaching ladder when they allowed me to take the reserves at Rangers. I was one of the more experienced players and I really appreciated the opportunity. It was when I stepped into that side that I realised how good a coach Walter was. I learned so much working with him and playing under him. Walter was always hands-on even when it came to the reserves. I remember I was in the dressing room and I was going back out in the afternoon to put the reserve team through their paces. Walter asked what I was up to and I told him I was going out to put on a crossing and finishing session. He then said, "Do you mind if I come out and put the session on?" I watched and he put on an amazing session. It was great for up-coming players like John Spencer and Gary McSwegan who were all hoping to push into the first team at that point. Walter has such a wealth of experience and you can just learn so much from him.

IAN DURRANT (RANGERS 1984–98)

Walter Smith deserves the world for what has done for Scottish football. He had a good schooling at Dundee United, working under Jim McLean and winning the Scottish title with just a squad of sixteen players. Then he went to Rangers and after stepping up from being Graeme Souness's assistant he has gone on to become one of the most successful managers in Ibrox history. He is right up there with the great Bill Struth. Walter is a great man. He always wants the best and is ultra-competitive. He wants to win even in training. The Gaffer has never changed in all his time at Rangers. He maybe took a wee step back when he became the manager but he is always a guy you could have a good crack and banter with – when the time is right, of course.

TERRY BUTCHER (RANGERS 1986–90)

Walter was always a man who goes about things with great dignity and is a real gentleman. Like Sir Alex Ferguson he is a man who is very demanding and certainly doesn't suffer fools gladly. It goes back to the old saying, 'Show me a good loser and I will show you a loser.' Walter hates to lose and that is because he has been so used to winning. Walter has also proved himself to be a great coach with a great tactical knowledge of the game. Some people might say he is more old school but if he is old school then he certainly has shown he knows how to thrive in the modern game. Away from the pitch he is a top man who is also extremely good company.

RICHARD GOUGH (RANGERS 1987–97)

I have to say that Walter Smith is the best manager I have worked under. The influence he had on my career certainly can't be overestimated. I was lucky enough to work with him at Dundee United, Rangers, Everton and with Scotland and I can't speak any more highly of him. You only have to look at his managerial record. Walter has been a success wherever he has been. When you look at Scottish football there have been three real godfathers of the game. There is Sir Alex Ferguson, Jock Stein and Walter Smith. He has earned the right to be placed in that top bracket with genuine legends of the game.

RAY WILKINS (RANGERS 1987–89)

Walter Smith is a real top geezer. As a person I absolutely love him. He is an absolute gentleman who loves a chuckle and a laugh. He might have been our assistant manager but he was also one of the boys. He is a top coach and manager who immediately gains your respect whoever you are. Walter is a true gent who also has a lovely wife, Ethel, and some great kids as well. He has had a great career and deserves all the success he has had because he really is a special guy. Walter certainly bucks the trend that nice guys never win. You only have to look at his record to know that certainly isn't the case. He is one of the greatest managers that Scottish football has ever had.

GARY STEVENS (RANGERS 1988–94)

Walter Smith was cute compared to other managers I had worked under. He had this ability not to say something he would regret in the heat of the moment. I had seen other managers go off on one and burn bridges between people but Walter would never do that. He was always quite cool and calculated. I am sure most of the players who have played under him will say the same thing – that his man-management is second to none. He knew how to gain the respect of people and also when to give you a bollocking or when you needed an arm around you.

JOHN BROWN (RANGERS 1988–97)

Everyone talks about Bill Struth but for me Walter Smith is up there as the greatest Rangers manager ever. Look at the success he had with the nine-in-a-row teams and even during that we could even have won the Champions League if it hadn't been for Marseille. Then his second spell has been just as good as he won titles and cups on a shoestring and also led Rangers to the UEFA Cup final. For me, when you talk about great managers then Walter should be up there in the same breath as Sir Alex Ferguson and Jock Stein. I have nothing but the utmost respect for the Gaffer. He treated me and every one of his players with total respect and because of that we would go that extra mile for him. I took a lot of injections to play in games I shouldn't have. I wouldn't have done that for Walter if I didn't have the utmost respect for him. Walter has also looked after me. When my career started to come to an end he gave me my first step into coaching. He allowed me to coach the under-18s and even when he came back to Rangers a second time he got me involved in the scouting, where I went to look and identify guys like Carlos Cuellar. I really appreciate everything Walter has done for me and I feel honoured to have called him my Gaffer.

IAN FERGUSON (RANGERS 1988–2000)

What the Gaffer has done during his time at Rangers has been nothing short of fantastic. From his time with Graeme Souness to becoming the main man, Walter Smith has been an absolute sensation for Rangers Football Club. Look at all the titles and trophies he won during his first spell at the club. You can't speak highly enough of his record during my time at the club but then he went back and was as successful in his second spell. It just shows what a great coach and man manager he is. The Gaffer always knew how to look after you and put an arm around you but he could also kick backsides when needed. He is definitely one guy you don't want to get on the wrong side of.

NIGEL SPACKMAN (RANGERS 1989–92)

What Walter Smith has done for Rangers and the Scottish national team is just amazing. He was obviously heavily involved in the nine-in-a-row teams but I would have to say what he has achieved in his second spell at Rangers has even eclipsed that. The first time around he had quality players and a fair bit of money to spend but in recent seasons he has hardly had a penny. He really has produced miracles on a shoestring. The club have had no money and he has had to constantly sell his best players and he has still produced titles, cups and Champions League football. Like a good Scottish malt whisky Walter certainly has mellowed and matured with age and has proved himself to be one of the greatest ever managers in the Scottish game.

TREVOR STEVEN (RANGERS 1989–91 and 1992–97)

I was fortunate throughout my career to play under some good managers and for some top teams. Walter Smith and Rangers definitely fall into those categories. Walter was in charge of a Rangers team who were very much a big fish in a small pond. I would say Walter was like the captain of our ship. We had a lot of leaders in our dressing room and some exceptional footballers back during my time at Ibrox. What Walter did was keep us all together and then steer us on to a very successful path. He has done that with great regularity and success during his two spells at Rangers. For that Walter deserves enormous credit and a massive place in the hearts of the Rangers fans.

MARK HATELEY (RANGERS 1990–95 and 1997)

Walter Smith is without doubt the best manager I have worked under. I have had the honour of playing under top managers like Arsene Wenger, Fabio Capello, Terry Venables and Bobby Robson but, for me, Walter tops them all. He has shown he can do it at any level. He proved he was a top manager when he had money during our nine-in-a-row years and now he has shown he can do it without a penny, as he's worked miracles at Everton and then back at Rangers again with next to nothing. As a manager I think he ticks all the right boxes when it comes to football management.

PIETER HUISTRA (RANGERS 1990–95)

I am now in management in my own right and a lot of what I saw under Walter Smith I have tried to take into my own jobs. Things like the importance of man-management and giving the players the right environment, so they feel relaxed and play their best football. Man-management was a big thing for Walter Smith. He certainly helped me because I was still a youngster when I moved to Glasgow with my now wife. It was a bit of a culture shock but Walter being the great man he was did everything he could to make me feel settled.

DAVID ROBERTSON (RANGERS 1991–97)

I played under Sir Alex Ferguson when I was younger. He was great but I have to say Walter Smith was the real inspiration in my career. He was the man who got me playing at the highest level. He took the gamble to pay near enough £1 million for me and showed faith in me. Even after the 'three foreigner' rule was lifted I was still the left back and that was a big thing for me, knowing I had the Gaffer's backing. The one thing that every player speaks about with Walter is his man management. I worked under him for six years and they really were six great years. Walter has this natural ability of turning good players into very good players. The other thing about Walter was that if you looked after him he would look after you. Even when I first signed and came down from Aberdeen he went out of his way to help me. If we were playing up at Aberdeen then he would tell me to go up on the Thursday night, do a wee bit myself on the Friday, stay with the family and then meet up with the team at the hotel before the game. Even at the other end he would sometimes give me another day or so off to spend extra time with the family. These were little things I really appreciated. It makes you want to give 110 per cent for him when you go out on the pitch and I think that is the reason why he has been so successful wherever he has been. Andy Goram is always 'The Goalie' and to me Walter will always be 'The Gaffer'.

ANDY GORAM (RANGERS 1991–98)

I played under Sir Alex Ferguson for Scotland and Manchester United and when it comes to management his record is second to none. He is the best manager Britain has ever produced. But what Walter Smith has achieved with Rangers and Scotland has also been massive. In terms of Britain's best ever managers I would put Walter second behind Sir Alex Ferguson. I don't think I can pay him a bigger compliment than that. That is how highly I rate the Gaffer. Walter is a great manager but he will admit that he has been lucky he has had good people like Archie Knox and Davie Dodds beside him and more lately Ally McCoist, Kenny McDowall and Ian Durrant. During our time it was Archie and Davie. With Archie it was like good cop/bad cop. If one gave you a bollocking then the other would come and pick you up and that was how it worked. The Gaffer's man-management skills were and still are second to none. He knows when to give players a cuddle or a kick up the backside. The only thing I would say is that when you see the Gaffer's right eyebrow raised then beware. That was when you knew he was angry. You still see it today on the television or in interviews. I have probably seen it as much as anyone but the Gaffer was first class to me and was also a terrific coach into the bargain as well. You don't have the success he has had throughout his career without having something special.

STUART McCALL (RANGERS 1991–98)

I have said it many times that Walter Smith is the best manager I have ever played under and I stand by that. His record in both spells at Rangers speaks for itself and he is quite rightly up there with all the Rangers greats. He also never forgets the players who have played under him. I remember he brought the nine-in-a-row team down to Bradford for my testimonial game. He didn't have to do that but he did and I really appreciated it. He also inspired Rangers to a 4–2 win, so even in friendlies he had a real will to win. It shows his will and desire to win.

DALE GORDON (RANGERS 1991–93)

People always ask me who was the best manager I ever worked under and I always tell them it was Walter Smith. The way he handled and managed players was and still is second to none. From a personal point of view the trust and belief he showed in me made me respect the guy even more. All the players during my time at Rangers looked up to Walter. He was such a presence and is very much a Rangers legend. That is why the likes of Ally McCoist and Ian Durrant will go on to have successful careers in management because they have had such a good education under Walter.

FRASER WISHART (RANGERS 1993–95)

Walter is definitely the best man-manager I have come across. I remember I played for Rangers in a reserve game at Alloa Athletic on a Monday night. None of the team had played on the Saturday. The team was Ally Maxwell, Gary Stevens, John Brown, Steven Pressley, me, Pieter Huistra, Ian Durrant, Charlie Miller, Alexei Mikhailichenko, then Gordon Durie and Duncan Ferguson up front. These were guys who couldn't get a game on the Saturday. Walter had a squad as strong as that and was able to juggle things and keep everybody happy. There aren't many managers who could deal with situations like that. There is definitely a presence about Walter. He gains everybody's respect and not in a fearful sort of way. It is a genuine respect. He knew when to mix with you and when not to mix with you. That presence is what struck me about Walter.

BRIAN LAUDRUP (RANGERS 1994–98)

I have said on numerous occasions that Walter Smith is the best manager I have ever worked with in my career. He just has this tremendous ability to make the players want to play for him. Walter would go to great lengths to make sure that everything was right for you. That and the fact he is a great coach are the main reasons for me as to why he has been so successful in his two spells at Rangers. It is no mean feat what Walter achieved in my time as a player during our nine-in-a-row spell and then again he has come back and worked hard to turn things around on his return. What Walter Smith has done for Rangers and Scottish football throughout his time has been nothing short of fantastic.

ALAN McLAREN (RANGERS 1994–99)

Walter Smith is a great human being. He is always pleasant and was really nice to me. Every time I go back to Rangers he can't do enough for me. His managerial record stands up against the best. He led Rangers to nine-in-a-row and then came back to Rangers for a second spell and dragged the club out of the doldrums and back where it should be, at the top of Scottish football. Archie Knox and Davie Dodds also played a big part in Walter's early success and I am sure Walter will be the first to agree with that. Davie and Archie were also top coaches and Davie, especially, was also a good link between the players and the management. I suppose Walter's managerial record is even more impressive when you look at what he has done for Scotland. We were at our lowest ebb under Berti Vogts but he came in, steadied the ship and then got things going again. Scottish football has an awful lot to thank Walter Smith for.

ALEX CLELAND (RANGERS 1995–98)

I played under Walter for three-and-a-half seasons which turned into seven-and-a-half when he and Archie followed me to Everton.

When you work for people like Walter and Archie that long it becomes more than professional. I now class them as friends. They showed faith in me during my career and for that I will always be really grateful to them. They were just two great guys and two great football people into the bargain. The one thing that struck me about Walter was that he was always fair and constructive with you even when he was angry. He would always try and help and encourage you but at the same time if you didn't play well or didn't do what you were told then you knew you would feel his wrath. Walter's strength was definitely the way he managed his players. It didn't matter if you were a £6 million player like Paul Gascoigne or Brian Laudrup or a £600,000 signing from Dundee United. Price tags didn't matter to Walter because he treated every single one of us exactly the same.

DEREK McINNES (RANGERS 1995–2000)

There is no doubt that Walter Smith is one of the greatest managers Scottish football has ever seen. He has achieved and won so much in the game. His record really is unbelievable and I fear it could be a very long time before we see somebody as successful as him again. He is an inspiration to every young manager in the Scottish game and really is one of our game's true greats.

GORDAN PETRIC (RANGERS 1995–98)

I knew Walter because I had played against his teams when I was at Dundee United. The first time I met Walter I recognised what type of person he was. People had always said the Gaffer was a nice person and a really honest guy. From the first day I walked into Rangers I could see that for myself. He was also a top coach and manager into the bargain. I have since met Sir Alex

Ferguson quite a few times in recent years and Walter is just like him. They both have a real will to win every game and to do the best for their respective teams. I was lucky to work with Walter, Archie Knox, John Brown and Davie Dodds.

JORG ALBERTZ (RANGERS 1996–2000)

I have to thank Walter Smith from the bottom of my heart for taking me to Glasgow Rangers. He signed me and introduced me to such a brilliant team and to Ibrox. It was the best period of my playing career and I can't thank him enough for that. If he had stayed at Rangers then I am in no doubt I would have finished my career at Ibrox. It just wasn't the same for me after Walter left. Dick Advocaat was a top coach and had great success at Rangers but I suppose our personalities clashed and we never really got on. That was never the case with Walter. He was the ultimate gentleman and a person who I had total respect for. For me he is a living legend. I just can't thank him enough for what he did for me and my career.

JOACHIM BJORKLUND (RANGERS 1996–98)

Walter Smith is a fantastic man and person. Whenever I speak about Walter and Rangers it always brings a great warmth to my heart. He is one of the best managers I have played under in my career. You could go and talk to him about anything whether it be football or anything away from the club. I have nothing but respect for Walter for what he did for me and how he helped me settle in Scotland. He is a great, great man. Also, Walter, like most of the Scottish guys we had in that dressing room, wanted the team to play hard but they also balanced things well away from the pitch. There were a good few parties and a lot of humour and fun in my time at Ibrox and that was a major part of our success and that came from the manager.

SERGIO PORRINI (RANGERS 1997–2001)

I have played under Marcello Lippi who has won the Champions League and the World Cup. He is a top coach and a great man and all I can say about Walter Smith is that he is right up there with him. He was a top coach but also away from the park he also knew how to look after his players and their families. That is something I will always appreciate. He is a top manager and one of the best the British game has ever had. I think Walter's success is even more remarkable because when Lippi had his success it was mainly with Italian players but with Walter he managed to fuse together so many different nationalities and still put a winning team out. He is a man and manager who I have nothing but total respect for.

LORENZO AMORUSO (RANGERS 1997–2003)

Walter Smith is a manager you could go and talk to about anything. I had never come across anyone like that in my time until I met Walter. He was the man who convinced me to come to Rangers. When I first met him I knew I wanted to play for him but unfortunately injury meant that Walter never saw the best of me. That is my one big disappointment of my time at Rangers. I wanted so much to help his Rangers team to make it 10–in-a-row but it wasn't to be. I think for what he has done for Rangers he deserved it. It was a shame the way his final season at Rangers went and that was why I was so glad he got the chance to return to Rangers again. He has gone back and done a truly remarkable job in truly testing times. He has brought Rangers out on top again and also taken them to the UEFA Cup final. He is one of the game's true greats.

NACHO NOVO (RANGERS 2004–10)

I have to say Walter Smith is one of the greatest people I have ever come across in football. I would say the Gaffer was like a father figure for me when I was at Ibrox. But he was like that for all the players who played under him. I owe Walter a lot for what he did for me at Rangers. He is just a great man and a brilliant person. I once had a really bad spell under him at Rangers. I was feeling very down but Walter was the one who picked me up. He spoke to me, put an arm round me and got me back to playing football with a smile on my face again. Walter made me feel great again and I have to thank him massively for that. I know I owe him a debt of gratitude and so do Rangers as a whole. He has done so much for the club and I don't think what he has done will be fully appreciated until the day he walks out of Ibrox. For me, Walter is Mr Rangers.

SASA PAPAC (RANGERS 2006–)

In my career there have been two coaches who have been hugely influential. One is Miroslav Cotic, who was my first coach when I was starting out in Mostar. He was like a second father to me when I was starting out in football. He trained me when I was under-17 and was really important for my development. The other one is Walter. He has been similarly influential in my career. He has given me the best coaching of my professional career, no doubt. I learnt a lot from Walter. You can work with him a long time and learn many things. But he has something special about him and the way that he goes about things is unique. He has a knack of knowing how certain things can help you win a game, or even win a league. You cannot learn these things from him. It's something in his heart that is quite extraordinary. I had never experienced that before in my senior career.

DAVIE WEIR (RANGERS 2007–)

I have to say Walter Smith has been absolutely brilliant for me and my career. Without doubt he has been the biggest influence on my career. He has given me opportunities that without him I may never have had. It was Walter who gave me the chance to play in the English Premier League and then again when things had gone wrong with me for Scotland. He then took me to Rangers and handed me the honour of becoming Rangers captain. What Walter has done for me means a lot and I know I have an awful lot to thank him for. When you are working with somebody like Walter Smith every day you tend to take things for granted. You think what he has done at Rangers in recent seasons is just the norm. It won't be until he goes that people will really appreciate the unbelievable job he has done. And I am not just talking about Rangers but also with Scotland and at Everton as well. You only have to look at what he did for Scotland and the way he turned things around there. Even down at Everton by keeping that squad in the English Premier League with all the problems behind the scenes was an achievement in itself. Walter has been successful wherever he has been although it will probably be for his Rangers days that he will most fondly be remembered. For me, Walter's record is unmatched. Willie Waddell and Bill Struth started the club ethos and there is no doubt Walter Smith has carried that on. There is no doubt Walter is now a Rangers great with everything he has done for the club.

LEE McCULLOCH (RANGERS 2007–)

When it comes to Walter Smith I really don't know where to start. His record in management speaks for itself and he has also attracted some really big players to Rangers. A lot of them I don't think we would have got if the Gaffer hadn't been there. People want to come and play for him and because of that he seems to get the best out of people. He is just a brilliant father figure and a real leader that everyone can look up to. He has won an amazing amount of cups and titles and his achievements really are phenomenal. Bill Struth might be the most successful Rangers manager ever but I am in no doubt that if the Gaffer had been in charge the same length of time then he would have even surpassed that record. For me, I still think our Gaffer is the best manager in Rangers' history.

KIRK BROADFOOT (RANGERS 2007–)

The one thing I would have to say about the Gaffer is that he is a really humble guy. He has achieved so much in the game but has time for absolutely everybody. He is also still so grounded and down-to-earth. I will always be thankful to him for giving me the chance to play for Rangers. It was a boyhood dream for me. Also to play under him just made it even more special. There is no doubt he will go down as an Ibrox legend and rightly so. What he has done for the club has been truly remarkable and every Rangers fan, including myself, has a lot to thank the Gaffer for. He has given us all so many happy times and led Rangers through two of the most successful periods in the club's proud history.

STEVEN WHITTAKER (RANGERS 2007–)

The Gaffer was been brilliant for me from the day I signed. I endured some hard times in the first couple of years but he showed faith in me. He is just brilliant the way he works with people. He gets the best out of everyone. Over my last couple of years under him he has definitely helped me on the mental side and my whole approach to the game. He gave me a real determination to be a winner and he has instilled that in every one of his players. That has been shown with the success he has had throughout his career.

There have been quite a few highlights under the Gaffer. Over his last four years we won at least two of the three domestic trophies every single season. Every one of these campaigns was special. Winning the championship is always massive. He made it three-in-a-row in titles out of the four years we were there. We also got to the UEFA Cup final. I dreamt about playing in a game like that and Walter and Rangers gave me that opportunity. I have had so many great times under Walter Smith and I can't thank him enough for everything he has done.

STEVIE NAISMITH (RANGERS 2007–)

I've not had a lot of managers in my senior career but growing up as a Rangers fan I was a massive fan of Walter Smith. He has managed so many top players like Paul Gascoigne and Brian Laudrup and so many great Rangers teams. So when I first heard that the Gaffer wanted to sign me that went through my mind and I felt in an honoured position. He had managed so many top players and now he had identified me as a player he felt could bring something to his Rangers team. It really was a massive thing for me.

KENNY MILLER (RANGERS 2000–01 and 2008–11)

The job Walter Smith has done in the last four-and-a-half years at Rangers has been nothing short of phenomenal. He has managed the club in one of the toughest periods in Rangers' history but has still managed to put out a team that was strong enough to win leagues and lift cups. There were periods where the club was in total turmoil but the Gaffer still managed to keep the team together on the pitch. He has managed to deliver two trophies per season over the last three campaigns and taken the team to a European final. What he has achieved has been absolutely incredible. I really enjoyed having played a part in that success and working under the best manager I have had in my career. Without a shadow of a doubt the Gaffer got the best out of me. I definitely played the best football of my career under him and I can't thank him enough for what he has done for me and my career.

CHRISTIAN DAILLY (RANGERS 2008–09)

I first came across Walter Smith when I was still a schoolboy training with Dundee United. Since then I have gone on to work under him with Scotland and Rangers and there is no doubt he is up there with the best managers I have had. There is no doubt about that. He has so many different attributes but the biggest one for me is the way he is always so calm and self-assured. He knows the game inside out and also how to deal with people, which is important in the modern-day game. These are some of the reasons why Walter has remained in the game for so long and also at the top of the tree.

PEDRO MENDES (RANGERS 2008–10)

Walter Smith is without doubt one of the top managers I have worked under. He is right up there in every aspect of the game. Every manager has a different way they want to work. One of Walter's main strengths is his skill in dealing with the players. The way the players are together around him is quite an achievement. Managers all have different approaches to the game and deal with players in their own particular ways. Jose Mourinho and Harry Redknapp have their own methods, but, for me, Walter is top in all aspects of the game. Walter has done a terrific job at

Rangers. We just need to look back and see what Rangers have won since he has returned. For sure, Walter is one of the top managers Rangers have had in the club's proud history.

KYLE LAFFERTY (RANGERS 2008–)

He is the manager who brought me here. I always dreamt of playing for Rangers and he gave me that chance. I have to thank him for that. To score three goals in his last game to win the title and the three-in-a-row was just amazing. The players were desperate to win it for Walter and send him off on a high. We managed to do that and it was great to see him pick up his last trophy for the club. It was a great achievement for him. He is a legend at the club. Everybody knows what he has done for Rangers and he deserves everything that comes his way.

MADJID BOUGHERRA (RANGERS 2008–)

Walter Smith is one of the best managers I have played under. You only have to look at the manager and see what he has achieved in the game. I think he is very similar to Sir Alex Ferguson in terms of what he has achieved and his standing in the game. I also owe him a lot. The manager showed enough faith to sign me from Charlton and he gave me the confidence to grow into the player I am today. He believed in me and that is a big thing. He has allowed me to improve and build as a player. Now my image and profile is quite high and that is all thanks to Walter Smith and my Rangers team mates.

It is absolutely fantastic what the manager has done in the game. He is always defending Scottish football. Players, past and present, the club and his family should all be very proud of him. He is a very special man.

GREGG WYLDE (RANGERS 2009–)

Walter Smith has done so much for me. I spoke to him after his final game to thank him for what he had done for me in my career so far. I just said: 'Thanks very much, Walter, for everything, putting me in against PSV, helping me along in my career.' He told me I had deserved it all, so I'm grateful to him for that. I couldn't have imagined what was going to happen to me that season. I was thrown in at the deep end against PSV. I thought that might be my last game and then I played against Celtic too. After that, I played a lot and I really enjoyed it. I enjoyed working for him. It is hard to think that he has now gone after everything he's done for the club.

VLADIMIR WEISS (RANGERS 2010–11)

Before I went to Rangers I knew Walter Smith was a big man in football. He was a coach with a lot of top-level experience that I knew I could really learn from. That was why I decided to join Rangers ahead of Celtic and thankfully that proved to be the case. Walter showed his qualities throughout the course of the season. He is a fighter who never knows when he is beaten. He never gives up because he has got this real will to win. I think that shone through in his final season. A lot of people wrote us off but we got back off the canvas and fought back. In the end we won the League Cup and the title and we proved we were the best team in Scotland.

I learned so much playing under him in Scotland. I returned to Manchester City a better player and a step closer to making the breakthrough there. I loved every minute of my time at Rangers under Walter and it is a time of my career that I will always have special memories from.

NIKICA JELAVIC (RANGERS 2010–)

Walter Smith is a great man. He might be a big manager but he speaks to you and treats you like a friend. He is somebody you can always talk to and he is also a man who commands huge respect. I am so appreciative of Walter. He was the man who took me to Rangers and gave me everything I now have in my career. If it hadn't been for Walter then there is no doubt I would probably have still been at Rapid Vienna. I remember when he first called me he was very persuasive. He told me that Rangers had been watching me for some time and he was very keen to sign me. He believed I could help the team. That gave me great confidence and right away I knew that Walter Smith was a manager who had faith and belief in me. You want to play for people like this. He explained how Rangers were a big club and a bit about their great tradition. He also employed my friend, Sasa Papac, to try and convince me to sign for Rangers. He basically told me what I had already found out for myself by speaking to Walter. He told me that he had been at Rangers five years and it had been the best spell of his career. He also told me that Walter was a top manager and that I should come and join Rangers. I took his advice and there is no doubt playing under Walter for a season has been massive and has been brilliant for my career.

WALTER SMITH'S
IBROX TROPHY CABINET

1990–91 – Scottish Premier League title.
1991–92 – Scottish Premier League title and Scottish Cup.
1992–93 – Scottish Premier League title, Scottish League Cup
and Scottish Cup.
1993–94 – Scottish Premier League title and Scottish
League Cup.
1994–95 – Scottish Premier League title.
1995–96 – Scottish Premier League title and Scottish Cup.
1996–97 – Scottish Premier League title and Scottish
League Cup.
2007–08 – Scottish League Cup and Scottish Cup.
2008–09 – Scottish Premier League title and Scottish Cup.
2009–10 – Scottish Premier League title and Scottish
League Cup.
2010–11 – Scottish Premier League title and Scottish
League Cup.

INDIVIDUAL AWARDS

SPL MANAGER OF THE YEAR: 2007–08, 2009–10.
SFWA MANAGER OF THE YEAR: 1991–92, 1992–93, 1993–94,
1995–96, 1996–97, 2007–08, 2009–10.
PFA SCOTLAND MANAGER OF THE YEAR: 2009–10.
OBE: 1997.